The New Dynamics of Development

Ding Yifan

The New Dynamics of Development

The Crisis of Globalization and China's Solutions

PETER LANG
Lausanne • Berlin • Bruxelles • Chennai • New York • Oxford

Library of Congress Cataloging-in-Publication Data

Names: Yifan, Ding, author.
Title: The new dynamics of development : the crisis of globalization and China's solutions / Ding Yifan.
Description: New York : Peter Lang, [2023] | Includes index.
Identifiers: LCCN 2023000371 (print) | LCCN 2023000372 (ebook) |
ISBN 9781433193200 (hardback) | ISBN 9781433193217 (ebook) |
ISBN 9781433193224 (epub)
Subjects: LCSH: China–Economic conditions–2000- |
Sustainable development–China–History–21st century. |
China–Economic policy–2000- | China–Foreign relations–21st century. | Globalization.
Classification: LCC HC427.95 .Y54 2023–(print) | LCC HC427.95–(ebook) |
DDC 330.951–dc23/eng/20230109
LC record available at https://lccn.loc.gov/2023000371
LC ebook record available at https://lccn.loc.gov/2023000372
DOI 10.3726/b19094

Bibliographic information published by the **Deutsche Nationalbibliothek.**
The German National Library lists this publication in the German National Bibliography; detailed bibliographic data is available on the Internet at http://dnb.d-nb.de.

Cover design by Peter Lang Group AG

ISBN 9781433193200 (hardback)
ISBN 9781433193217 (ebook)
ISBN 9781433193224 (epub)
DOI 10.3726/b19094

This edition is an authorized translation from the Chinese language edition
Published by arrangement with CITIC Press Corporation
(B&R Program)

Published by Peter Lang Publishing Inc., New York, USA
info@peterlang.com - www.peterlang.com

This publication has been peer reviewed.

Contents

Part II The Crisis of Globalization and China's Solutions

Preface

China's response to the problems raised by Globalization, is now being recognized by more and more countries. When globalization is in crisis, China is willing to help it get back on track—regression is not the right solution anymore. It is impossible to return to a development model based on the framework of nation-states because the market would be too narrow to spread and develop technology and productivity. Beyond the economy, the nation-state framework cannot solve the many global issues facing the world today, such as global climate change and terrorism. For China, globalization is about building a community of shared future by all human beings, or a community of sovereign states—countries who are willing to voluntarily unify under the principles of consensus, co-building, and sharing, so they can strengthen their cooperation and jointly address challenges and crises.

However, some leaders from developed countries hold different views. Some politicians believe that by disrupting the global value chain, the industrial production process could be brought back to their countries, thereby boosting domestic employment and economic growth. Meanwhile, some even claim that global warming is a deliberate lie invented to slow down their countries' development. For example, in 2017, the U.S. announced it would withdraw from the Paris Agreement and lift restrictions on greenhouse gas emissions.

Although China cannot force all countries to participate in global governance, we can make all countries aware of the benefits to the world of stronger global governance. If some countries are unwilling to uphold multilateralism and improve global governance, China will have to take on the task of global governance itself. For those countries that want to disengage from global governance and return to unilateralism, they will eventually realize that they are also disengaging from the track of this era—they will lose their competitive advantage and in the end isolate themselves. Only countries that actively contribute to the world can share the benefits of its global development.

In 2013, China proposed the Belt and Road Initiative (BRI) with the core ideas as followed: "multilateral cooperation, consensus, co-building, and sharing". The BRI has provided a new impetus for world economic growth, where the emerging economies are playing an increasingly important role. This Initiative continues to be open to all, China's wishes desire is to involve countries that can provide additional innovative development models and solutions. Collectively these innovations could diversify the world's development and therefore provide more models for the references of each country.

The main content of this book is my analysis of the development of globalization in recent years, some of which have already been scattered in some publications. I hope to string all the beads into an integral necklace through editing and modifications, which could provide some comprehensive reflections on contemporary globalization. I would like to acknowledge the help of all those who provided me with comments during the editing process, which made the logic and analytical framework of this book clearer and more explicit. I also want to express special thanks to CITIC Press and the Taihe Institute, for having absolute faith in my project and for their willingness to publish this book in Chinese version. I want to thank warmly my friend Einar Tangen who suggests me to add a few comments to each chapter, to explain the purpose and background, why I wrote on this topic. That way, my readers outside of China can better understand in what context the chapter was written. I'm also grateful to Peter Lang for their willingness to publish this English version.

I am responsible for any errors and mistakes in this book, and I would like to invite readers to give me their precious comments.

Ding Yifan

Haidian District, Beijing, China, May 29, 2023

Introduction

In recent years, globalization has been blamed for being the origin of all misfortunes in Western countries. Politicians with anti-globalization slogans take the opportunity to emerge as the biggest winners in various elections.

The most prominent winner was US President Trump. He was elected under the slogan of "America First", and he wanted to put the slogan of America First into practice. The United States withdrew from the TPP and threatened to reshuffle the North American Free Trade Agreement and renegotiate the free trade agreement with the European Union. The Trump administration has also imposed unilaterally tariffs on China's exporting goods to the United States in the name of America First.

The United States has always been a believer in free trade and the main driving force behind the promotion of free trade around the world. And globalization has grown through the ethos of global free trade and cross-border investment liberalization. Globalization has a huge impact on the world economy. In terms of GDP, the world economy got its fasted growth from the 1990s to the financial crisis in 2008, and international trade also grew the fastest. That was the golden age of globalization.

In fact, the biggest beneficiaries from globalization are large multinational companies in developed countries. They take advantage of the opportunities of trade and investment liberalization to allocate resources and production globally, increasing their investment returns exponentially. However, liberalization has made the social redistribution system of developed countries seriously inclined towards the wealthy, resulting in a rapid widening of the gap between the rich and the poor populations. The Occupy Wall Street movement claimed that 99 % of Americans did not benefit, and only 1 % of the wealthy people benefited from this globalization.

Many developing countries (including China) actively participated in globalization, and took advantage of the opening of the global market to develop rapidly and realize industrialization. They are also beneficiaries of globalization, but not at the cost of enlarging social disparity and environmental pollution. Taking China as an example, globalization has also brought about the polarization of the gap between the rich and the poor people. Coastal areas were the first to receive foreign investment, and they developed rapidly. However, the central and western regions do not have these regional advantages, and few foreign companies decided to invest there. The development gap between them and the coastal regions is widening rapidly. Foreign investment is concentrated in cities, and China's urban-rural income gap is widening amid globalization. However, the Chinese government has not sticked to the "Washington Consensus" and has not fully followed Western experts' advices to privatize its economy and liberalize its capital market. In this context, the government still has the ability to guide economic development, invest in infrastructure construction, improve people's quality of life and use the government's "visible hand" to intervene in the market. Regions and social groups that are not "favored by globalization" have been allowed by government assistance to realize a better development and allow hundreds of millions of people get out of poverty.

When globalization is in crisis, China is willing to use its own power to help globalization return to the right track, because China believes that going backwards is not the right way to solve the problem. It is impossible for us to return to the development model based on the nation-state framework, because the market is too narrow, it hinders the dissemination of technology and the growth of production capacity; that kind of nation-state framework cannot solve many global problems facing the world today, such as global climate change or the proliferation of international terrorism. China wants to promote its own version of globalization, which is to build a community with a shared future for mankind. It can also be said to be a community of sovereign states. Under the principle of "mutual consultation, joint construction, and sharing benefits", China wants to bring the international community together to strengthen cooperation and jointly deal with the challenges and problems facing our planet.

During those years of globalization crisis, I wrote many papers commenting international events. This time, I put them together and reedited them according to my own logic. My purpose is to give ordinary people, and scholars, a sense of how people, like me, in China, were thinking about important issues and times, as they happened. For each issue there was some question, event and/or issue, that prompted me to write. Sometimes, the questions we ask and attempt to answer are more important than the answers themselves. Putting these questions and events into context may be of use to those who want to understand China's development during the period covered. I hope you find it useful.

This book has two parts. The first part analyzes China's unique development model, including China's choice of development path, the characteristics of its governance system, the reform and development of the financial system, and the reflections on how its economy can cope with challenges during the medium- and high-speed development phase after the completion of high-speed development. The first part also discusses China's position in the international arena and how China uses its national power.

The second part analyzes the crisis of globalization and some of the dilemmas China faces during this process. This part starts with China's complex relationship with the United States, such as the long-standing issues of entangled currency exchange rate between China and the United States. Then it discusses how China can work with emerging economies to build a new type of international relations and push globalization in a healthier direction. This part culminates in the issues of China's proposal to build a community of shared future.

The essays presented cover topics that people now, and years from now, will want to understand. While I am just one voice, I can by presenting these issues in terms of chronology, and context, give some indication of what and how some of us were thinking.

Part I

China's Unique Development Path

1 What Drives China's Economic Growth under the "New Normal"?

In 2012–2013, China's GDP growth started to slow down, as external markets shrank, due to the global recession. From 2001 to 2011, China had had very fast economic growth, the average annual growth ratio was above 10%, with a peak of 13% in 2013. This fast economic growth is supported by an even faster export growth ratio. Indeed, during those golden years of globalization, China's export growth was above 20% almost every year. So China's growth model was labeled "export led growth". Unfortunately, after the international financial crisis of 2008/09, which was followed by a global recession, starting in 2010 China's export experienced a dramatic drafter which, China's GDP growth slowed down.

In response the Chinese government issued a new development strategy named "New normal", acknowledging that China's economy has come into a new period of growth characterized by a moderate growth ratio but also a better quality growth. While under the "new normal", Chinese people can experience more progress in the quality of their daily life, because of environment improvement, infrastructure progress, new forms of economy, including electronic payment and sharing economy, etc... This was interpreted by some of the international media that China had come to the realization that its economic growth was slowing down, they reasoned that China would be facing a series of challenges, such as, an aging society, competition from other emerging economies, etc.. .

> *As someone who was being interviewed numerous times by various domestic and international media groups, as well by fellow res*earch colleagues from abroad, I wrote the following articles and papers for Chinese media in response to those questions mainly in 2016. I present them now to show how I interpreted what China was thinking about and responding to, in the post International Financial Crisis period of time.

In 2017, rumors spread about the slowdown in China's economic growth in international financial markets, as two U.S. rating companies downgraded China's sovereign credit ratings[1]. However, the International Monetary Fund forecasted stronger China's economic growth at the same time[2]. This contrast reflects the confusion about China's growth prospects.

Indeed, a series of challenges for China's economic growth is still ahead. Many industries still struggle with overcapacity, and some manufacturers have been losing money because they could only utilize 65 % to 70 % of their machinery and equipment for production. The average bad debt ratio in some banks is between 6 % and 7 % due to the increasing losses of enterprises, and the ratio of some regional commercial banks is even higher. Additionally, local governments have been struggling with their financing channels to borrow new money, and some resource-producing provinces even experience an economic decline due to the plummeting resource prices.

Meanwhile, economic growth in some provinces has improved already, especially in the coastal regions. After having experienced the contraction in exports from traditional industries, Chinese coastal provinces have found a new development path with a more than 7 % growth rate, which signals the effective beginning of China's economic transformation. Many high-end manufacturing industries have made great progress in those coastal provinces, such as robotics, drones, and smart manufacturing. However, these industries are still not large enough to be the engine for the overall acceleration of the current development of the national economy.

However, the Chinese central government has various tools to deal with the economic downturn, as fiscal policy still has a lot of room for maneuver. Today, many developed countries have to repeatedly rely on monetary policy and even apply negative nominal interest rates as they have run out of fiscal policy under a huge burden of fiscal deficit[3]. On the contrary to these developed countries, the debt levels of the Chinese government remain manageable, and it could issue additional treasury bonds. Treasury bonds are a popular investment product for both the public and financial institutions, and we could also allow foreign central banks and other institutions to invest in Chinese treasury bonds to lower the exchange rate risk and promote the internationalization of the RMB. China could increase public investment more flexibly to stimulate important areas of the economy and drive overall economic growth. By taking short-, medium-, and long-term development into account, China needs to adapt its population policy more actively, accelerate the upgraded version of urbanization, and improve support services (including the reform of the household registration system).

As international investment and trade have been growing fast under the Belt and Road Initiative (BRI) in recent years, China could accelerate the development of economic projects in BRI regions in the future, expanding outward investment and exports to new markets. With the economic structural transformation, industrial upgrade, and outward investment boom, the Chinese economy will greatly leap forward after the completion of the 13th Five-Year Plan.

Consumption Growth Contributes to China's Sustainable Development

In recent years, China's economy has undergone significant restructuring, with the share of the three major industries in GDP changing significantly, along with the ratio of investment to consumption. All the changes happen in the context of the development of a socialist market economy with Chinese characteristics—the socialism with Chinese characteristics not only "adheres to the basic principles of scientific socialism, but also gives it distinctive Chinese characteristics according to the conditions of the times"[4]. China's economic growth is realized while sticking to the main features of socialism that prioritize fairness and look after the interests of the majority of people.

Along with gradually improved social security system and rapidly increased consumption levels, Income per capita has grown faster than GDP in China. Over the past five years, more than 60 million people have been lifted out of poverty, and the Chinese government has provided more than 13 million families with subsidized housing. These achievements have led to the expansion of the consumer base, the rising purchasing power, and the healthier development of the Chinese economy. In the first three quarters of 2017, consumption contributed as much as 64.5 % to China's economic growth—the service sector now accounts for more than the combined scale of primary and secondary sectors, and becomes the strong backbone to support economic growth.

Since the 21st century, China's rapid growth is closely related to exports in the first decade. However, after the outbreak of the international financial crisis in 2008, China's largest export markets—Europe and the United States—have fallen into recession. Although the developed economies have been gradually recovering, their growth is much slower now. As China can no longer rely on large-scale exports to drive economic growth. How does it find a new impetus for economic growth?

Under its stimulus package, China's economic growth is also mainly supported by infrastructure construction and the real estate market. Although China's economy is one of the biggest stabilizers of the world economy before and after the financial crisis, its surging debt rate and financial risks associated with the booming investment are now challenges that cannot be ignored. Therefore, the Chinese government has put into strong effort to stabilize the real estate market and eliminate excess production capacity. However, what will be the future driving force for China's economic development?

Often overlooked by some less optimistic Western media toward China's economic growth, huge consumption potential still needs to be released in the biggest single market with a 1.4 billion population. Consumption seems to have become the main driving force for China's economic growth, given its transformation of economic structure and improvement of the social security system. In fact, China's structural transformation will impact itself and the rest of the world as well.

On the 10th anniversary of the international financial crisis, Financial Times commented on the possibility of another financial crisis in the United States. The authors even pointed out the potential trigger—"loan insurance bonds", a new financial collateral product. China's structural transformation provides itself and other countries more resilient to external shocks against the risk of another global crisis, as it is now largely dependent on the domestic market.

The efforts to expand the consumer base have been effective over the years, as consumers have become the backbone of sustainable economic growth. However, to release the maximum potential of the Chinese market, better product quality and more options for consumption are still expected. Now, it is the sharing economy that offers the new "option".

Sharing Economy Improves People's Welfare

In recent years, sharing economy booms with the endless emergence of new business models, such as bike-sharing, car-sharing, and home-sharing all over China.

Sharing economy provides more convenience for users, improves the efficiency of resource distribution, and creates financial rewards for those who share. This new economic model of sharing reflects not only the great potential of China's manufacturing industry but also showcases the improved civility of Chinese people.

Just imagine, what would have been if we promote bike-sharing in China 30 or 40 years ago? China's manufacturing industry was quite backward then, and commodities were rationed due to short supply in general. To buy a bike, people would need the purchasing permit or wait in a long queue. If bike-sharing had been available then, few people would have returned the bikes for others to continue using, let alone cars being shared. However, as Chinese people's living standard improves, the once-popular bikes have become a niche commodity. Today, only people who ride bikes as sports would care about owning the expensive ones, while normal people have shifted to bike-sharing. Besides, the advent of bicycle sharing brought the old bike manufacturers back to life, which has not only boosted GDP growth but also created more jobs.

Amazed by the ubiquitous and colorful bikes on Chinese streets, we must notice that few countries could afford to allocate tens of millions of bikes into society in a short period. The bike is not complicated to manufacture, but to produce a gigantic number of bikes require enormous production capacity. Besides bike-sharing, sharing economy, in general, composes an essential part of the supply-side reform in China, which becomes an important path toward long-term development.

New problems are incurred in sharing economy as well. Many sharing bikes are intentionally vandalized, and sharing cars are used for illegal racing—no individual property, no moral responsibility; unorganized sharing bikes also occupy too much public space in some cities, which even block some roads for pedestrians to pass. All these phenomena could be regarded as a matter of personal ethics, but also reflect institutional loopholes.

To healthily develop sharing economy, several following aspects shall be addressed:

1. Improve the civility of all population
   The core of the sharing economy is the sharing of goods. If these shared goods are deliberately destroyed or irresponsibly used, they would become junk and huge wastes eventually and end the circulation within this economic model. Sharing economy provides convenience for everyone, and everyone is obliged to take care of this model.

2. Government administration should be more humane
   The new-emerged sharing economy will certainty cause and encounter many new problems. Administrators should not use simple nor arbitrary approaches as solutions—they could not just abruptly ban or prohibit all trials once problems occur. On the contrary, administrators are supposed to research and explore new management methods to adapt to the new form of consumption. For example, cooperation between industry associations and communal administrations could be built to find ways to facilitate people's lives without disrupting community order.
3. Establish a social credit system
   It's necessary to register individual information to get the permission of using shared goods. However, the regulators should emphasize the protection of users' privacy, as they reserve and evaluate individual credit using internet technology. If personal information is not well guarded, people's mistrust in sharing economy will be detrimental for future development.

The Chinese government attaches great importance to the healthy development of sharing economy. As stated in an executive meeting of the State Council chaired by Premier Li Keqiang in June 2017, developing sharing economy is China's adaption to the new round of global technological revolution and industrial change: "(sharing economy) could apply internet platforms to optimize resources allocation, eliminate excess production capacity, and cultivate new growth dynamics, and the new model is an important measure to promote the structural reform on the supply side while pushing mass entrepreneurship and innovation to a wider scope and higher level, so that to create more jobs and provide more economical, diverse and convenient services for people's daily life[5]."

If sharing economy can promote economic development while facilitating the cultivation of social morality and the establishment of a social credit system, it will become an important grip for China's economic development in the next phase. As the rapid development of various forms of sharing economy has also caused diversified public opinions, some argue that sharing economy causes social disorder while others think it is the right direction for future development. Chinese leadership might take a more inclusive and prudent approach for future regulation[6]—sharing first and regulating second. With a more tolerant environment for new technologies and business models, new driving forces of economic growth could survive and thrive.

Humans are inert and are reluctant to accept new things after getting used to old things and old technologies. As a result, innovative behavior is often overlooked and perishes at the early stages. When the American inventor Bell tried to sell the telephone to the Western Union Telegraph Company, he was rejected because the company thought that the telegraph was enough; the president of IBM once thought that the world needed only five computers at most and did not need to invest much in personal computers at all; Steve Jobs was severely laughed by other company executives while researching on touch-screen phones, as others believe that phones must have keyboards. Many technologies would have been permanently buried without the tolerance from consumers and the persistence of inventors; many technologies did not survive because of human ignorance, and we know only the survivors.

New industrial and business models are faced with doubts and criticisms from conservative people as well. When DiDi was first launched amid strong cynicism, and even Beijing's usual congestion could become an excuse to blast Didi; the bike-sharing was also splashed with cold water when it first appeared. However, most Chinese city administrators have become more open-minded toward new industries despite serious problems that might still occur sometimes. For example, they are happy to witness and cultivate the "last-mile" convenience for the public brought by bike-sharing. However, in some small cities, less tolerant administrators would directly ban bike-sharing or simply locked them up.

In the future, more innovations will emerge with the deep combination of artificial intelligence and internet technology. The lack of tolerance for new ideas and changes will impede China's technological progress compared to other innovative states; there is no need to panic in front of the uncertainty and disruption brought by changes, as we could always find solutions and reestablish order. During increasingly fierce technological competition among states and enterprises, higher tolerance of innovation is required by China.

Self-Reliant Innovation and Foreign Talents

While Chinese government insists on self-relian innovation, we should not exclude foreign talents from our technological innovation endeavor. Once at Los Angeles airport, while I was waiting for my flight, I heard a lot of announces made in French. I was so curious that I went to Information desk. I has been told that in Silicon Valley, there is a very important French community, of several hundreds of thousands people. That made me think about China's autonomous technological innovation strategy. So I wrote my own experience in a paper in 2017, to warn Chinese authorities not to exclude foreign talents who can be invited to participate in China's technological endeavor.

As China's economy enters the "new normal", innovation, instead of large-scale investment would be the main driver for the long-term economic development—the famous slogan "mass entrepreneurship and innovation" by Premier Li Keqiang summarized the paradigm shift.

Chinese companies have made great progress concerning innovation, not only with the emergence of technologically innovative companies such as Huawei and Tencent but also with the companies such as Alibaba that are constantly innovating in business models. China's innovation used to chiefly depend on domestic companies and scientists, but foreign talents are also an essential part of China's strategy to develop capabilities of self-reliant innovation.

A vivid example of using foreign talents to promote science and technology innovation can be found at the San Francisco airport in the United States, where the travelers could hear the airport announcement in both English and French. Located in California next to Mexico, San Francisco airport might prioritize English and Spanish, but why would French be used instead? The strategy staff would tell you that hundreds of thousands of French people live near Silicon Valley, and they are important participants in the revolution of communication technology in the US. To facilitate their travel, the San Francisco airport has made French the second language of the airport.

In the 1970s, the French were the first to develop Minitel technology, which uses telephone lines to transmit information and present it on a screen[7]. However, the French domestic market was too small and venture capital was not developed yet, so it was quite unlikely to apply the technology immediately then. In the 1990s, internet technology developed rapidly in the United States and quickly took over the world market, but the communication application of internet technology was not developed enough there. Meanwhile, French researchers soon developed some new internet technology applications such as IP phones, which greatly saved the cost of cross-border communication. Trapped by limited French venture capital market, those French researchers were lured to Silicon Valley by American investors. Of course, the new products and technologies were pocketed by the United State as well. Silicon Valley has perhaps concentrated on the smartest brains in the world, with a large number of talents from China, India, the Middle East, and other countries and regions, who sustains and drives the most dynamic innovation center since the 1990s.

The Chinese market has both disadvantages and advantages over the United States. The market size in China is several times larger, and many technologies developed in China can quickly become profitable projects, which represents an unparalleled opportunity for many new technologies; meanwhile, China's venture capital is still underdeveloped. Therefore, a growing number of financial institutions are becoming interested in investing in new technologies, especially as many private equity funds are now partially playing the role of venture capital.

It is now a perfect time that China could leverage outside talents to foster innovation. First, many researchers in developed countries strongly wish to direct their newly invented technologies into the market, which brings them both more income and a sense of accomplishment. Since the 1990s, many new technologies invented in Europe and North America were hoarded by multinational corporations (MNCs). These technologies usually came out by accidence or out of personal interest of researchers in small companies, and the inventions were bought out by the MNCs before they became matured products. However, the MNCs would rather squeeze more profit from their "ancient" products than replace them with their newly-purchased technologies. Therefore, the researchers are interested in soliciting Chinese investors who would help transform their inventions into final products.

Second, as many government-subsidized projects lost their funding due to budget cut in the West, researchers started to globally search for investors for technology transfer since the financial crisis in 2008—all they need is the one last push to turn their researches into products, and the global researchers are looking at the Chinese market. In the past, Chinese companies were only responsible for the manufacturing part of the international industrial division of labor, always following the lead of large MNCs. To transform into an innovative economy in the future, China needs to turn to small enterprises and researchers with innovative ideas. If China could take advantage of new technologies and lead in one or two industries, it would continue to attract more talents to China and develop new technologies there. At that point, foreign talents will become a new source of innovation in China.

The Grassroot Foundation of China's Technological Innovation

Once I has been invited to attend a national 3D contest in Yunnan. I was surprised to witness so many students from 2nd and 3rd tier universities, they may not be as well known as Chinese prestigious universities students, but they can still make perfect 3D design projects. That reminds me that when the US has been surpassing European countries in late 19 century and early 20 century in terms of manufacturing power, its development was not supported by those Ivy League universities, but by numerous State universities. Although State universities had only trained mechanical engineers and agronomists, the formation of massive engineers have improved tremendously US industrial productivity, so that the US became quickly the biggest industrial power in the world. So China's industrial and technological progress may not rely only on Chinese top universities, but on numerous 2nd and 3rd tier universities. When president Obama visited manufacturing enterprises on the Western cost, he had an interesting conversation with Steve Jobs. President Obama asked him why he made all his products in China, instead of in the US. Steve Jobs responded that he cannot afford to bring back this manufacturing parts in the US, because he needs more than 4000 engineers who accept to work on 3 shifts, 24 hours a day, on the first front of production, to adjust machines and control the quality. But he cannot find this type of engineers in the US. This aspect is by and large neglected both by Chinese media and international media. So I wrote down my experience in 2017.

While speculating whether China will fall into the "middle-income trap", western media seems to have overlooked the foundation of economic development for a country. Those media, usually out of ideological bias, tend to believe that huge bubbles exist within China's rapid development. China's development has the same recipe as most western countries—technological progress and significant productivity increases.

So, can China's technological progress continue to support its economic development in the future? Only by clarifying this question can we know whether China will fall into the "middle-income trap", and people could find the answer while watching the National 3D Digital Innovation & Design Competition in December 2018. In this competition kicked off in the small city of Yuxi in Yunnan Province, the audience would feel the enthusiasm for technological progress among young Chinese innovators and users.

The competitors present exquisite products and novel designs made with new 3D craftsmanship, such as 3D printing and 3D design. However, these new objects were inaccessible to normal people before the emergence of 3D technology, when industrial designs were done on flat paper endless trials were necessary to get a product to a satisfactory result. The traditional industrial design could have ignored many unthought problems and the final products could not match the design. Besides, the traditional industrial design and production process causes more waste of labor, materials, and time.

3D technology makes the design and production process much simpler—industrial design is done on the computer, where 3D imaging technology can vividly delineate the appearance of the product. Time and materials would be saved as many assembly trials could be excluded from the production process.

3D technology will revolutionize manufacturing, and China is not left behind in this major transformation. Although entering into the era of 3D technology at the same time as other developed countries, China's manufacturing industry still needs to gain more competitive advantage by greatly develop of this new technology.

An interesting phenomenon in this 3D competition is, in front of the judges who are all professors or industrial gurus from top institutions, most participant students were from the 2nd or even 3rd tier universities. While Chinese students in prestigious universities are occupied with cutting-edge scientific researches and academic paper publications, other students find their vocation in technological development that could significantly improve China's manufacturing industry. This technological R&D might seem trivial in the beginning, but in the future, they can take China's manufacturing industry to the next level and make it invincible in the world market.

National competitiveness cannot only be shaped by those top universities or companies; the key relies on the enthusiasm of the general public to participate in nation-building. When the United States rose to prominence in the early 20th century, its manufacturing and agricultural productivity quickly surpassed that of the European industrial nations. It was not the Ivy League universities that brought the US to the center of the world stage, but the state universities. At that time, state universities were established everywhere, and most of them had only two disciplines in the beginning—mechanics and agronomy. These state universities trained a large number of engineers and agronomists who contribute to the overall productivity increase, and the strong foundation helped the United States quickly caught up with the industrial powers of Europe.

These second-and third-tier universities in China are like the state universities in the United States back then, where the talents might not be able to compete in the field of cutting-edge science but would become the solid foundation to upgrade China's manufacturing industry. These students with an innovative spirit and active participation are the true future of China.

Green Development Has Become the Main Theme of China's Economic Development

In recent years, China has increasingly emphasized the idea of green development. The zeal to be the GDP champion is now replaced by the pursuit of high-quality sustainable development. China's green development is mainly reflected in several major progress: restoration of the ecological environment, promotion of forestry industry, innovation in renewable energy and clean energy industry, development in green finance, and international cooperation to promote the idea of green development.

After decades of efforts, China has made world-recognized achievements in restoring the ecological environment. Today, desertification is a common problem faced by many countries, and global climate change and excessive exploitation of nature are the reasons for its aggravation. However, China has made remarkable achievements in afforestation and oases recreating to combat desertification.

For more than 30 years, through the efforts of several generations of "desertification combaters", nearly one-third of the Hobq Desert in Inner Mongolia has been effectively treated. Today, this region conceals more than 24 billion cubic meters of water, where a 500-billion RMB economic cluster of desert tourism, food, and photovoltaics are forming along with the gradual restoration of the ecological environment.

Not far from Beijing, the miracle happened in the Sekhangba as well. Because of excessive logging and poor management, the once hunting ground for the Qing Dynasty royal family was turned into a wasteland in the 1950s, with no original forest left. After 60 years of hard work by two generations, Sekhangba is now a popular vacation destination, with thousands of hectares of the forest again.

On the border between Shaanxi and Inner Mongolia is the Mawusu Desert, with a total area of 42,200 square kilometers. After decades of a treatment since the 1960s, 30 % of the Mawusu Desert is now covered with vegetation, 80 % of the area has been treated, and soil erosion has ceased while reducing the annual sediment flow into the Yellow River by 400 million tons. The newly reclaimed farmland has reached 1.6 million acres[8], generating tremendous economic benefits for local farmers.

Erik Solheim, the UN Under-Secretary-General and UNEP Executive Director, once spoke highly of China's active exploration in desertification control and dust storm prevention. Solheim was quite impressed by the high-tech ecological technology used in Hobq Desert Sand Control Project and the eco-tourism projects developed by local herders, and "the development model of the ecological economics of the Hobq Desert provides experience for other countries and regions that are facing desertification problems". In the Hobq model, science and technology drive the development of enterprises, industrial development drives the scale of sand control, and ecological improvement drives people's livelihood. Solheim believes that China's experience in sand control can also spread to

Africa, the Middle East, Latin America, where more people along with the Belt and Road Initiative would be benefited from sustainable development[9].

China's forests, grasslands, and wetlands are all expanding, which brings a hugely beneficial impact on the overall climate. In northern China, especially in Beijing, the yellow sandy sky in spring is no longer a common sight. Since the launch of the Return of Farmland to Forest Project in 1999, China has accumulated return more than 500 million acres of farmland to forest and grassland, with a total investment of more than 500 billion RMB. In 2018, the National Forestry and Grassland Administration was established along with the National Park Administration, which unified the management of national parks and other types of nature reserves. In Pilot sites such as Qilian Mountain, Northeast Tiger, and Leopard National Park, Sanjiangyuan, Shennongjia, and Qianjiangyuan, natural resource monitoring platforms have been initially built with the foundation to eventually realize a 3D natural resource and ecological environment monitoring pattern system. Each national park pilot area has launched projects such as forest (ginseng) land clearing and forest restoration, ecological corridor construction, alien species removal, special remediation of tea mountains, and ecological treatment of bare mountains.

The logging industry was once an important part of China's industrial system, but the disappearance of large areas of the forest also causes dramatic climate change. How can China meet the demand for raw materials during industrialization and urbanization, while protecting valuable forest resources? Bamboo could the solution. China has a tradition of growing bamboo forests and using moso bamboo for economic development. In recent years, some regions have begun to experiment replacing wood with moso bamboo. Anji County in Zhejiang Province typically represents the successful development of the bamboo industry in recent years. Bamboo grows quickly, and generally, two- or three- year old moso bamboo can be cut down for raw material; the large bamboo forests are also important tourism destinations. Today, Anji County receives about 500,000 tourists every year, and the tourism industry generates more than 30 million RMB. Besides, bamboo has become a cultural symbol of Anji County as well, with the native folk performances such as Anji Bamboo Orchestra and the "Bamboo Dragon" dance of Shangshe Village featuring various arts and cultural exhibitions in China and beyond.

Farmers could not only plant mushrooms along with the bamboos, but also raise chickens, goats, and other livestock in the bamboo forests. Bamboo-related industries have also flourished in Anji County, such as furniture, fiber, fabrics, flooring, charcoal, and other industries that use bamboo as raw material. Many new jobs are created, and the import of moso bamboo from other provinces is even sometimes required to meet the demand of local production.

China's achievements in the field of renewable energy and clean energy are also remarkable. The Chinese government pledged at the Paris Climate Conference that China will vigorously strengthen the development and use of renewable energy sources, aimed at increasing the share of non-fossil energy in primary energy consumption to about 15 % by 2020 and reducing CO2 emissions per unit of GDP by 40 % to 50 % compared to 2005. China will become the largest producer and consumer of renewable energy.

Hydropower occupies an important position while developing renewable energy. Since the 21st century, with the reform of China's energy system, the whole society was mobilized to participate in the development and construction of hydropower, which has greatly accelerated hydropower development. In 2004, with the commissioning of Unit 1 of Gongboxia Hydropower Station, China's installed hydropower capacity exceeded 100 million kilowatts, surpassing the total capacity of the United States. In 2010, the installed hydropower capacity exceeded 200 million kilowatts after the commissioning of Unit 4 of Xiaowan Hydropower Station. At present, China not only owns the world's largest hydropower capacity but also has the largest and fastest construction projects of hydropower units. China is the global center of hydropower innovation.

Solar energy is another focus of China's renewable energy development. In recent years, China has invested heavily in the research and development of solar power technology, which rapidly increases the production capacity of its solar-related industries. China's solar panel production accounts for about 60 % of the world's total production; in 2007, its photovoltaic panel production value was 15 billion RMB, with a photovoltaic power generation capacity of about 820,000 kWh. In 2009, the Chinese government implemented the milestone Golden Sun Demonstration Project, and many provinces accordingly developed their tailor-made plans for solar industries as well. China has a comprehensive spectrum of solar power technology, and it also leads in the fields of photovoltaic panels and thin-film solar cells.

China's wind power industry has also grown rapidly in recent years. Since 2005, China's installed wind power capacity has doubled for five consecutive years. In 2009, its installed wind power capacity reached 25.8 million kilowatts, surpassing Germany and ranking second in the world. In 2010, 16 million kilowatts of new wind power capacity were added, allowing China to surpass the United States. China has established large wind power bases in Xinjiang, Inner Mongolia, Gansu, Hebei, and Jilin, while megawatts offshore wind power bases are built in coastal provinces such as Jiangsu, Shanghai, Shandong, and Zhejiang. According to a report by the Global Wind Energy Council at the 8th Asian Wind Energy Conference and International Wind Energy Equipment Exhibition in June 2011, China's installed wind power capacity is expected to reach 250 million kilowatts by 2020 and more than 500 million kilowatts by 2030.

The nuclear power industry grows rapidly in China as well. By the end of 2017, China had 37 nuclear power units in commercial operation, with an installed capacity of about 35.81 million kilowatts; meanwhile, 19 nuclear power units are under construction, with an installed capacity of about 22 million kilowatts. According to the 13th Five-Year Energy Plan, China will have 58 million kilowatts of nuclear power in operation and 30 million kilowatts under construction by 2020. To accomplish this goal, China's installed nuclear power capacity should grow at a CAGR of 17.43 % from 2018 to 2020. The development potential of China's nuclear power industry is huge in the long term, as the installed capacity of its nuclear power pipeline and reserve projects was about 164 million kilowatts, according to the World Nuclear Association.

Green development requires more financial support, and China has also made efforts in recent years to explore various channels to promote green finance. Currently, China's green credit has exceeded RMB 9 trillion and has established the world's largest green bond market.

China's green finance is characterized by several "most". First, the growing fastest speed. The issuance amount and stock value of China's green bond have been ranking the first since 2016, and the balance of green loans has been constantly growing, comprising nearly 10 % of total corporate loans; second, the most comprehensive policy framework. The Guidance on Building a Green Financial System, the top-level institutional documents, was jointly issued by the People's Bank of China and others in 2016, along with a series of specific policies on green bonds, green credit, assessment, and information disclosure, which provides institutional safeguards for the standardized development of green finance. According to the top-level institutional design, provinces and cities have also introduced many specific implementation measures to provide guarantees for green loans and interest subsidies. Third, the most cutting-edge regional pilot projects. The pilot zones in five provinces (regions)—Zhejiang, Jiangxi, Guangdong, Guizhou, and Xinjiang—has accumulated abundant practical experience for the future construction of the national green financial system.

While realizing long-term domestic achievements, China looks forward to sharing its experience with other developing countries. As a result, China is actively cooperating with the international community in all aspects of the green economy. In 2007, the African Union launched the "Great Green Wall" program, planning to plant a 15-km-wide and 7600-km-long forest belt across West and East Africa to prevent further expansion of the Sahara Desert. In 2017, the Xinjiang Institute of Ecology and Geography of the Chinese Academy of Sciences formally participate in the Great Green Wall program. Besides, China is also transferring its technological experience to Mauritania in combating desertification to Africa.

China has taught mycorrhiza cultivation technology to other African countries as well. The newly-trained technical personnel effectively manage the forestry damage caused by the growth of mycorrhiza in some parts of Africa, and they also protected slopes and prevented soil erosion. China has exported a large number of solar and wind power generation products to countries around the world, helping many of them reduce the price of solar power generation and making great contributions to global sustainable development. In many developing countries in Asia, Africa, and Latin America that lack technical capacity, China has helped them build a large number of renewable energy power facilities with a donation and low-interest loans, solving technical and financial problems and allowing these developing countries to participate in the global action to reduce CO2 emissions.

China is also actively promoting global cooperation of green finance. In 2016, China included issues about green finance in the G20 summit for the first time. In 2017, China established the network of green finance regulators as one of the initiating countries. in 2018, the Green Finance Committee of the China Society of Finance and the Financial City of London jointly released "Green Investment Principles in 'One Belt, One Road' ". During the implementation of the Belt and Road Initiative, China and many countries have signed memorandums of cooperation on green finance, and China hopes that the investment projects along the BRI regions will become a model for the development of the green investment.

China has made evident progress in green development over the year, and it is praised as a model by relevant UN organizations. China could better summarize its previous experience and share them through international cooperation so that green development can become an important part of China's contribution to the global economy in the 21st century.

Notes

1 Translator's note. https://www.barrons.com/articles/china-s-p-downgrades-debt-rating-citing-financial-risks-1505998287

2 Translator's note. https://www.reuters.com/article/us-china-economy-imf-idINKBN1950KR

3 These approaches have created skepticism in the market, and the negative interest rates policy in developed countries even caused widespread panic for the investors and consumers. Usually, the market would react in the opposite way to what the central banks expected, for example, investors would pull out the money and transfer the capital to other countries.

4 Central Literature Research Office. Selected Important Documents Since the 18th Plenum of the Chinese Communist Party: Volume I. Beijing: Central Literature Publishing House, 2014

5 Li Keqiang hosted an executive meeting of the State Council to deploy the healthy development of sharing economy [EB/OL].(2017-06-22). http://www.cac.gov.cn/2017- 06/22/c1121187321.htm.

6 Li Keqiang: regulation of e-commerce and mobile payments should be inclusive and prudent [EB/OL].(2017-06-27). http://www.xinhuanet.com/money/2017-06/27/c129641944.htm.

7 Minitel is a national network built by the French in 1982, was established and operated before the Internet, with 25 million users, but was eventually replaced by the Internet due to high operating costs and outdated technology, and was officially closed on June 30, 2012.—Editor's Note

8 1 acre ≈ 666.67 square meters—Editor

9 Solheim: China's experience in sand control is worth learning from the world [EB/OL]. (2017-07-05). http://www.xinhuanet.com/tech/2017-07/05/c_1121270605.htm.

2

Core Competitiveness of China's Equipment Manufacturing Industry and National Economic Growth

I was once asked in 2015 by a Western journalist about the rapid progress of Chinese high speed train industry. The subtext was that China had borrowed heavily from technologies from Japan and Europe, a reoccurring topic which comes up frequently in regards to China's progress. I explained that behind China's fast progress, there are a number of factors which are usually ignored by outsiders. For instance, China's high speed train's locomotive is created in one piece, by a massive hydraulic press compared to that of Japan which is created in two pieces and then welded together. China's one piece design is stronger and can therefore withstand higher speeds. The heavy industrial equipment and engineering that went into creating Chinese high speed train allow Chinese manufacturing sector to produce remarkable dividends, both in terms of lower costs, faster production and superior performance. Responding to the reporters questions prompted me to reflect on China's economic development and how it is seen by many outside China.

The dominant narrative of various countries and media groups is that China's economic progress is due solely to foreign investment in China. That China's industrial basis was a product solely of outside innovation and funding. While foreign investment certainly was a major factor in creating more jobs, opportunities, and increasing China's industrial production capabilities, without China's own innovations and adaptions of processes and industries China would have been but a poor shadow of what it has actually achieved.

In recent years, the export of China's high-speed rail has attracted many attentions. However, few would ask why and how China's high-speed rail has grown so fast. What are the forces driving China's large, and still growing, annual exports? Behind the impressive figures is the development of China's equipment manufacturing industry, to which people pay fewer attention behind this eye-catching news. Only after understanding China's equipment manufacturing industry can people understand the major drivers in the development of the Chinese economy.

The Difficult Start of China's Equipment Manufacturing Industry

Since the founding of the People's Republic of China in 1949, the Chinese government has always attached great importance to the development of the equipment manufacturing industry. In 1961, China produced its first 10,000-ton hydraulic press, which was a huge technological breakthrough at that time. Today, China can produce a wide range of presses, and its technology in this area is quite mature. However, at the beginning of the reform and opening up, if China wanted to significantly improve the level of equipment manufacturing, it was supposed to use a lot of foreign exchange to import equipment. At that time China's foreign exchange was very tight, so it soon became unsustainable.

China's development has somehow gone through a process of reform first and then opening up later. China used to widely open its market to foreign investment because China's equipment manufacturing industry could not meet the needs of economic development, so it had to invite others to invest. At that time, China did not have foreign exchange to import advanced equipment nor have the ability to produce that equipment.

It is very rare, in the world economic history, that a country as large as China to use a completely open market approach to promote development. When Westerners talk about the rapid development of East Asian economies, they often compare China with Japan and Korea—China's development model is very different. Japan's and Korea's development relied on something other than openness; they both relied on borrowing money in international capital markets, importing technology, and then exporting products abroad to make money to pay off their debts. In fact, the 2 Eastern Asian tigers have much closed economy. According to American economist Nicholas Lardy, China's economy is more open than Japan's. China's open development policy is "really open" at the early stage of reform and opening up.

It was difficult for China to issue bonds in the international market, and with the shortage of foreign exchange, China had no way to introduce key technologies to develop its equipment manufacturing industry. Therefore, China's equipment manufacturing industry had a very difficult start, and it used to develop very slowly despite having the government prioritized support.

The Rapid Development of China's Equipment Manufacturing Industry

The "Eleventh Five-Year Plan" and "Twelfth Five-Year Plan" have delineated the modernization process of China's equipment manufacturing industry in detail, and remarkable achievements were achieved after the combined 10 years of development. Today, China's infrastructure construction has exceeded many developed countries, and this astonishing speed can not be separated from the development of the equipment manufacturing industry.

For example, every year Beijing has one or two new subway lines opened; meanwhile, subway system in Paris, London, and New York have taken hundred years of construction to reach their current size. In 2016, Beijing's subway has become one of the largest subway systems in the world—within just 20 years. However, people should also remember that Beijing had only two subway lines for a long time, and that was also a period of slow development for China's equipment manufacturing industry. Infrastructure construction must be based on the development of equipment manufacturing.

In the 1990s, I visited the construction site of the English Channel Tunnel and found that there were only two brands of shield machines for digging the tunnel, one was Siemens and the other was Mitsubishi. With the development of China's equipment manufacturing industry, today many Chinese companies are also able to produce shield machines, which have greatly contributed to the construction of infrastructure projects such as subways. In addition to Beijing, many other cities in China (such as Chengdu, Kunming, and Hangzhou) are also building subways. Without the progress of China's equipment manufacturing industry, not to mention the fact that German and Japanese companies cannot produce the amount of equipment to meet China's needs, China cannot afford to pay their exorbitant price neither. China's high-speed rails must go through the mountains, and the construction of high-speed rail need for large-scale industrial equipment are mainly made in China. Without the development of China's equipment manufacturing industry, all of this would never have been possible.

In the rescue of some major international disasters in recent years, machinery and equipment produced in China can be found. In Japan's Fukushima nuclear accident rescue site, people could find the machinery and equipment marked with Sany Heavy Industries. In the mining accident in Colombia, Chinese enterprises rushed ahead to provide a huge pipe for the rescue of miners and used mechanical equipment to beat the pipe into the ground. It can be seen that China's equipment manufacturing industry has made great progress over the years, which is not only reflected in China's domestic infrastructure construction, but also in the rescue operations of major international accidents, which greatly enhanced the image of China's equipment manufacturing industry, expanding China's influence in the world.

In recent years, China has exported more and more machinery and equipment, and China has surpassed Germany and the United States to become the world's largest exporter of machinery and equipment. The export of machinery and equipment has ensured the growth of China's trade volume and also changed the structure of China's foreign trade, bringing huge profits to Chinese enterprises. To give a simple example, Jinan No. 2 Machine Tool Factory makes automotive molds. One mold costs 80,000 RMB in China, but the market price for export to the United States is 58,000 USD. The United States Ford Motor Company recently replaced two sets of assembly lines from the Jinan Second Machine Tool Factory. All of this demonstrates the progress of China's equipment manufacturing industry. The export trade of China's equipment manufacturing industry has helped Chinese companies to gain a lot of profits and has contributed to the reform of China's foreign trade structure.

The export of China's railroad technology has also made great progress and opened up huge markets. Some of China's railroad technology has been acquired through purchases, some from Japan, some from France, Germany, and Canada, and has been absorbed and adapted to form China's technology. What supports the progress of China's railroad technology is also the equipment manufacturing industry, for example, the streamlined head of high-speed rail is formed in one press. China has an 80,000-ton hydraulic press that can form the front end of the Harmony in a single press. The technology of Japanese Shinkansen is also very advanced, but the front end of the Shinkansen train is not as good as the front end of Chinese high-speed rail, because Japan does not have such a large hydraulic press, the front end of the Shinkansen train is pressed into two pieces and then welded. China's equipment manufacturing industry is more advanced than Japan's, the competitiveness of China's high-speed rail is stronger than

Japan's Shinkansen, and the ability of China's one-shot headstock to resist wind is stronger. These technological developments are supported by the equipment manufacturing industry.

Massive Market for China's Equipment Manufacturing Industry

Urbanization and the development of the equipment manufacturing industry go side by side in China: urbanization creates a massive market for industrial development, while China's self-dependent innovation in the equipment manufacturing industry accelerates its urbanization.

China has constructed more than half of the skyscrapers in the world. The core lying under the glass, concrete, and steel is China's state-of-art civil engineering technology and equipment manufacturing industry. Mr. Liang Wengen, chairman of Sany Heavy Industry, was once in a TV show being asked about "In how many international megaprojects have Sany participated", and the global equipment manufacturing tycoon rhetorically responded, "I am wondering if you could tell me, how many international megaprojects have not Sany's equipments?" In fact, from the Burj Khalifa Tower to Hong Kong-Zhuhai-Macao Bridge, Sany is everywhere.

China has made a significant breakthrough in smart construction with an independently designed product, called the "Aerial Construction Machine". This intelligent equipment comprises a construction platform and other supporting technology, which enables in-place casting of reinforced concrete in high-rise buildings through mechanic operation and smart control, both efficiently and intelligently. The significant "aerial" feature means that the whole construction process would be completed on the platform of each floor in the air. By setting up a mobile "construction factory", the machine could replace human labor in terms of integrating the casting of reinforced concrete in the construction of the high-rising (or super high-rising) buildings. The erection of skyscrapers in China has been significantly accelerated by such an "aerial construction machine".

In recent years, China has rapidly knitted the biggest national high-speed railway network, crossing the varied topography from mountains to waters. The accelerating development is inseparable from a special kind of equipment—the tunnel crossing bridge girder erection machine. This machine has at least halved the construction period of the 345.5-kilometer-long Chongqing-Guiyang railway to the shortest period of 5 years, during which 209 new bridges were constructed amid the endless mountainous region.

The tunnel crossing bridge girder erection machine combines both the functions of transportation and bridge erection. This giant "bumblebee" is 72-meter long and 9-meter high and has 64 large radial tires, which could diligently carry the bridge girder along the railway route and directly install it at the end of the road. Based on the real-time data such as speed, direction, and collision detection synthesized from more than 100 incorporated sensors, the machine operators could be informed of the precise construction situation and perform the exact control and operation needed.

Computer numerical control (CNC) machine tools belong to the cutting edge of equipment manufacturing, serving as the "mother machine" to make other important equipment. As the manufacturing technology of CNC machine tools used to be monopolized by few developed countries, it could cost China a fortune to purchase the machines and become a "stranglehold" due to export control.

China has made significant breakthroughs in the CNC machine tools industry in the past years, among which the most remarkable progress is the manufacturing technology of the heavy-duty machine tools. Nowadays, the annual output and sales of the Chinese-made heavy-duty CNC machine tools rank first in the world, including the heavy-duty CNC gantry boring and milling machines, heavy-duty CNC floor-type boring and milling machines, heavy-duty CNC horizontal lathe machines, and heavy-duty CNC vertical lathe machines. The output value of Chinese CNC machine tools is almost the sum of the output of the German and Japanese, maintaining its first place in the world for many years.

Another "national treasure" in the heavy industry is the closed-die hydraulic press forge, as this strategic equipment is an important measurement of China's national (military) industrial strength. There are just a few countries in the world that can develop this symbolic creature. Only four countries have the forges that can exert more than 40,0000 tons of pressure, including China, the United States, Russia, and France. In 2014, the Chinese 80,000-ton closed-die hydraulic press forge broke the 51-year record maintained by the former Soviet Union in one fell swoop, which terminates the time when Chinese large forgings were controlled by foreign countries.

Besides, Tsinghua University has developed a 160,000-ton hydraulic die forging press, whose magnitude greatly exceeds the current capacity in the manufacturing industry. In comparison, the Russian die forging hydraulic press is 75,000 tons, and that of the United States is 45,000 tons.

The essence of "Made in China" is not just about the size of equipment but also the ingeniousness of the machine. The machining accuracy of Chinese heavy-duty machine tools is 0.008 mm, about 1/10 of the diameter of a hair. This precision-level significantly contributes to the power generation capacity and the manufacturing capability of ocean-going vessels. China's "aircraft carrier" machining center is 15-meter high, 22-meter wide, 39-meter long, which weighs 900 tons. It can process steel materials as the size of a basketball court into any shape, such as the low-pressure inner cylinder and high-pressure outer cylinder of the million-kilowatt class nuclear power unit.

The quiet performance of submarines is the core indicator of its combat capability, and the Chinese Navy has been criticized for its poor performance in this regard. The US military even once claimed that they would be able to detect the position as soon as the Chinese submarine left the port. Today, this hyperbole has become history because of China's remarkable technological breakthrough. At present, China could manufacture quieter propeller after the commissioning of the seven-axis six-linked propeller processing machine tools.

The seven-axis six-linkage processing machine tool is currently the largest and most complex machine tool in the world, and its successful production symbolizes the international competitiveness of China's machine tool companies.

For example, CITIC Heavy Industries has successfully developed a CNC heavy-duty machine tool for crankshafts with full-function and high-precision. The independent intellectual property of this manufacturing technology enables China to get rid of heavy reliance on the imported large-scale marine crankshafts, making it the third country that can independently design and manufacture crankshaft processing equipment after Germany and Japan. Another Chinese industrial giant, Qiqihar Heavy CNC Equipment, has also independently developed the first heavy-duty CNC multi-tasking milling machine tools for crankshafts in China, which manufactured the first full set of marine engine crankshaft that is made in China.

More than 70 % parts of the mid-to-high-end machine tools are developed and manufactured domestically. The five-axis CNC machine tools made in China are recognized overseas as well. When Chinese companies export advanced CNC machine tools to Germany, it signifies the end of the technological monopoly of the developed countries, which guarantee the robust technical support and equipment supply for the development of Chinese defense industry.

China's Equipment Manufacturing Industry Goes to the World

With the globalization of China's economy, more and more brands of the Chinese equipment manufacturing industry have gone to the international market. In recent years, among the machinery and equipment exported from China, there are three most popular ones: locomotives, port equipment, and advanced CNC machine tools.

China produces locomotives for the construction of railroads and subways in many countries around the world. The two leading companies in China's locomotive manufacturing industry are China Southern Railway (CSR) Group and China Northern Railway (CNR) Group, which have become more competitive after their merger to form the CRRC Group. CRRC Group not only takes advantage of the development of China's high-speed railway to develop new locomotives and carriages but also promotes its products globally under the "One Belt, One Road" initiative. At present, locomotives and carriages produced by CRRC Group have been exported to 105 countries and regions worldwide, and 83 % of the countries with railroads in the world are using CNR Group's products.

In the process of international development, CSR Group has built an international strategic platform of products, technology, service, capital, and management. CNR Group has established the largest manufacturing base in South Africa in the southern hemisphere, realizing the overall export of products, technology, services, and materials. By utilizing its rich experience in high-end equipment manufacturing, CSR Group provides customized and integrated solutions for customers to build six transportation systems of safe transportation, green transportation, intelligent transportation, convenient transportation, tourism transportation, and value transportation so that people in all countries can enjoy the convenient travel brought by CRRC solutions.

The CRRC Group has established advanced localization bases in the United States, Australia, South Africa, Malaysia, and other countries, and actively implements the working mode of localized manufacturing, localized labor, localized procurement, localized maintenance, and localized management, and continuously promotes the rearrangement of the global value chain, industrial chain and supply chain of high-end equipment manufacturing. The subway manufacturing base invested and built by The CRRC Group in Boston, USA has won wide praise from all circles.

By investing in new construction, mergers and acquisitions, capacity cooperation, and other forms, CNR Group has continuously participated in the global high-end market competition. At present, CSR Group has set up 83 overseas subsidiaries and 15 overseas R&D centers in 26 countries and regions around the world, forming a global business system.

The business system has been established all over the world. The overseas assets of CSR Group have increased from RMB 3 billion in 2013 to more than RMB 34 billion in 2018, and the order volume in the overseas market has increased from USD 3.5 billion in 2013 to USD 6.3 billion in 2018. These overseas subsidiaries can not only operate effectively but also truly integrate into the local society and become a respected enterprise by local people.

CSR Group has great respect for the cultural traditions of each country. The subsidiary in Malaysia has designed a special vehicle for women, which is suitable for the local culture and religious beliefs and is very popular among the locals. Through the method of "taking in" and "going out", CNR Group has trained many high-end talents for Malaysia's equipment manufacturing industry and strengthened the foundation of talents. Besides, by supporting local enterprises and recommending domestic suppliers to build local factories, CNR Group has also promoted the transformation and upgrading of Malaysia's rail transportation industry. When natural disasters occur, the staff of CSR Group also donate to the Malaysian people for disaster relief and dedication. Because of this, the order volume of CSR Group in Malaysia has accumulated more than 10 billion yuan, which is a model of China-Malaysia trade cooperation.

In May 2018, the first batch of 4 cars tailored by CNR Group for the Boston Orange Line subway was tested online at Wellington Station. Massachusetts Governor Charlie Baker said that this is the first time in nearly 40 years that Boston's Orange and Red Line subways to have been updated to a new generation. The 152 Orange Line cars and 252 Red Line cars ordered by the Massachusetts Bay Transportation Authority from CNR will replace the existing older cars on both lines and will be put into service gradually.

The Boston subway is the first subway system in the United States and has been in service for more than 100 years since 1897. CRRC Group has the full intellectual property rights of the new subway vehicles, which are the first batch of subway vehicles produced in China according to U.S. standards. These subway cars not only meet the high requirements of the United States in terms of technology, localization, and laws but also use a more user-friendly design to improve the travel experience of passengers. The new Orange Line trains will be operated in 6-car sets, and if all of them are put into service, the interval between trains during peak hours will be shortened from 6 to 7 minutes to 4 and a half minutes, which means that the passenger volume per hour will be increased by about 40 %.

The first manufacturing facility in the U.S., the Springfield plant, is already in operation. The Springfield plant will be responsible for the assembly of hundreds of subway cars and the local production of subsequent Boston subway cars. Currently, the Springfield plant has 156 employees. The Springfield plant currently employs 156 people, and CNR is committed to hiring another 150 or so local employees by 2021. We are already ahead of schedule," said Jia Bo, vice president of CNR's Massachusetts office. By 2021, we expect to employ 260 people." Other projects built by CNR Group in the United States include the Los Angeles subway project and the Philadelphia double-decker bus project.

China provides 80 % of the machinery and equipment for ports worldwide. Over the years, when looking at ports in Europe, the Americas, and elsewhere, one can see that most ports have bridge cranes nearly 10 meters high, and most of them are marked with the ZPMC logo, from Rotterdam to Hamburg, from San Francisco to Busan. These "steel giants" have witnessed the rapid development of China's equipment manufacturing industry.

In 1992, Deng Xiaoping issued the famous "Southern Talk", which opened a new climax of China's reform and opening up. At that time, Guan Tongxian, who was the deputy director of the Water Transport Department of the Ministry of Communications, was greatly impressed by the enthusiasm of this round of reform and came up with the idea of founding a harbor machinery manufacturing enterprise[1].

At the end of the 1980s, the core technology of port machinery was in the hands of Western countries, Japan and South Korea, which controlled large orders for key port equipment and occupied 95 % of the world market at that time. market. As a "latecomer", Guan Tongxian had a keen observation of the future of the port machinery industry and firmly believed that it was necessary to establish a port machinery manufacturing enterprise in China.

To enable the rapid development of Shanghai Zhenhua Heavy Industries Co., Ltd. (ZPMC), Guan Tongxian used talents without any restriction. He implementated the incentive-based management mechanism and set up the "ZPMC Meritorious Minister" award with more than 1 million RMB bonus—the winners will only be judged by his or her contribution, regardless of position, education, identity—all the changes were totally new to the Chinese state-own enterprises. This incentive mechanism not only enhances the staff's enthusiasm for learning, but also allows ZPMC to train a large number of English-speaking skilled welders. Therefore, ZPMC occupies a linguistic advantage when entering overseas market, and receives consistent praise from enterprises in various countries. Until today, the nearly 10,000 welders of ZPMC still form the basis of the competitiveness of the company, which cannot find the second one in the world. The perfect talent incentive mechanism maintains the enthusiasm of employees. The encouragement of innovation has enabled ZPMC to have dozens of world top technologies with independent intellectual property rights; in product innovation, Guan Tongxian has set the goal of "at least one world firstborn technology every year", and ZPMC has gradually occupied the leading position of port machinery manufacturing technology.

In 1998, the United States launched six international tenders for port machinery, ZPMC was the only five; in 2000, ZPMC with fully automatic port machinery, the first time entered the German market; in 2004, ZPMC signed a large order across the year and occupied the largest global market share; in 2008, ZPMC has controlled more than 70 % of the global port machinery market share, becoming the undisputed "king of port machinery".

In just a few decades, Guan Tongxian has won purchase orders from 76 countries and regions, and ZPMC has been invincible in the international market competition and won many battles, which is a model of the Chinese machinery manufacturing industry. Guan Tongxian also finally achieved the ambition of the year: "Where there is a container port in the world, there must be ZPMC container cranes in operation."

According to the statistics of the British authoritative magazine *World Cargo News*, between June 2015 and June 2016, 222 out of a total 271 orders for shore bridges were signed by ZPMC, accounting for 82 % of global market share. This is the 18th consecutive year that ZPMC ranked first in the world in the global port machinery market. In 2016, the output value of ZPMC reached the highest peak since its establishment in 1992, and the market share of ZPMC's port machinery products reached more than 80 % worldwide[2].

ZPMC was founded with only a dozen employees, but today has nearly 40,000 employees and is one of the world's largest manufacturers of large cranes. Today, ZPMC's products not only cover the major container ports in China but also enter major ports abroad. About 78 countries and regions around the world, more than 150 ports have the figure of ZPMC port machinery. For example, Vancouver in Canada, Miami, Long Beach, Oakland, Tacoma, Seattle, and New York on the east and west coast of the United States; countries in South America such as Brazil, Venezuela, and Colombia; countries in Asia such as Singapore, Thailand, Malaysia, Indonesia, Myanmar, Oman, and the United Arab Emirates.

ZPMC has more than 20 world-leading core technologies, 28 national key new products, 16 Shanghai key new products; applied for 223 domestic patents, including 103 invention patents, 113 utility patents, 7 design patents; applied for 24 valid international patents, 10 valid international authorized patents.

In addition to port machinery, China's ability to manufacture machine tools has also made leaps and bounds. High-precision CNC machine tools made in China have been exported to European countries.

China has been developing its machine tool manufacturing industry in a planned manner since the 1950s. However, for a long time, the progress of China's machine tool manufacturing industry was too slow to meet the rapid development of China's economy, and the Chinese manufacturing industry relied heavily on imported machine tools. In recent years, the demand for heavy industrial products such as national defense, aviation, high-speed rail, automobiles, and molds in China has increased significantly, driving the rapid development of the machine tool industry. in 2010, the market sales of CNC machine tools in China reached 360,000 units, which grew to 627,000 units in 2016. Driven by the national plan to revitalize the equipment manufacturing industry and the transfer of the international industrial chain, the investment in the acquisition of equipment and tools in China has grown steadily and is expected to remain at an annual growth rate of about 20 % in the next 5 to 10 years, and the demand for machine tool industry will still maintain high growth. With the deepening of China's economic restructuring, CNC machine tools and the CNC system industry will continue to maintain rapid development.

Most CNC machine tools produced in China have primary intelligent functions. However, for a long time, China's independent production of CNC machine tools are mainly low-end products, high-end CNC machine tools still have to rely on imports. 2017 January to September, China's imports of CNC machine tools amounted to 18.7 billion yuan, and the annual imports of CNC machine tools amounted to 22 billion yuan, showing a continuous downward trend. In terms of exports, according to statistics of CCID Consulting Group, China's CNC machine tool exports will maintain a rapid growth trend in the next few years[3]. 2017, China's CNC machine tool exports exceeded imports for the first time. Behind the continuous growth of the export value of CNC machine tools and the continuous decline of the import, value is the steady improvement of the technical level of China's CNC machine tools.

As the comprehensive strength of China's CNC machine tool industry continues to improve, there are more and more large foreign companies choosing to enter the Chinese market. in October 2016, EMAG Group, a leading global metalworking solutions provider, held an opening ceremony in Yongchuan, Chongqing, officially announcing the establishment of EMAG (Chongqing)

Machinery Co. Previously, the EMAG Group had already invested in two plants in Jiangsu Province, China, one in Taicang in 2003 and the other in Jintan in 2014.

Western countries as well as Japan and South Korea used to occupy the high-end market for CNC machine tools. The "Made in China 2025" science and technology development plan lists CNC machine tools and basic equipment manufacturing as the strategic development direction of China's manufacturing industry. In recent years, China has made some remarkable achievements in the manufacturing of CNC machine tools.

In 2013, the high-precision five-axis vertical machine tool was manufactured by Dalian KD NC Co. This is a milestone for China's machine tool manufacturing industry. The innovative equipment manufactured by Dalian KD not only broke the technological monopoly of western countries but also its machining efficiency was more than double that of imported similar machine tools.

Qiqihar No.1 Machine Tool Factory was one of the first projects introduced from the Soviet Union during the first five-year plan and made great contributions to China's machine tool manufacturing. 2007, after the restructuring of Qiqihar No.1 Machine Tool Factory, it was renamed Qiqihar Heavy-duty CNC Equipment Co. (Qi Heavy). The SMVTM1600×30/250L-NC CNC single column moving vertical turning and milling machine and HT250×280/180Y-NC CNC heavy-duty horizontal lathe developed by it were accepted by German and Italian customers. Now, Qi Heavy have already made great progress in both European and American markets.

At present, developed countries in Europe and the United States actively advocate the use of green energy to replace traditional energy. As a result, CNC turning and milling machine will be used in the field of wind power generation machinery processing. The CNC machine tool exported to Italy will be used for the processing of large hydraulic turbine spindles, power station rotors, support rollers, motor-generator shafts, and rotors, with a maximum processing diameter of 2.5 meters, a maximum load weight of 180 tons, a spindle accuracy of 0.025 mm, a total machine length of 38 meters, and a maximum processing length of 28 meters, which is the longest CNC machine tool developed by Qi Heavy CNC, and the It is the longest CNC machine tool developed by Qi Heavy CNC, and also the first CNC machine tool with processing length over 28 meters.

At present, China's production of CNC machine tools in some segments have reached the international advanced level. With the growth of domestic manufacturing demand for CNC machine tools, Chinese companies producing

CNC machine tools have greater market and development prospects to become an important supplier of CNC machine tools in the world market.

Grow Economy Through the Development of the Equipment Manufacturing Industry

The biggest threat to China's economic development is the so-called "middle-income trap". Will China fall into this trap? The key to the answer lies in how China responds to the disappearance of the demographic dividend. The disappearance of the demographic dividend will lead to a decline in productivity, and some industries in China are already moving out of the country. One of the important reasons why manufacturing in some of China's coastal provinces is starting to move overseas is that the price of labor in China is rising. As low-end manufacturing moves out, whether China's manufacturing industry can remain competitive depends largely on whether the equipment manufacturing industry can be upgraded and become stronger.

There are some good signs now, such as the rapid development of robotics related to industrial manufacturing in China. China has become the world's largest user and producer of robots. Although China has not yet fully mastered the most advanced robotics technology, it is still a leading country in the development of related technology. There is still a lot of room for investment in the use of robots and in R&D in China. Especially with the development of artificial intelligence, it will combine with robotics to create stronger intelligent productivity, giving China's manufacturing industry better prospects for growth. If this momentum continues, even if China's demographic dividend disappears, industrial robots can make up for this loss, allowing China's economy to remain highly competitive in the future.

Notes

1 Development history of Shanghai Zhenhua Heavy Industries Co., Ltd. (ZPMC) http://www.zpmc.com/lishi.aspx

2 World Cargo News. *ZPMC STS crane market share.* 01 Aug 2017 https://www.worldcargonews.com/news-in-print/zpmc-sts-crane-market-share-36058

3 CCID Consulting, Series Report on the CNC Machine Tools in China https://www.sohu.com/a/377941725_378413

3

The Reform and Development of China's Financial System

I was asked by a French media group to write two papers about China's financial reform and its currency's internationalization in 2017.
In reviewing China's financial reforms, I noted that the reform had involved both, Chinese financial systems, and financial institutions, and reflected an important change in China's thinking about its development model.
My desire in writing these papers was to help readers understand not only the financial system reforms, but also the changes that occurred in our financial institutions and the thinking and planning behind these decisions.

Historically, China has been a major financial power and has made significant contributions to the development of the global financial system. For example, China invented paper money in the Song Dynasty and was the first country in the world to issue paper money. Paper money played an important role in solving financial shortages and promoting economic development. After the Mongols occupied the Central Plains, the Yuan government tightened its control over the economy and paper money became the main currency in circulation. Marco Polo, who came to China from Europe to do business, also recounted how Venetian merchants had to exchange their gold coins for paper money to make purchases in the market.

However, the excessive expansion of finance had also brought disaster to successive Chinese regimes. At the end of the Western Han Dynasty, Wang Mang usurped the throne, established a new dynasty, and introduced currency reform, but the failure of the reform led to the rapid collapse of the new dynasty. There are few examples of regime overthrow due to mismanagement of monetary and financial affairs. A recent example is an issuance of gold yuan notes by the Kuomintang government in the 1940s, which led to financial and monetary chaos, soaring prices, and the eventual collapse of the financial system, and the loss of the Kuomintang government's popularity.

After the founding of New China, under the planned economy, the financial system was part of the planned economy, highly coordinated by the government, developed relatively slowly. After the reform and opening-up, China's financial system had to be reformed, which laid the foundation for China's economic prosperity. The future reform and development of China's financial system will have a significant impact on the future economic development of China.

Building a New Financial System

From 1953 to 1979, China implemented a "grand unified" financial system in which the People's Bank of China (PBOC) was in charge of all financial operations. The People's Bank of China exercised central banking functions and handled all specific banking operations; it was both a financial administrative organ and an economic entity operating financial services. The People's Bank of China set up branches throughout the country according to administrative divisions, and they unified according to the directive plan of the head office and practiced the separation of deposit and loan, and unified deposit and loan.

At the end of 1978, the Third Plenary Session of the Eleventh Central Committee of the Communist Party of China decided to reform and open up the country, shifting the focus of government work to economic development. The corresponding reform of the financial system began in late 1979, with the core idea of limiting government behavior to only exerting macro-control while letting the markt gradually play the role of resources allocation.

From 1979 to 1992, the construction of a new financial system, the gradual opening of the financial market, and the establishment of a macro-financial control system were the three aspects of financial reform. As the reform progressed, a multiform, multifunctional, and multi-level financial system with Chinese characteristics was initially formed with the People's Bank of China as the leader (exercising the function of the central bank), the four major state-owned specialized banks as the main body, and other banks and non-bank financial institutions co-existing. At the same time, China's financial market (including money market, securities market, and foreign exchange market) was initially established and achieved certain development.

In September 1983, the State Council decided that the People's Bank of China would exercise the functions of the central bank of China, and in January 1986, the State Council promulgated the Provisional Regulations on Banking Administration of the People's Republic of China, which established the People's Bank of China as the state organ under the leadership of the State Council to manage the financial affairs of the country, and as the central bank of the country. The Chinese government actively explored various means to improve the financial macro-control system.

Subsequently, China has established four major state-owned specialized banks with the nature of economic entities operating independently, namely Industrial and Commercial Bank of China, Agricultural Bank of China, Construction Bank of China, and Bank of China, among which Bank of China was originally specialized in foreign exchange and foreign trade.

In 1986, with the approval of the State Council, the Bank of Communications was established as a joint-stock bank. Since then, some national or regional commercial banks have been established, including CITIC Industrial Bank, China Merchants Bank, Everbright Bank, Guangdong Development Bank, Shenzhen Development Bank, Fujian Xingye Bank, Huaxia Bank, and Shanghai Pudong Development Bank.

In October 1979, China International Trust and Investment Corporation was established by the State Council to engage in the comprehensive operation of financial and trade technical services. China Everbright International Trust & Investment Corporation and China National International Investment & Trust Corporation were also established one after another. In 1987, China's first securities company, Shenzhen Special Economic Zone Securities Company, was established, followed by Shanghai Shenyin Securities Company, Shanghai Wanguo Securities Company, Haitong Securities Company, Huaxia Securities Company, etc. In November 1990, Shanghai Stock Exchange was established. In November 1990, the Shanghai Stock Exchange was established, and in December of the same year, the Shenzhen Stock Exchange was established. Besides, enterprise group finance companies, leasing companies, pawn companies, etc. also emerged.

The interbank market is the earliest, fastest-growing, and most representative market in China's money market, which developed along with the formation of the new financial system.

From 1986 to 1988, the interbank lending market was established in different parts of China, and the lending business developed rapidly. At the same time, commercial paper began to replace registered credit, and the state vigorously promoted commercial paper and developed banknote acceptance and discounting business, bringing commercial credit into the orbit of bank credit. The bill discounting market in China was then formed. Besides, since 1983, all the liquidity of Chinese domestic enterprises was supplied by bank loans. Due to the control on the scale of credit, these loans could hardly meet the short-term financing needs of enterprises, which promoted the formation of the short-term quick-impact securities market for enterprises.

In April 1988, China allowed the official listing of Treasury bills issued in 1985–1986, and since then trading has been very active, fundamentally changing the situation where there was no market for Chinese government bonds. Since 1981, some Chinese enterprises began to raise funds through the issuance of shares; from 1984 to 1985, Chinese enterprises began to carry out shareholding reforms, and as the scope of the reforms gradually expanded, China's stock market gradually developed and improved. Later, intermediary service companies such as securities registration companies were established, and a more regulated secondary market finally took shape in the early 1990s. Besides, a medium to long-term bond market for Chinese enterprises began to take shape with the issuance of three-year bonds by the Shanghai Petrochemical General Factory in 1987.

In October 1980, China started the foreign exchange transfer and quota lending business, and the foreign exchange market emerged. 1986, the foreign exchange transfer business began to be supervised by the State Administration of Foreign Exchange, and it was also the time when the foreign exchange transfer business between foreign-invested enterprises and the quota transfer business of domestic enterprises' retained foreign exchange were started. From 1988 onwards, foreign exchange transfer centers were set up in various provinces and cities, further expanding the scope of foreign exchange transfer.

Improving Financial Markets

In early 1992, Deng Xiaoping issued the "Southern Talk", and in October of the same year, the 14th National Congress of the Communist Party of China explicitly set the establishment of a socialist market economy system as the goal of China's economic system reform. In December 1993, the State Council issued the Decision on the Reform of the Financial System, starting a new round of reform of the financial system. This reform involved the transformation of the functions of the central bank, the transformation of the national specialized banks into state-owned commercial banks, the formation of policy banks, the formation of urban and rural cooperative banks, the reform of the monetary policy system (including the interest rate system), and the reform of the foreign exchange system.

First, the functions of the central bank are becoming clearer. The goal of China's monetary policy is to "maintain the stability of the currency and thus promote economic growth", which makes monetary policy much simpler, the goal is to stabilize the currency. In the past, monetary policy had a dual objective—"to stabilize the currency and to develop the economy". At the same time, the intermediary and operational objectives of the central bank's monetary policy shifted from controlling the size of credit to controlling the money supply, total social credit, interbank lending rates, and bank reserve ratios.

The Law of the People's Republic of China on the People's Bank of China, adopted in 1995, legally defined the five instruments of monetary policy as deposit reserves, central bank benchmark interest rate, rediscount rate, central bank loans, and open market operations, while the rest were included in the category of other monetary policies.

From 1996 to 1999, the People's Bank of China lowered interest rates seven times in a row, and in 1998 it made a major reform of the deposit reserve system and abolished credit scale control. This shows that the macro-financial regulation of the central bank has entered a historical period of mainly indirect regulation and control. Since the end of 1998, the People's Bank of China has set up nine major cross-provincial and municipal branches nationwide according to economic zones, completely changing the framework of setting branches according to administrative divisions in China for decades. This has far-reaching implications for reducing administrative intervention, promoting regional economic and financial development, and strengthening the central bank's financial supervision.

Second, the four major state-owned banks have also undergone commercialization reforms. The main content of the new round of reform was to transform wholly state-owned commercial banks into modern commercial banks, and the Law of the People's Republic of China on Commercial Banks promulgated in 1995 clarified that wholly state-owned commercial banks should operate on the principles of efficiency, safety, and liquidity, and should be autonomous, risk-bearing, self-financing and self-restraining. To make the four wholly state-owned banks responsible for their future operations, under the guidance of the government, these four banks cleared some of the bad debts caused by past policy requirements and undertook financial restructuring. In 1998, the Ministry of Finance issued 270 billion yuan of special treasury bonds specifically to replenish the capital of state-owned banks, bringing the capital adequacy ratio of the four banks to 4 % by 1996 standards. In 1999, the four major banks divested 1.4 trillion yuan of assets (of which 980 billion yuan were non-performing assets) to four newly established asset management companies. Besides, the four major banks further strengthened the first-tier legal entity system and implemented a strict authorized credit system; the state formally abolished loan size control, implemented asset-liability ratio management, and included operational efficiency and asset quality in the assessment of the managers of the four major banks, thus realizing a shift from administrative to economic evaluation. In addition to the above-mentioned reforms, the four major banks have also carried out many internal reforms, streamlined their organizations and personnel, and introduced some advanced management concepts and methods from abroad.

While reforming state-owned commercial banks, China also formed some policy banks and urban and rural cooperative banks. 1994 saw the establishment of three policy banks, the China Development Bank, the Export-Import Bank of China, and the Agricultural Development Bank of China, creating the necessary conditions for wholly state-owned banks to divest themselves of policy business. At the same time, the direct link between policy loans and base money was severed, which ensured the People's Bank of China's initiative in regulating base money.

Since September 1996, more than 50,000 rural credit cooperatives and more than 2,400 county federation societies have been delinked from the Agricultural Bank of China, and the business management and financial supervision of rural credit cooperatives have been assumed by county federation societies and the People's Bank of China respectively. City credit unions in each city were also merged to form city cooperative banks in 1996 and renamed as city commercial banks in 1998.

Again, in March 1997, the PBOC established the Monetary Policy Committee, and in April of the same year, the Regulations of the Monetary Policy Committee of the PBOC were officially promulgated, and the PBOC's system of formulating and implementing the monetary policy was gradually improved. In the same year, the interbank bond market was established, and the operational means of monetary policy changed from direct control of loan size in the past to the use of various monetary policy tools to regulate base money, and the financial supervision function of the central bank was gradually strengthened. The year 1998 witnessed the abolition of loan size control in China.

After the reform and opening-up, China's financial institutions have gone through several stages: primary mixed operation, strict separation, and co-existence of separate operations. The period from the early stage of reform to the opening up of 1995 was the stage of primary mixed operation. Except for the four major banks, other financial companies such as Bank of Communications, CITIC Industrial Bank, and other non-banking financial institutions were all mixed operated.

From the late 1980s to the early 1990s, specialized banks not only broke through the boundaries of the professional division of labor but also began to break through the boundaries of industry division of labor and developed into securities, insurance, investment, trust, real estate, etc. In 1990, Shanghai Stock Exchange and Shenzhen Stock Exchange were established one after another, and banks played an important role in the development of the securities market. The main form of commercial banks' participation in the securities business is the establishment of wholly-owned or equity-invested securities companies or trust and investment companies, whose main business is the issuance, agency trading, and operation of corporate securities.

These financial practices enlivened the financial market, but also led to many problems: first, there was serious irregularities and financial disorder; second, an imperfect financial regulatory system posed great risks; third, the massive transfer of bank credit funds triggered serious inflation, with China's inflation rates reaching 13.2 % and 21.7 % in 1993 and 1994, respectively. In 1995, China adjusted its regulatory regime, and the Commercial Bank Law of the People's Republic of China stipulated that commercial banks were not allowed to engage in trust investment and stock business or invest in real estate and not allowed to invest in any non-self-use real estate; commercial banks were not allowed to invest in non-bank financial institutions and enterprises within the country.

With the establishment of the China Insurance Regulatory Commission (CIRC) and the promulgation of the Securities Law of the People's Republic of China in 1998, China's financial sector separation system was perfected. In 1995, the People's Bank of China Law was promulgated, allowing qualified securities dealers and fund management companies to enter the interbank lending market. in October 1999, the China Securities Regulatory Commission (CSRC) and CIRC agreed to allow insurance funds to enter the stock market; in early 2000,

PBOC and CSRC allowed eligible securities firms to use their stocks and securities investment funds as collateral to borrow from commercial banks.

Finally, since April 1, 1994, China has made significant reforms to its foreign exchange management system. The foreign exchange retention system, the foreign exchange surrender system, and the approval system for foreign exchange use plans were abolished; the settlement and sale of foreign exchange were made compulsory for domestic enterprises to achieve conditional convertibility of the RMB under the current account, and the foreign exchange transfer centers in provinces and cities were abolished to establish a unified national interbank foreign exchange market. In January 1996, the new balance of payments declaration system was formally implemented, and in June of the same year, foreign-invested enterprises were given the right to settle and sell foreign exchange at will, and foreign banks became designated foreign exchange banks at the same time, and in December of the same year, the convertibility of RMB was realized. In 1997, China approved a few foreign banks to operate RMB business on a trial basis in Pudong, Shanghai, and Shenzhen.

In 1998, the number of foreign banks operating RMB business on a trial basis was increased, and the scale of business was increased from RMB 30 million to RMB 100 million; in 1999, the geographical restriction for foreign banks to establish additional branches in China was lifted. The number of foreign banks operating RMB business in Shanghai and Shenzhen continued to increase, and the scale of business further expanded.

The World Trade Organization and the Reform of China's Financial System

On December 11, 2001, China joined the WTO (World Trade Organization) and formally participated in the division of labor in the world economy, which accelerated the flow of international capital in the Chinese market and the process of globalization. This has brought great challenges to the reform and development of China's financial industry. Since the beginning of China's accession to the WTO, the Chinese financial industry has undergone tremendous changes.

In 1998, the Securities Commission of the State Council and the China Securities Regulatory Commission were merged to form the China Securities Regulatory Commission at the ministerial level. On November 8 of the same year, the China Insurance Regulatory Commission (CIRC) was established to supervise the insurance market, and in April 2003, the China Banking

Regulatory Commission (CBRC) was established to perform banking regulatory duties. After three reforms, the People's Bank of China (PBOC) has separated its monetary policy from its securities, insurance, and banking regulatory functions, focusing on its three core functions of "formulating and implementing monetary policy, maintaining financial stability and providing financial services". At the same time, the CBRC, together with the Securities Regulatory Commission and the Insurance Regulatory Commission, has built a tight regulatory system covering all three markets: banking, securities, and insurance.

Second, China's financial intermediaries were reformed, and in 2002, the Second National Financial Work Conference was held, making it clear that the reform of wholly state-owned commercial banks was the top priority of China's financial reform, and that the direction of reform was to transform them into joint-stock companies by the attributes of modern financial enterprises. With the idea of strengthening financial supervision and reforming state-owned banks further deepened, the central government decided to form the Central Huijin Company to lead the restructuring and listing of China's banking industry. On December 16, 2003, the Central Huijin Company was established to exercise the rights and obligations of a financier on behalf of the state for key financial enterprises such as the Bank of China and the Construction Bank. The Party Central Committee and the State Council decided to select Bank of China and China Construction Bank for pilot shareholding reform, and injected US$45 billion through the Central Huijin Company on December 30, 2003, paving the way for the shareholding reform of the two pilot banks.

ICBC, Bank of China, and CCB all decided to introduce foreign strategic investors before going public, with ICBC introducing Goldman Sachs, Express, and Allianz; Bank of China introduced Swiss Bank, Li Ka Shing Foundation, and Royal Bank of Scotland; and CCB introduced Bank of America. The main purpose of introducing foreign strategic investors is to solve the institutional and mechanical problems that restrict the development of state-owned commercial banks and to achieve the improvement of corporate governance structure and the transformation of corporate culture through diversification of equity and public ownership of the listing. Construction Bank was listed on the mainboard market of Hong Kong in October 2005 and on the Shanghai Stock Exchange on September 25, 2007. On June 1, 2006, the shares of Bank of China Limited were officially listed and traded on the Hong Kong Stock Exchange, making Bank of China the third commercial bank in China to be successfully listed in Hong Kong. On July 5, 2006, the A-share of the Bank of China was listed. On October 27, 2006, the A+H shares of ICBC were successfully listed on the Shanghai Stock

Exchange and the Hong Kong Stock Exchange. Agricultural Bank A shares and H shares were listed on July 15 and 16, 2010, respectively, and after exercising the over-allotment option, Agricultural Bank raised US$22.1 billion, making it the largest IPO in the world at that time.

On December 31, 2006, with the approval of the State Council, the CBRC approved the opening of China Postal Savings Bank. At the same time, progress was made in China's rural financial reform. The CBRC relaxed the access policy for banks and financial institutions in rural areas at the end of 2006, and the policy was extended from a local pilot to the whole country in October 2007. Under this policy framework, domestic and foreign bank capital, the industrial capital and private capital can invest, acquire and set up various banking financial institutions in rural areas of China, such as village banks, community-based credit cooperatives, and commercial banks can set up "lending only" loan subsidiaries. This policy has further opened up China's rural financial market, increased the number of new rural financial organizations, and fundamentally changed the original thinking on the stock reform of the rural financial system.

As of the end of June 2009, 118 new rural financial institutions—including 100 village banks, 7 loan companies, and 11 rural capital mutual aid societies—were operating in China.

After joining the WTO, China chose to gradually open up its capital market. The Chinese government selected a group of foreign institutional investors to enter the Chinese market and limited the size of their investments. In May 2003, UBS became the first QFII to be approved in China, and now QFIIs have become an important institutional investor in the Chinese stock market. The QFII mechanism can not only optimize the investor structure and investment philosophy of the capital market, but also strengthen the capital market, enhance market dynamics, and promote the convergence of the Chinese capital market with the international market, improving their corporate governance structure, business management, accounting system, and transparency.

On September 8, 2006, the China Financial Futures Exchange (CFFE) was established in Shanghai, the first financial derivatives exchange in mainland China and the first exchange to adopt a corporate structure. On April 16, 2010, China's stock index futures were officially listed for trading. Stock index futures have not been around in the financial market for long, only about 20 years, but they have become one of the major financial products. After 20 years of development, stock index futures have become an indispensable hedging tool for foreign securities companies, investment funds, and other institutions, and one of the most important products of the international capital market system. The listing of stock index futures has greatly improved the competitiveness of China's capital market.

On October 23, 2009, China's GEM market was officially launched. The GEM market provides a new financing channel for China's independent innovative and growth-oriented enterprises, creating opportunities for private investment and further improving the structure of China's capital market.

Besides, there have been some changes in the RMB exchange rate and interest rate formation mechanism. On July 21, 2005, China implemented the reform of the RMB exchange rate formation mechanism and implemented a managed floating exchange rate system based on market supply and demand, adjusted by reference to a basket of currencies. As of July 21, 2008, the RMB has appreciated by 21 % against the USD.

As the most important indicator of the price of funds in the financial market, interest rates play an important role in both the allocation of financial resources and the allocation of resources in the real economy. In recent years, China's interest rate market reform has steadily advanced. Since 1996, China has liberalized the interest rates in the interbank lending market, the bond market, the issuance rates of treasury bonds, and policy financial bonds in the interbank market. China also liberalized the interest rates on domestic and foreign currency deposits and loans and tried to handle RMB long-term large deposits under the agreement, gradually expanding the floating range of RMB loan rates. At present, China's interest rate market has achieved the milestone of "lower limit for loan rates and upper limit for deposit rates". The focus of future interest rate marketization will be the further liberalization of these two limits.

Future Trends in China's Financial System Reform

Looking ahead, China's financial system will undergo significant changes. China's economy cannot continue to develop without the support of the financial sector, which faces many challenges as well as opportunities in its next development.

First, China needs to build a balanced financial system in the future. International economists have divided countries into two categories according to the characteristics of their financial systems: bank-dominated countries and financial market-dominated countries. The United Kingdom and the United States are financial market-dominated countries, while continental European countries and Japan are bank-dominated countries. Many Chinese scholars, such as Chen Yulu and Ma Yong, believe that China's financial system also belongs to the bank-dominated type[1], which is determined by China's cultural traditions, the legal system, and social preferences. In terms of the legal system, China is a civil law country with an incomplete and poorly enforced legal system, so it would be more efficient to have a bank-led financial system in China. In terms of cultural traditions, the Confucian ethics formed in the course of history still influences Chinese people's social relationships, and Chinese people value kinship credit over contractual credit, so this credit culture is also more suitable for a bank-led financial system. In terms of social preferences, Chinese people are more reluctant to take investment risks and are therefore more supportive of a bank-led financial system. In the future, China will build a financial system with a balanced development of banks and capital markets, but banks will still play a major role in the development of the financial system for some time.

Second, the mixed operation of financial institutions will be gradually promoted, and a unified financial regulatory system will be established. The development of China's contemporary financial industry has gone through several stages: primary mixed operation, strict separation, and co-existence of separate & combined operations. After China accedes to the WTO, China's financial institutions not only need to reform their historical legacy, but also have to face the fierce competition brought by multinational hybrid financial institutions. Therefore, it is a necessary choice to steadily promote the mixed business operation and strengthen the competitiveness of Chinese financial enterprises. The most likely way for China to do this is to establish a financial control company in the form of a "mixed group and separate subsidiaries". This form can take into account the advantages of mixed and separate operations and better maintain a dynamic balance between efficiency and stability. The subsidiaries operating different financial businesses have relative independence, and there are different firewalls within the financial holding company so that the failure of individual companies will not bring a devastating blow to the whole group.

If China's financial institutions are to adopt a mixed business model in the future, China's financial regulatory model will also need to be adjusted accordingly, as the current "one bank, three councils" model is based on the separation of financial institutions[2]. Separate operations and regulations are conducive to risk control. However, with the development of financial globalization and the emergence of large financial conglomerates, competition in the financial industry has become increasingly fierce.

In this context, the development of China's financial industry has become a mixed industry, and the trend is to unify the regulation of the financial industry. The future unified regulatory landscape can be roughly divided into three lines of defense. The first line of defense is the internal control of financial institutions, through strengthening self-monitoring and management, to achieve self-identification and control of risks. The second line of defense is external supervision, which is the core line of defense of the entire regulatory system. Chinese financial institutions have insufficient internal control technology and experience, and in the process of marketization, homogeneous competition is serious: each financial institution tends to put the pursuit of profit in the first place and has insufficient motivation to implement internal control. Conflicts of interest and ethical issues may arise in the process of mixed business operations of financial institutions, which require strong external regulation to impose constraints. The third line of defense is social intermediaries and public supervision. Social intermediaries include accounting firms, auditing firms, rating agencies, consulting agencies, etc. Exposure and coverage by the mass media are also an important part of informal supervision.

Finally, the opening of the capital account should be promoted in an orderly manner to realize the internationalization of the RMB. Since the 21st century, especially after 2002, China has significantly accelerated the pace of opening the capital account in the face of the pressure of RMB appreciation and the rapid growth of foreign exchange reserves. The establishment of QFII and QDII (Qualified Domestic Institutional Investor) is also intended to allow the Chinese market to gradually adapt to the process of capital account liberalization. According to the IMF's definition, there are 40 capital items in 7 major categories, among which 5 are fully convertible, 8 are convertible, 17 are partially convertible, and 10 are completely non-convertible in China. In other words, more than 75 % of China's capital items are fully or partially convertible, and the degree of capital account opening is medium.

The dollar-dominated international monetary system has many inequities. Peripheral countries are in a weak position in this system and bear most of the costs. According to the American economist Stiglitz, the accumulation of foreign exchange assets in non-reserve currency countries means that the richest countries in the world have access to cheap money, while poor countries not only do not get cheap money but also bear the investment risks of reserve currency countries.

In response to the financial crisis, the United States wanted to stimulate economic recovery, by implementing several rounds of quantitative easing, resulting in a flood of liquidity in the international market. Prices of oil, precious metals, and other commodity futures rose sharply. As a result, the level of global inflation is rising, and asset bubbles appear frequently, which is mostly harmful to emerging economies.

The international monetary system needs to be adjusted, and there will be a variety of currencies playing a more important role in this system in the future. In addition to the two major currencies, the euro and the U.S. dollar, the British pound, the Japanese yen, and the Chinese yuan will play a bigger role. Therefore, the internationalization of the RMB is an integral part of the future reform of the international monetary system.

In November 2015, the International Monetary Fund decided to include the RMB in the SDR currency basket, and this decision officially took effect on October 1, 2016. The RMB's weight in the SDR currency basket is 10.92 %, surpassing the Japanese yen (8.33 %) and the British pound (8.09 %) and ranking behind the US dollar (41.73 %) and the euro (30.93 %).

Following the inclusion of the RMB in the SDR currency basket, the use of the RMB in international markets has gradually expanded. China is the largest trading partner of more than 130 countries worldwide, so many of China's trading partners have chosen to use the RMB to settle some of their bilateral trade items. This will soon make the RMB the third largest international trade settlement currency after the US dollar and the euro. With the establishment of the offshore RMB market, the number of RMB bonds issued overseas is also increasing, creating new demand for RMB. China's "One Belt, One Road" initiative has received a positive response from many countries, which are willing to work with China to increase infrastructure investments and enhance trade and information connectivity between countries, some of which are also settled in RMB, contributing to the internationalization of the RMB.

The internationalization of the RMB will certainly go through a process, from a transaction currency to a pricing currency, and from an investment currency to a reserve currency. For other countries to reserve RMB, the capital account must be opened up so that other countries can invest in China's capital market and make profits.

It has taken many countries years to move from current account opening to capital account opening. Japan, the UK, and Germany took 16, 18, and 20 years respectively. The sequence of capital account liberalization in China is: "capital inflows before capital outflows; direct investment before indirect investment; portfolio investment before bank credit; long-term investment before short-term investment; institutions before individuals; debt instruments before equity instruments and financial derivatives; issuance market before trading market; and liberalization of transactions with the real background before opening up transactions without real background ."

The international financial crisis of 2008 has left developed countries in the United States, Japan, and Europe with a heavy debt burden. Against the backdrop of a lack of fulcrum for economic development, slowing technological innovation, and slow economic growth, the debt of these countries is likely to continue to grow. There is a tried and true way out of the debt crisis, which is to rely on inflation and currency devaluation to write off most of the real debt, and it seems that these developed countries will not be able to break out of this historical circle in the future. This approach, while effective, can seriously affect the credibility of these countries' currencies. In the process of emerging from this international financial crisis, if the RMB stays strong, it will certainly contribute greatly to China's price stability and economic growth. At that time, the RMB may become a popular international reserve currency compared to the dollar and the euro.

Notes

1 Chen Yulu, and Ma Yong. *Megatrends in China's financial system.* China Finance Press, 2011.

2 The term "one bank and three commissions" is an abbreviation for the four financial regulatory authorities, namely the People's Bank of China (PBoC), the China Banking Regulatory Commission (CBRC), the China Securities Regulatory Commission (CSRC) and the China Insurance Regulatory Commission (CIRC). In March 2018, the 1st meeting of 13th session of the National People's Congress resolved to merge the CBRC and the CIRC into the China Securities and Insurance Regulatory Commission (CBIRC).—Translator's note

4

How to Better Use China's Massive Foreign Exchange Reserves

During the golden age of globalization, China's GDP growth is driven to a large extent by a fast export growth, which had contributed to the rise of China's huge foreign currency reserve. But that huge foreign currency reserve caused some troubles to China's macro-economic management, because it might be the origin of Chinese imported inflation. Chinese central bank has taken some measures to alleviate the inflation pressure, but with some costs. So Chinese researchers held a series of discussions to talk about Chinese huge foreign currency reserve. Is it a hot potato? I have been invited to write a few articles on this issue around 2016, and I tried to give my answers.

China is the world's largest foreign exchange reserve holder, reaching a peak of \$3.99 trillion in July 2014 in dollar terms, falling to \$2.99 trillion in 2016, and stabilizing at around \$3 trillion in 2017. Not many countries in the world have a GDP of \$3 trillion, and the size of China's foreign exchange reserves, which exceeds the GDP of many countries, is indeed incredible.

However, the huge amount of foreign exchange reserves also seems to pose some problems. Foreign exchange reserves are made up of foreign currencies, and if foreign currencies depreciate, China's reserves will shrink. Some have questioned the ability of China's central bank to manage its foreign exchange reserves as they have fallen from nearly \$4 trillion to less than \$3 trillion. Others have questioned the use of foreign exchange reserves to buy financial products such as U.S. Treasuries as a one-way street. Are these views correct? How should we rationally understand China's huge foreign exchange reserves?

The Rapid Growth of Foreign Exchange Reserves and the Macroeconomic Risks

The growth rate of China's foreign exchange reserves is a miracle in the history of the world economy. In 2001, when China joined the WTO, foreign exchange reserves were just around $200 billion. However, in 2011, China's foreign exchange reserves exceeded $3.1 trillion. Within 10 years, China's foreign exchange reserves have grown more than 10 times.

The rapid growth of foreign exchange reserves has indeed brought some inconvenience to China since China had faced a shortage of foreign exchange for a long time. In the past, the goal of Chinese business development was to earn foreign currencies via export, because China was unable to purchase vital machinery and equipment due to the shortage of foreign exchange at that time.

Recently, excessive foreign exchange reserves can be troublesome sometimes, which the Chinese could never have imagined 10 years ago. With the growing debt of developed countries, international financial markets may be in turmoil, and the trend of China's export growth and growing foreign exchange reserves seems unlikely to change in the short term. In this context, the excessive growth of foreign exchange reserves may affect the stability of China's macroeconomy and needs to be noted.

Instability in the International Bond Market Could Lead to Losses in China's Foreign Exchange Reserves and Currency Mismatch on Debt for Companies

Since 2009, the international market has been unstable for dollar bonds, euro bonds, and yen bonds, mainly because the debt of these countries is growing too fast and investors suspect that the risk of buying their treasury bonds will increase. This has led to a rapid rise of costs of funds for the U.S., Japan, and European countries, and the risk of debt default has followed.

In 2009, Japan's newly issued national debt surpassed 50 trillion yen, which is a high record. In 2018, Japan's government debt as a share of GDP was the highest in the world at 238 %. At that time, interest on the debt alone already cost 1/5 of Japan's annual fiscal budget. This trend will continue to develop in the future as Japan's population ages. Japanese government debt is mainly purchased by the Japanese people, and Japan's savings rate is so high that a debt crisis has not yet erupted in Japan, but the outlook for yen debt is not good. The debt of the Eurozone was lower than that of Japan and the United States in the past because the "Treaty on European Union" stipulates that the fiscal deficit of Eurozone countries cannot exceed 3 % of each country's GDP and the ratio of each country's government debt to GDP cannot exceed 60 %. However, after the financial crisis broke out in 2008, the bad debts of banks in some countries in the Eurozone increased rapidly, and the governments took out fiscal money to bail out the banks, making the fiscal situation deteriorated rapidly. In the past, the interest difference between the government bonds of these EU member states and the German 10-year government bonds was negligible, but after the outbreak of the financial crisis, the interest difference between them has rapidly widened. In the case of Greece, for example, the spread between Greek and German bonds increased to 274 basis points.

The non-core countries in the Eurozone are facing a structural recession: to prevent the debt crisis from worsening, they have to cut their fiscal deficits significantly. These countries cannot rely on increased public spending to stimulate their economies, which will only make the recession worse and last longer. These countries may also experience debt deflation: as nominal prices and wages continue to fall, the real debt burden in euro terms will increase. This could lead to a new wave of private (and even public) sector defaults.

Germany, the core country of the Eurozone, is also unhappy with the way the euro has evolved. In the 10 years since the euro was launched, Germany has been limiting its wage growth and even cutting social welfare spending to control debt growth. After the outbreak of the debt crisis in Greece and Ireland, European public opinion exploded with statements such as "Greeks can retire early" and "Ireland has a super-low corporate tax". Such public opinion makes the Germans feel indignant, as they think the other countries in the Eurozone took advantage of Germany, and Germany's tax revenue is used to subsidize those countries' government spending.

In the Eurozone, Spain and Portugal's financial systems also have many problems. Spanish banks have a lot of investments in Latin America, especially in Brazil. If the investment bubble in Brazil burst, Spanish banks will have a lot of bad debts. If the Spanish government bails out the banks, the sovereign debt will climb rapidly. If these countries in the Eurozone keep having a debt crisis, other countries in the Eurozone will be affected, the German confidence will be shaken, so they will fear that the EU loans to the economically weaker member states will never be repaid. Because of these "divisive factors", the euro will continue to fall against the dollar until the Eurozone finds a way to further integrate its finances.

To diversify the risk of foreign exchange reserves, China still bought some euro bonds and yen bonds after the financial crisis. However, for these reasons, the yen and euro exchange rates are likely to decline against the dollar in the short term, so China's foreign exchange reserves could see a contraction.

The most troublesome part is the foreign exchange debt of enterprises. In recent years, the trend for Chinese companies to "go global" has become more pronounced, with many of them investing overseas with borrowed dollars, and the low exchange rate of the dollar and low-interest rates in the U.S. over the years have helped these companies invest and expand overseas. However, if the dollar strengthens in the future, the debt of these companies could grow rapidly. Note that there is a negative correlation between the U.S. dollar and commodity futures prices, as a stronger dollar will lead to lower commodity futures prices. Chinese companies are investing heavily in the development of raw materials overseas, and if the dollar reverses and the price of raw materials fall in the future, Chinese companies' dollar-denominated debt could become a heavy burden.

In the Medium to Long Term, a Depreciation of the Dollar Is Inevitable, and the Outlook for Global Inflation Is Worrisome

The dollar exchange rate is likely to rise in the short term, and China's foreign exchange reserves will not shrink rapidly. But the depreciation of the dollar seems to be a general trend, as it is the only way for the U.S. to get out of its huge debt. According to the Congressional Budget Office, the U.S. deficit for fiscal 2009 was more than $1.4 trillion—about 11.2 % of GDP—setting a new high for the U.S. deficit in nearly 60 years and slightly higher in relative terms than the deficit in 1942. In 2010, the U.S. government debt was 98 % of GDP, and if the interest rate on this credit was 5 %, in 20 years the government would have to pay as much interest as the amount of the credit. In 40 years, the U.S. government would be paying twice as much interest as the amount of the credit, and in 60 years, the amount of the credit would be equal to a threefold increase, while the debt would still be outstanding. As a result, the Congressional Budget Office estimates that by 2020, interest payments on the U.S. government's debt will rise from the current 9 % of revenues to 20 %, to 36 % by 2030, and 58 % by 2040. With such high debt pressure, the U.S. will never get ahead.

Historically, there have been numerous examples of currency devaluation to reduce government debt. For example, the British pound was once the hegemonic currency of the international monetary system, and the U.K. enjoyed this "money-issuing privilege." In the second half of the 19th century, because it could print money at will, the British government spent lavishly, and the country's debt burden grew heavier. When the British government realized that the debt was unsustainable, it took many measures to reduce spending and control the size of the debt. However, because the British pound was on the gold standard and could not be devalued at will, the British government's debt continued to increase, accounting for nearly 100 % of GDP, despite the government's tightening of finances and the people's suffering. It was not until the end of World War II when the U.S. dollar took the place of the British pound, and the pound was decoupled from gold and devalued for five consecutive years, that the level of British debt gradually declined, and the British government was relieved of nearly 40 % of its debt after the pound was devalued.

Therefore, the ultimate solution for the United States could only be a decent "default". That is, by printing money to trigger inflation and write off part of the debt. In 2010, the Federal Reserve launched its second quantitative easing policy, issuing $700 billion in banknotes, after the first quantitative easing in 2009.

The first quantitative easing in 2009 had already issued $1.7 trillion in bills, adding up to a total of $2.4 trillion. The U.S. plan is to issue $4 trillion, so it will continue to do so in the future. And U.S. public opinion is spreading the news that the core price index (CPI) in the United States has reached its lowest value in nearly 20 years.

During the financial crisis, the European Central Bank also bought some problematic bonds of countries in crisis, which in a way is also printing money. Besides, the possibility of money printing in Japan is also increasing, and with the Japanese government intervening in the exchange rate market, they will issue more money. However, there is a time lag between inflation and money printing. According to the history of hyperinflation caused by massive money printing during the Weimar Republic in Germany, there is a time lag of 3 to 4 years.

The international market has already reacted to the expected future depreciation of the dollar. Commodity futures prices, represented by gold and oil, have been moving higher. Because the dollar is the pricing currency of commodities, the depreciation of the dollar will cause the commodity futures prices to rise

The loose monetary policy of the U.S. did not promote the growth of domestic investment in the U.S. because of the high risk and low return of investment in the U.S. As a result, U.S. easy money policy has turned the dollar into an arbitrage currency, like the Japanese yen in previous years. U.S. companies borrowed from the Federal Reserve at low-interest rates and then invested in other markets. U.S. firms became the main force behind speculation in the Eurozone and the source of economic bubbles in emerging economies.

To guard against the risk of foreign exchange reserves and to encourage Chinese companies to invest abroad, it was the only option to use up some of China's foreign exchange. However, when investing abroad, Chinese companies should not only invest in energy or resources. Although it is good to invest in resources or energy, as it can preserve and increase value in times of inflation, a future change in monetary policy in the U.S. could cause resource prices to plummet. The crisis in Latin American countries in the early 1980s was caused by such. Chinese companies should invest in the sales networks of some developed countries at the right time to grasp the pulse of consumers and ensure that Chinese export, which can maximize their benefits in the future.

The loose monetary policies of the United States and other developed countries have led to excess liquidity in the market, with large amounts of capital chasing exchange rate differentials and interest rate differentials, creating economic bubbles wherever these hot money flows go.

According to China's regulations, all foreign currency entering China will be bought by the Foreign Exchange Bureau and an equal amount of RMB will be issued. If these RMBs are allowed to enter the market, it is equivalent to issuing more money and inflationary pressure will increase. In recent years, the People's Bank of China has increased its flushing efforts by issuing additional central bank notes without converting too much hot money into RMB into the market. However, such activities have increased the central bank's operating costs and, if sustained over the long term, will not be conducive to balancing the central bank's books.

The Fed's interest rate is low, so if China and its interest rate differential will be too large to attract more hot money into China, China's interest rate can only be maintained at a lower level. But this will cause the problem of economic overheating, and meanwhile, the public's expectation of inflation has become a major hidden danger. The rush to buy property has become a trend, and the rapid growth of housing prices has exacerbated the discontent of low-income groups in society and increased social instability.

At a time when the dollar is depreciating, the euro is in crisis and the yen is unreliable, the call for the internationalization of the RMB has become louder and the impulse to implement it will increase. However, western public opinion believes that the internationalization of the RMB must be predicated on China opening its capital account, so the pressure on China to open its capital account is very strong. This is a very dangerous move because Western capital has released a lot of liquidity, and they are looking for markets. Once China's capital market is opened and a large amount of external capital flows in, a huge bubble will appear in the Chinese economy and when it bursts, it will cause a serious recession.

Currently, due consideration should be given to using exchange rate and interest rate policies to stabilize prices. RMB appreciation is a long-term trend because of China's strong economic growth and the fact that RMB appreciation can increase purchasing power. As the inflation may continue for a longer period in the future, our policy choices should first prioritize stabilizing prices. Although China has a large surplus in exports, this is mainly the surplus of processing trade by foreign companies and joint ventures. Excluding this portion, China has a deficit in general trade. In other words, when the nominal exchange rate appreciates and the price of imported goods decreases, RMB appreciation will not cause trade imbalance but will be beneficial to curbing imported inflation. Therefore, we should not be afraid of RMB appreciation, but the rate of appreciation should be controlled by China itself to avoid a sharp rise and fall, as well as to avoid an easy monetary policy and a generous fiscal policy after the exchange rate appreciation for fear of affecting economic growth, which could easily lead to an economic bubble. Price stability is good for the population, but an appreciating nominal exchange rate can put businesses under more pressure. At this time, the government should implement measures to support enterprises, such as subsidizing their R&D projects, giving them export tax rebates, and increasing policy loans for small and medium-sized technology enterprises. Besides, subsidizing low-income groups is also necessary to maintain economic and social stability in times of inflation.

The appreciation of the RMB exchange rate facilitated the internationalization of the RMB in the context of global inflation. The 1970s was also a time of global inflation. The deutsche mark appreciated, but interest rates in Federal Germany were consistently higher than in neighboring countries, and thus inflation was significantly lower than in other Western European countries. As a result, the purchasing power of the deutsche mark was stronger than that of the currencies of other Western European countries. In the absence of an open capital account, the deutsche mark has become the reference currency in Western Europe, and later the deutsche mark became the core of the European Monetary Union, and the euro was established on the basis of deutsche mark. If in the future China can use exchange rate policy and interest rate policy to stabilize prices so that China's inflation rate is lower than that of other countries, the advantage of

RMB's purchasing power will be more obvious, and even if China does not open its capital account, RMB will naturally become the reference currency in Asian region. In this way, after the financial crisis, the internationalization of the RMB can be accomplished and China can avoid the dilemma of rapidly opening the capital account or the inability to internationalize the RMB.

The Increase and Decrease of China's Foreign Exchange Reserves

In the first quarter of 2011, China ran a slight deficit in foreign trade. A slight deficit in foreign trade is not a bad thing, given China's yearly surplus in foreign trade, the huge pressure on the appreciation of the RMB exchange rate, and the increasing foreign exchange reserves. However, the strange thing is that when there is a deficit in foreign trade, China's foreign exchange reserves have gone up against the trend and increased a lot. In other words, this increase in foreign exchange can be defined as hot money. Of course, not all foreign direct investment is hot money, but some of it is certainly hot money that enters the Chinese market for arbitrage under the banner of direct investment. Hot money enters China in three main ways: first, under the banner of direct investment; second, with the opening of private equity; and third, when Chinese companies borrow cheap dollar capital abroad and then return to invest at home. The third way has accumulated the biggest risks and will be the most damaging in the future.

As inflation rose, the People's Bank of China began to tighten monetary policy, raising the reserve requirement ratio and interest rates several times to curb liquidity. Theoretically, the tightening monetary policy is detrimental to those low value-added companies, as continued production will lead to losses. In the end, these firms have to choose to switch to other products, which is in line with the goal of optimizing the structure of the economy.

However, because of the easy monetary policy in the United States, Japan, and some European countries, the international market is full of liquidity, and many Chinese companies go to overseas Chinese financial institutions to borrow money and then exchange it into RMB in the name of export credit, which not only meets their own needs for borrowing and investment but also raises cheap capital. With the appreciation of RMB, these enterprises can also earn an exchange rate difference when they repay the loan. Chinese financial institutions, with their strong strength and reputation, can borrow very low-interest dollar funds in the international market, and then add an interest rate to re-lend them to Chinese companies, who can also earn a lot of revenue every year. This seems to be a good deal for both Chinese companies and financial institutions. However, from a macroeconomic perspective, the combination of favorable factors may create a "synthetic fallacy".

The U.S. dollars that enter China through these channels are converted into RMB and then go to the Foreign Exchange Bureau, where they become part of the foreign exchange reserves. But China's foreign exchange reserves are already too large, and this inflow of hot money increases the management risk of the Foreign Exchange Bureau and does not bring additional benefits to China's development. This hot money increases the systemic risk to the Chinese economy in two ways. First, the money is borrowed from overseas. The Fed's interest rates are low now because the U.S. wants to encourage investment and consumption, but if in a while the Fed decides that inflation is the enemy, it will change its monetary policy and raise interest rates. At that time, if the Chinese companies have not yet repaid their loans, they will have to pay a huge price as a result. Second, the money undermines the effectiveness of China's monetary policy, making it impossible to fully implement the government's efforts to promote economic transformation. Moreover, many of our industries are facing the problem of overcapacity. The government's policy was supposed to limit the development of these industries and even eliminate some enterprises, but the constant flow of cheap money into these industries will allow excess capacity to continue to accumulate. When the market becomes averse to the excess products, their prices will fall, which will lead to the deterioration of the financial system and even lead to financial crisis and recession.

China used to pay less attention to the problem of overcapacity because the problem it faced for a long time was shortage. But as the economy and the market develop, overcapacity should be a matter of great concern to China. China should not forget that Marx's most powerful analysis of the economic crisis is that it is caused by overproduction.

Those—who try to find a basis in economic fundamentals to explain the change of RMB exchange rate—ignore an important factor that causes the change of exchange rate: the appreciation and depreciation of the currency are caused more by the change of capital flow. Although changes in capital flows are influenced by people's expectations of economic fundamentals, they are not always so. For example, in recent years, changes in the RMB exchange rate have not been caused by changes in economic fundamentals.

After the outbreak of the international financial crisis in 2008, central banks in developed countries, led by the Federal Reserve, injected large amounts of liquidity into the market to prevent capital markets from freezing or even collapsing due to panic. At that time, all central banks had zero interest rates, and the annual interest rate of commercial bank loans was only about 3 %. The financial crisis led to a sharp decline in the exchange rate of the U.S. dollar and an appreciation of the RMB relative to the U.S. dollar. The financial crisis led to an economic recession in Western countries and a sharp drop in demand, which also caused a precipitous fall in China's exports, with export processing enterprises in a state of mourning. Some import and export enterprises in China's coastal provinces see hope for survival in the interest rate differential between overseas and China. Import and export enterprises can finance themselves overseas, and many of them borrow 3 % annual interest dollar loans in overseas markets and bring the money into China in the name of export advances and so on and invest it casually in some financial products and properties to get a return of more than 10 %. And with the appreciation of the RMB, they can get an annual interest spread of about 20 %. According to the Bank for International Settlements, from 2009–2014, more than $1 trillion in one-year dollar loans flowed into China in this way. The massive inflow of hot money into China drove up the yuan's exchange rate, so the yuan kept appreciating during those years.

However, the Federal Reserve withdrew from quantitative easing at the end of 2014, and public opinion generally expected the Fed to officially enter an interest rate hike cycle soon. They expected that interest rates on future dollar loans would keep rising, and the dollar exchange rate would also rise. Due to such expectation, hot money, consisting of short-term foreign debt borrowed by companies, began to rapidly withdraw from China starting in 2015. At that time, if companies did not repay their short-term loans soon, the future debt burden would grow as interest rates on the debt rose and the dollar appreciated.

In 2015, roughly more than $800 billions of hot money left China. The massive capital outflow put significant pressure on the RMB exchange rate to depreciate, and the RMB did depreciate slightly. In 2016, there were increasing expectations of RMB depreciation, and many people exchanged RMB for foreign currency to reverse real estate overseas. A massive outflow of Chinese savings could cause a financial crisis. Against this backdrop, the People's Bank of China began to tighten capital controls, which soon curbed the trend of capital flight.

In 2017, many people thought that the trend of RMB exchange rate changes would be the same as in 2016, so they were still ready to use RMB for USD to arbitrage. But this time, expectations of a stronger dollar did not exist. Since the Federal Reserve changed its monetary policy, the force of the dollar appreciation has been released. The Fed hesitated to raise interest rates again and again, rather than entering a rate hike cycle as quickly as before, indicating that the U.S. economy was not recovering as expected and that raising rates too quickly could trigger a new round of bubble bursting. These changes made international investors doubt the prospect of dollar appreciation and started to move away from the dollar, and the dollar exchange rate started to decline. In contrast, the Chinese economy has seen showing new growth signs, with business activities represented by the "Internet +" starting to take off and the sharing economy emerging. These trends have attracted U.S. capital flows to China and contributed to the rise in the RMB exchange rate. Over the next few years, as China's economic restructuring deepens, and as the "Belt and Road" initiative leads to increased outbound investment in RMB, the RMB exchange rate will become even stronger.

The U.S. Is Not a Haven for China's Fleeing Capital

Since 2016, some rich Chinese people have been trying every possible way to move their earned money to the United States. On the one hand, probably because China's anti-corruption storm was getting fierce, some people's money cannot be seen under the sunlight, and they want to run away. On the other hand, some people calculated that the Fed has entered the interest rate hike cycle, the dollar will appreciate in the future, so if they transferred out the RMB assets, they could use the exchange rate difference to earn income in the future. However, there are always some people who thought themselves smarter but ended up losing their wealth.

People who transfer their assets to the United States often think: the United States is the most powerful military country in the world, and the United States believe in liberalism, the sanctity of personal property, so it is the safest choice to transfer assets to the United States. However, if we look at history, it shows that such a way of thinking is wrong.

The United States is a very politically correct country, and if it is at war with any country, immigrants from that country in the United States often suffer unfair treatment. The Japanese began immigrating to the United States early on, and there were many Japanese immigrants in the United States before World War II. During World War II, the United States put Japanese immigrants in internment camps and confiscated their property.

After the outbreak of the Korean War, China sent volunteer troops to fight against the United States, and the United States froze all the assets of Chinese people in the United States. Europeans had many assets in the United States, and when they saw this situation, they began to worry about the safety of their assets in the United States. They were afraid that the United States would freeze European assets in America, accusing European countries had trade relations with China. As a result, Europeans began to leave their dollar assets in Europe, creating the Eurodollar market.

These examples show that it is not very safe for the Chinese to keep their assets in the United States. Many strategists in the United States see China as the greatest potential threat to the United States and believe that sooner or later war will break out between China and the United States. The "Thucydides Trap" is a way for these people to rehash ancient Greek history to set the stage for a potential conflict between the U.S. and China. In this context, shouldn't those who transfer their assets to the United States fear that their assets will be confiscated one day?

Even if there is no war between China and the United States, the anti-corruption cooperation between China and the United States has thrown a wet blanket on those who want to transfer their assets to the United States. Since Trump took office, the U.S. government has tightened controls on capital that has fled overseas. At the G20 Hangzhou summit, leaders agreed to strengthen anti-corruption cooperation and set up a mechanism for anti-corruption cooperation. Governments have a common interest in dealing with capital flight, and those who think it is safe to move their assets to the U.S. may have made a mistake.

Those who want to exchange RMB for USD for arbitrage may not see the general trend of world economic development. It is a general rule that when the Federal Reserve withdraws from quantitative easing and enters the interest rate hike cycle, U.S. bond yields follow, and the exchange rate of the U.S. dollar should also follow. However, this time the Fed raised interest rates, but the dollar exchange rate did not rise for a long time. Just carefully studing the U.S. economic data, you can find the fishy. Since the outbreak of the financial crisis, the U.S. stock market once plummeted, but now it has risen to a level far higher than before the crisis. But in terms of labor productivity, the U.S. economy has not made much progress over the years, and employment rates in manufacturing and other industries have not changed much. So, is such a brilliant achievement of the U.S. stock market another round of financial bubbles? If the Federal Reserve continues to raise interest rates, will it triggera new bubble burst? In this context, international investors began to worry about the consequences of the Fed's rate hikes. Therefore, the new round of Fed rate hikes did not cause the dollar exchange rate to rise, but rather caused the exchange rate to fall. And the U.S. government may not want the dollar to be too strong. In Obama's administration's 8 years, the U.S. government debt doubled to nearly $ 20 trillion. As the Fed raised interest rates, and the interest rate on U.S. Treasury bonds rose, the U.S. government needs to pay more interest each year. If the dollar appreciates too quickly, the U.S. government's debt burden will become even heavier. In this context, to transfer the yuan into dollars and ship to the United States for making money from the interest difference, it is worth taking the risk?

How to Dialectically View China's Foreign Exchange Reserves

China's foreign exchange reserves have been increasing since 2017. According to data released by the People's Bank of China, China's foreign exchange reserves stood at US$3,109,213 million at the end of October 2017, some US$700 million increase from the end of September 2017, maintaining the increase during nine consecutive months. The data indicates that the pressure of RMB depreciation is rapidly decreasing, and capital inflows into China are accelerating and export trade is achieving growth.

Among many factors, the reduced pressure of RMB devaluation is probably the most important concern of the Chinese public. The growth of China's foreign exchange reserves is relatively increasing compared to the foreign exchange reserves in the previous two years. And on this issue, Chinese domestic public opinion has formed an incorrect perception, as if the decrease of foreign exchange reserves is China's loss. It is impossible for foreign exchange reserves to only grow without decreasing, and too much foreign exchange reserves will make China "bound by itself". China already has the largest foreign exchange reserves in the world, and we need to have a clearer understanding of this fact.

China's foreign exchange reserves peaked at $3.99 trillion in 2014 and were on the verge of surpassing the $4 trillion mark. 2015–2016 saw a rapid decline of nearly a trillion dollars. Some argue that the decline in foreign exchange reserves is due to mismanagement.

In fact, in late 2009, China's foreign exchange reserves were just over $2 trillion, nearly doubling within less than five years. At that time, we did not worry about the inflow of hot money, but since 2015, we have started to worry about "capital flight".

Since the outbreak of the international financial crisis in 2008, central banks in many developed countries have used unconventional monetary policies of zero interest rates and quantitative easing to pour a lot of liquidity into the market to ease the market panic. At that time, the interest rate for a one-year commercial loan overseas was only 3 %. Because of the shrinking export market, many Chinese exporters started to raise money in the overseas market and then transfer it back to China to arbitrage in the form of foreign trade advances. If the business is well run, the profit is much more than 10 %, greatly exceeding the return of the real economy. During the second half of 2014, the Federal Reserve withdrew from quantitative easing. Many predicted that the Fed would soon enter a cycle of interest rate hikes and that the dollar exchange rate would rise, meaning that these companies would have more debt to repay. As a result, many companies made large debt repayments, leading to capital outflows from China, a reduction in foreign exchange reserves, and rising pressure on the RMB to depreciate.

After 2015, as China's foreign exchange reserves rapidly decreased, some believed that RMB depreciation would become a long-term trend, and some Chinese savers joined the capital flight. Others moved their funds overseas to speculate in real estate in the name of various investments.

In 2016, the pressure to depreciate the RMB eased when China's foreign exchange authorities tightened capital controls, and the Ministry of Commerce strengthened its review of outbound investments, fearing that a significant reduction in foreign exchange reserves would lead to a fragile Chinese financial system.

In 2017, capital flows reversed and China's foreign exchange reserves rose again in succession. This was caused by a combination of external and internal factors. Externally, the Federal Reserve had been very cautious in raising interest rates, with small and long intervals between each increase, which has weakened expectations of dollar appreciation. At the same time, the emerging sectors of the Chinese economy were developing strongly, attracting some foreign capital and growing foreign exchange reserves. Besides, as the global economic situation improved, China's export trade picked up, and the foreign exchange settlement increased. Foreign exchange reserves grew along with it. In China's foreign exchange reserves, U.S. dollar assets account for the highest proportion. As the Federal Reserve returned to normal monetary policy slowly, people started to let down their guard and stopped worrying that the U.S. stock market bubble would burst. U.S. dollar assets performed well, the portion of China's foreign exchange reserves for the U.S. financial markets grew.

While the growth of foreign exchange reserves is not a bad thing, the high level of public opinion on foreign exchange reserves has created a dilemma for the institutions that manage the reserves. There is a strong voice in China that argues that a decrease in foreign exchange reserves means a loss. Foreign exchange reserves are highly liquid and therefore foreign exchange reserves are not suitable for investment in long-term products. From an investment point of view, too many foreign exchange reserves indicate that we are not using capital smartly enough, which is not necessarily a good thing.

Calculating foreign exchange reserves is not easy. It is too risky to hang on to only one tree, the U.S. dollar. If you want to diversify your investment risk, you have to invest in more financial products denominated in other currencies. But when we calculate the size of foreign exchange reserves, we have to convert assets in other currencies into dollars or yuan. Therefore, when the dollar appreciates, the size of foreign exchange reserves shrinks because the assets in other currencies depreciate. However, when the dollar depreciates, foreign exchange reserves denominated in dollars may instead increase. U.S. dollar assets still account for the largest share of China's foreign exchange reserves, so when the dollar exchange rate is unstable, there is a great deal of volatility in the statistics on foreign exchange reserves. Our estimates of foreign exchange reserve shrinkage are not necessarily accurate when exchange rates are volatile.

Foreign exchange reserves are a tool for sovereign countries to play games in the international arena. But if we only allow foreign exchange reserves to grow and not to decrease, we are "nullifying" ourselves and giving up the right to use foreign exchange reserves as a tool. The U.S. dollar is still the hegemonic currency in the international system, and European countries have used it heavily but suffered from it. For example, some years ago the United States imposed large fines on French and German banks, a fine of several billion dollars because the banks of these European countries traded in dollars with the countries sanctioned by the United States. As a result, European countries also began to promote the diversification of foreign exchange reserves, using the yuan instead of the dollar in the bilateral trade settlement between China and Europe, and increasing the yuan reserves. In the first two years, the RMB exchange rate slumped. If European countries only focus on the size of foreign exchange reserves, wouldn't this strategy be troublesome?

China's foreign exchange reserves are already the largest in the world, and we should no longer hold the view that foreign exchange reserves are only beneficial if they keep increasing. China has become a net capital exporter, with rising investments in developed countries, emerging countries, and countries along the "Belt and Road" route. Except for some specific projects that can be settled in RMB, overseas investments still consume a lot of hard currency (i.e. foreign exchange reserves). In this context, as China's outbound investment grows, foreign exchange reserves will naturally decrease. But this decrease is not a bad thing, as it can bring more gains, not only financial but also strategic gains.

Therefore, we need to think more dialectically about the change in the size of China's foreign exchange reserves.

Increase Foreign Investment and Be Wary of Investment Traps

The financial crisis has caused the U.S. government debt to climb rapidly, and the debt of the U.S. federal government is now equal to the U.S. GDP, not to mention that the debt of all state governments in the US is not small. Japan's government debt is even heavier, accounting for more than 230 % of Japan's GDP. If these debts were not basically held by the Japanese people, and if the Japanese people still had great trust in the Japanese government, Japan would have had a debt crisis long ago according to the general laws of the international economy. The government debt of the EU member states is around 80 % of the EU GDP, which is better than the US and Japan. But the EU is a confederation of sovereign countries with huge differences in debt levels between the trade surplus and deficit countries, and the trade deficit countries have been under huge debt pressure for the past two years, which has affected the credibility of the euro. Therefore, we have to analyze the debt situation of these hard currency countries to judge the risk of shrinking foreign exchange reserves that we face. As far as the debt situation of the United States is concerned, the outlook is not good.

According to Fred Bergstein, director of the Peterson Institute for International Economics, if this trend is allowed to develop, the U.S. current account deficit will rise to 13 % of GDP by 2030, while the U.S. net debt to other countries will reach 140 % of GDP. In this scenario, the U.S. would have to pay 7 % of its GDP to other countries every year in the future due to its huge external debt.

However, there are few solutions to the debt crisis, one is to tighten the spending and squeeze out money to pay off the debt; the second is to start a war and pay off the debt with looted wealth; the third is to inflate and write off the debt. In the era of paper money and the so-called "sovereign money" era, the third approach is the easiest, because the government can print money at will, which will certainly trigger inflation, the real debt will be diluted.

The Federal Reserve has already implemented its second quantitative easing policy, with a plan to buy $4 trillion in bonds. American public opinion is spreading the news that the CPI (Consumer Price Index) in the United States has reached its lowest value in nearly 20 years. As a result, the Fed could continue its quantitative easing policy without causing inflation. In fact, in any sense, a country's central bank buying its Treasury bills is equivalent to issuing banknotes, and the Fed's purchase of U.S. treasury bills is intended to cause inflation, devalue the dollar, and ultimately reduce the U.S. debt burden.

Meanwhile, since 2012, the European Central Bank has also injected nearly €1 trillion in three-year loans into European commercial banks. Besides, the ECB has bought up a large number of troubled bonds of countries in the debt crisis. These methods are all equivalent to issuing banknotes. Japan also issued many more yen to intervene in the exchange rate market. Therefore, there is a clear trend of excess liquidity in the international capital markets.

However, because of the shadow of recession, the excess liquidity has not yet caused significant inflation, but the commodity futures market has reacted somewhat, and the prices of raw materials such as gold and oil have started to rise. There is a time lag between inflation and the issuance of banknotes, and it will take several years for the impact of these measures to become apparent.

The dollar is the reserve currency in the international monetary system and the pricing currency for commodity futures such as oil and food. There is a mechanical link between the devaluation of the dollar, which inevitably causes commodity futures prices to rise. As China has become a major importer of various raw materials, a sharp rise in commodity futures prices in the international market will cause imported inflation, which will have a huge impact on China.

In some recent years, Chinese companies have been investing abroad, not only in Europe, the United States, and Japan, but also in some developing countries in Africa and Latin America, and these investments have become one of the important drivers of economic growth in some developing countries. Converting a large number of foreign exchange reserves into an outbound investment can reduce the risk of foreign exchange reserve shrinkage, and also use the outbound investment to obtain more technology that China desperately needs, as well as to get more return on investment. This may be the best way to hedge the risk of foreign exchange reserves.

However, there are also many risks associated with the outbound investment, and China needs to take early precautions and layout to prevent falling into investment traps. On a macroeconomic level, strengthening outbound investment can alleviate many problems. For example, greater outbound investment by Chinese companies can use up some of the foreign exchange, ease the pressure on the appreciation of the RMB caused by foreign exchange inflows, free the Chinese central bank from the burden of being forced to intervene in the market and remove a factor that contributes to macroeconomic instability.

At the microeconomic level, enterprises can invest in developed countries to acquire new technologies or open new markets, and in developing countries to reduce costs and hedge against the risk of diminishing marginal returns on investment. At present, it is a good time for Chinese enterprises to increase foreign investment. Since the outbreak of the financial crisis, European and American countries require fresh capital. Financial institutions in Europe and the United States used a lot of "high leverage" operations before the outbreak of the crisis, and then entered a round of "deleveraging" process after the outbreak of the crisis, which has caused banks and other institutions to "credit crunch" phenomenon. Although the Federal Reserve and the European Central Bank have injected a lot of liquidity into the market, it is difficult for industrial enterprises in Europe and the United States to loan. Many industrial enterprises in Europe are very willing to open their capital accounts to Chinese enterprises, allowing them to buy their shares and become their shareholders. In the past, it was difficult for Chinese capital to enter these companies because they were worried about leaking technology secrets, but now they are desperate for capital and are willing to let Chinese companies participate. Chinese companies can use this opportunity to enter the European market, learn more about the technologies that China desperately needs, and improve their products.

Likewise, many developing countries are in desperate need of Chinese capital. Many developing countries used to rely on aid and investment from developed countries to maintain their economic growth, but after the financial crisis, the flow of funds from developed countries was interrupted and many developing countries became the "forgotten corner", so they are eager to receive investment from Chinese companies. China's domestic infrastructure investment has been somewhat excessive and turns to invest in infrastructure in developing countries in Africa, Latin America, and other regions. Such foreign investment can not only improve the local investment environment, provide residents with a more convenient and comfortable living environment, but also can use China's excess capacity.

Besides, it is in the interest of Chinese companies to move certain production lines to other developing countries. This can make Chinese enterprises' exports to Europe and the United States no longer subject to China's export quotas, and also allow Chinese equipment investments to have a longer payback period and take full advantage of other countries' markets and cheap labor.

However, Chinese companies going abroad and investing overseas also need to guard against various risks. First of all, to invest in developing countries in Africa and Latin America, certain political risks should be taken into consideration. These countries used to be colonies of European powers, and the division of national borders was unnatural, hiding many conflicts. After the trend of national independence in the 1960s, these contradictions were ignored and covered up under the rule of strongman politics. When Chinese companies participate in the economic development of these countries, especially in the exploitation of certain resources, some of these contradictions are exposed and used by various forces to marginalize Chinese companies. The split in Sudan is a case in point. Although the ethnic conflict between the north and the south of Sudan has always been sharp, the immediate trigger that led to the split between the two sides was the oil development in Sudan. This is a new test for China, testing both Chinese traditional diplomatic wisdom (the principle of non-interference in internal affairs) and how they can help local development in exchange for residents' support for Chinese companies and avoid being caught in a whirlwind of entanglement with various forces.

Secondly, we need to avoid cultural conflicts when investing in Europe and America. While Chinese companies are concerned about interpersonal relationships when doing business in China, in Europe and the United States, interpersonal relationships are important, but compliance with various procedures (including laws and regulations) is more important. In the past, some Chinese companies ignored the cultural differences and had cultural adaptation problems after merging with some European companies, and finally failed to make full use of the influence of the original brand and the sales channels of foreign companies to import Chinese products into the European market.

Once again, Chinese companies investing overseas should also prevent price risks. The prices of many commodities in the international market, especially commodity futures, fluctuate greatly, and they are all priced in U.S. dollars. Therefore, when the exchange rate of the U.S. dollar changes under the influence of U.S. monetary policy, the price of commodity futures will follow. If you don't pay attention to this, your investment can become more than worthwhile when the price trend suddenly turns. For example, two oil crises occurred in the 1970s, triggering economic stagnation. Some Latin American and African countries took advantage of the low dollar exchange rate and low-interest rates to borrow dollars from international capital markets to develop oil exploitation. But by the 1980s, the Reagan administration changed U.S. monetary policy and raised interest rates sharply to curb inflation. As a result, the dollar exchange rate strengthened, interest rates rose, and oil prices plummeted. Those countries that borrowed cheap dollars to develop oil immediately fell into a debt trap and suffered huge losses. Then, for example, when the Japanese yen appreciated sharply in the mid-1980s, it opened up its capital account so that Japanese companies and people could exchange the yen for various currencies to invest around the world. When the real estate bubble in Japan was too big, Japanese companies went to the U.S. to invest in real estate. in the early 1990s, the U.S. real estate bubble burst, Japanese companies suffered huge losses, and Japanese banks had a "credit crunch". Japanese companies had to painfully withdraw funds from the U.S., and the Japanese economy has been in ruins ever since.

Therefore, when Chinese companies increase overseas investment, they should be wary of falling into a similar investment trap. After World War II, former U.S. Secretary of State Marshall proposed the famous European Recovery Plan, and while the U.S. gave large sums of aid to Western European countries, it also cultivated the habit of using the U.S. dollar among Western European companies, laying the foundation for establishing the hegemonic position of the U.S. dollar in the Western European region. In the process of investing overseas, if Chinese companies can encourage foreign parties to accept RMB as an investment currency, it will play an important role in the internationalization of RMB.

Finally, the Chinese government needs to regulate the investment behavior of Chinese companies overseas. In 2015, Chinese outbound investment exceeded foreign direct investment for the first time, and since then Chinese companies have been investing overseas at a high rate. We need to have a rational understanding of such a development trend.

The General Office of the State Council had forwarded the Guidance on Further Guiding and Regulating the Direction of Overseas Investment by the National Development and Reform Commission, the Ministry of Commerce, the People's Bank of China, and the Ministry of Foreign Affairs in 2017, which clearly stated that investments in real estate, hotels, cinemas, entertainment, sports clubs and other projects abroad by Chinese domestic enterprises should be restricted. Meanwhile, European countries such as France, Germany, and Italy are worried that Chinese companies investing in European companies through mergers will master the latest technology of European companies. Therefore they suggest the European Commission strengthen the review and monitoring of mergers of European companies by companies from other regions.

Chinese companies have developed and are capable of investing abroad, expanding overseas markets, and acquiring new technologies through mergers and other forms. These are all welcome changes. But we also need to prevent the "swarm" approach and avoid the phenomenon of Chinese companies running abroad for the sake of foreign investment. In the process of development, Chinese enterprises have suffered a lot of "rush in business" and "all at once" losses.

By summarizing the growth of Chinese enterprises' outbound investment in the past few years, NDRC pointed out that some enterprises failed to accurately grasp the strategic direction of the country's "going out", lacking systematic planning and scientific proof to carry out overseas investment: some enterprises made blind decisions, resulting in difficulties in follow-up operation and large losses; some have focused their overseas investment on real estate and other non-real economy fields, which not only failed to boost domestic economic development, but also led to a significant increase in cross-border capital outflow and affected China's financial security; some enterprises ignored the standards and requirements of environmental protection, energy consumption and safety in the recipient countries, which led to conflicts and disputes.

The "Guidance on Further Guiding and Regulating the Direction of Overseas Investment" forwarded by the General Office of the State Council does not stop Chinese enterprises from investing overseas, but encourages them to invest more actively in some fields: focus on promoting overseas investment in infrastructure that is conducive to the construction along the "Belt and Road" and the interconnection of neighboring infrastructure; steadily carry out the overseas investment that drives advantageous production capacity, energy consumption, and energy efficiency. The Chinese government has also encouraged Chinese enterprises to make more active overseas investments in some fields: focus on promoting overseas investment in infrastructure that is conducive to the construction along the "Belt and Road" and the interconnection and sharing of neighboring infrastructure; steadily carry out an overseas investment that leads to the export of superior production capacity, high-quality equipment and technology standards; strengthen investment and cooperation with overseas high-tech and advanced manufacturing enterprises and encourage the establishment of R&D centers overseas; participate in the exploration and development of overseas oil and gas, mineral and other energy resources based on the prudent assessment of economic benefits; make efforts to expand foreign cooperation in agriculture and carry out mutually beneficial investment in agriculture, forestry, animal husbandry, and fishery. China will promote overseas investment in commerce, culture, logistics, and other services in an orderly manner, and support qualified financial institutions to establish branches and service networks abroad and conduct business in compliance with the law.

The overseas investment of Chinese companies is certainly a good thing. But if you do not pay attention to the details of the investment, sometimes a good thing can turn into a bad thing. For example, although Chinese companies are investors and can bring more jobs and tax revenue to other countries, but if they become complacent and bossy, they will not only cause resentment among the leaders and people of the countries receiving Chinese investment but also cause low labor productivity and end up with the result of "losing money". Remember, they are operating on other people's land, under the management of other countries, earning the money of the local people, and should take care of the psychology (face) and interests of the local people. Chinese enterprises should respect local culture, local laws, and regulations, and treat local people and ordinary residents well. Only in this way can Chinese companies ensure a return on their overseas investments and achieve long-term development in overseas markets.

Of course, the Chinese government should also work together with Chinese companies to build China's soft power and create a good international image, so that Chinese companies can compete for more profits and markets in their overseas investments, and also add to China's soft power building. The Chinese government has done a lot of work for Chinese companies going abroad in recent years. The Ministry of Commerce has also provided training funds for employees of Chinese companies in Africa, allowing African employees to visit China and increase their perceptual understanding of the country. Chinese companies should also cooperate more actively with the Chinese government and contribute to building a positive image of China.

5

China's International Discourse Power

China's development in the 21st century is obviously the most successful in world history. But China's successful development nevertheless caused a lot of criticism in Western media. Theories bout "China threat" followed theories bout "China collapse". Different qualification of China's development made Chinese public opinion puzzled. As I have been often questioned by students of graduate school of Chinese academy of social sciences on Western media's specific description of China's development, when I was lecturing at this school, I decided to write down my analysis on international discourse power around 2016, because the qualification of China's development is not neutral.

In recent years, China's GDP has continued to grow; the quality of economic development has continued to improve; industrial upgrading has steadily advanced; new economic models have emerged. At the same time, China's disposable income per capita has grown faster than China's GDP, and the number of poor people has gradually decreased, so that by 2020, China could become a country with no *absolute poverty*. For a less populous country, these accomplishments could be achieved by a sudden discovery of underground resources of great economic value; however, as a country of more than 1.3 billion people, China's development could be regarded as a miracle in the economic history of the world.

We can hear some criticism of China's rapid development from both domestic and foreign public opinions. It is easy to understand that the foreign opinion on

China's rapid development can be scornful, but it is puzzling that some Chinese people find such criticism quite appealing. I believe that the international discourse power has huge impact to this phenomenon. The power to evaluate China's development is not yet in Chinese people's own hands, while foreign media have a great influence on the evaluation of China's development. Therefore, it is necessary to sort out how a country's international discourse is established—only by establishing China's international discourse can domestic and foreign public have a clear and objective understanding of China's development.

The Concept of Discourse Power

While the original meaning of discourse is "the right to speak", in modern society, discourse power (or "discourse") also refers to the ability to control public opinion and the direction of social development. Whoever holds the right to speak is in control of the direction of social opinion. Gramsci was an Italian thinker and an early leader of the Italian Communist Party. In current studies and discussion of the international monetary system and the theory of hegemony, we often have to quote Gramsci's definition of discourse. According to Gramsci's analysis, social groups usually use two kinds of power to maintain their position: the domination of the superstructure (or the "state apparatus"), and the intellectual and moral leadership. Discourse is the second type of power. The French thinker Foucault also defined discourse as a form of knowledge—he argues that power and knowledge belongs to a symbiotic pair, and all human knowledge is acquired through discourse. Discourse means that a social group transmits certain meanings to society based on *stereotypes*, thereby establishing its social status and becoming known to other social groups. The "self-evident" truths in our thoughts are in fact subliminally inculcated, and these "truths" may not necessarily be true. Foucault argues that discourse is the values and opinions that can be accepted as truth.

In addition, discourse is related to soft power—something can be interpreted as the ability to guide others to think and act according to one's will. Soft power changes as the dominance of a country changes. Such as France in 18th century, Britain in 19th century, and United States in 20th century, these countries created and possessed great soft powers. When a country is relatively strong, its soft power is sturdy; and if the soft power of one country is vigorous, its international discourse will be robust, as other countries will follow the dominant countries' values and way of thinking to consider any problems.

For example, in the 18th century, France had a strong international voice. At that time, French was the *lingua franca* of the world. For example, when we read Russian novels today, many passages are written in French. Tolstoy's novel "War and Peace" has long dialogues in French. Later on, Britain began its industrial revolution and gradually rose to power, colonizing the world and becoming the *"Empire on which the sun never sets"*, and English became a universal language. Finally, with the rise of the United States, the United States took over the international discourse from Britain. Soft power is related to hard power, but not necessarily correlated. When China was weak in hard power, its soft power was relatively stronger. For example, in the 1950s, when the national liberation movement was flourishing, China's Five Principles of Peaceful Coexistence became an important principle that governed relations between all major Asian and African countries; in the 1970s, China's "Three Worlds Theory" influenced the development of the world landscape. Since the 1990s, China's hard power has gradually increased, but its soft power has not achieved a corresponding development. There are several reasons for this: China is a socialist country, and the international socialist movement was at a low ebb from the late 1990s; China's "Three Worlds Theory" emphasized the global influence of the Third World, but as China focused on economic development and a low profile diplomacy, it became less vocal in the international political arena.

Countries that have the power of discourse will try to construct a discourse system. The discourse system changes in different periods and context, but it also has the components of inheritance. The discourse we are talking about today is inherited, so as the human civilization is inherited.

For example, we often talk about democracy and dictatorship nowadays. Democracy is actually a very old word, and democracy in its historical context is not the same thing as the politicized "democracy" today. Democracy in ancient Greece was a lotting system, while today's democracy is synonymous with civil rights and good governance.

In the 18th and 19th centuries, democracy was sometimes synonymous with the tyranny of the majority. In the second half of the 18th century, the American Revolution and the French Revolution occurred at the same time in history, and the Founding Fathers of the US were concerned that the tyranny of the majority would affect the development of the United States, so they devised a system of check and balance between powers. According to the American federalists, democracy and tyranny of the majority were almost equated. So, when the United States was founded, the framers of the political system devised the "separation of powers" system to prevent tyranny of the majority or the abuse of democracy. However, the American "separation of powers" system was later pictured as a standard form of democracy. This shows that the meaning of political vocabulary is constantly changing.

It was only after the 19th century that democracy became synonymous with universal suffrage and a slogan for women's right to vote and for people's social progress. Since then, democracy has slowly become a "good thing". After World War II, democracy was also the slogan of socialist countries. In the 1950s and 1960s, democracy was the slogan of the Third World countries against Western domination. After World War II, the Western countries wanted to restore their rule over the former colonial countries. But the peoples of Asia, Africa and Latin America demanded nation building, and their independence was achieved through democratic movements. At that time, the socialist countries actively supported the democratic movements of the former colonial peoples and even supported their armed independence movements. Until the 1960s, the Western countries' foreign policy for Asian, African and Latin American countries was to support dictatorial regimes—such as in Korea for Seung-han Lee, in Iran for King Pahlavi, and in Nicaragua for the Somoza family.

Politicians sometimes inherit slogans to arouse people's feelings, such as Bush Jr.'s "axis of evil"—a clear inheritance of Reagan's "evil empire" phrase. Because the collapse of the Soviet Union was considered a success of U.S. diplomatic strategy, Bush Jr. inherited and developed the discourse of the cold war, which led the public to believe that he was "on the right side of history". As we can see, discourse is also a right of interpretation, and the same discourse can be interpreted differently at different stages of history. There is a process of inheritance of discourse.

Discourse Building

Discourse is part of the international strategy of a great power and is driven by the state. However, the state basically only plays a driving role behind the scenes, and most of what we can see is the activity of some media people, industry experts and scientists.

The discourse in today's world is dominated by the United States. U.S. dominance of international discourse is accomplished through a dedicated strategy, not by accident. For example, one of the responsibilities of the U.S. government is "well-functioning communications and engagement," meaning that U.S. national strategic communications is a targeted, planned, and systematic global strategy that is one of the most important means of achieving its dominant international order and maintaining and asserting its global leadership position. The implementation of this strategy has a threefold significance for the United States:

- promoting domestic unity as a mobilizing factor for foreign expansion;
- strengthening relations with allied countries; and
- weakening the governments of non-allied countries and polarize their political and social systems.

These strategic goals are overtly stated in U.S. government documents. Obama also has a strategy with his own set of priorities, first, to get foreign populations to recognize the relationship of interest between their countries and the United States; second, to convince foreign populations that the United States plays a constructive role in global affairs; and third, to get foreign populations to see the United States as a respectable partner in addressing global challenges.

Film industry is a significant part of the U.S. strategic communication system, an important part of U.S. soft power, and a tool for the U.S. to spread its "mainstream values". The U.S. often makes movies themed with global issues, such as "2012". In the movie, when the world faces a disaster, it is always the Americans who save the whole mankind in the end. Hollywood plays a huge role in this, subliminally making audiences around the world agree that the United States is the most reliable and respected partner in dealing with global challenges. When you look at American entertainment programs through this lens, you will understand that they are in fact carefully planned, and they are subliminally instilling American values into the audience.

U.S. Department of Defense's *Strategic Communications Linkage Integration Concept* has several important elements to promote U.S. credibility and legitimacy:

- directing attitudes and behavior in favor of the United States; t
- degrading the credibility and legitimacy of adversaries by, for example, discrediting their ideology or policies and exposing their mistakes and lies;
- persuading specific audiences to take specific actions in support of U.S. objectives;
- directing adversaries to take or abandon specific actions.

Such work by Americans is done meticulously by observing intellectuals in other countries. Americans act purposefully to get some intellectuals to support U.S. goals, and they steer their opponents to take or abandon taking particular actions. If the U.S. finds that authors from some countries have written articles against the U.S., they will even invite these people to the U.S. and exert some influence on them. The United States relies on information operations to implement these tactics, known as "controlled information dissemination". These works include:

- "white propaganda"—infiltration through public government activities, such as public diplomacy led by the U.S. State Department and government media represented by the Voice of America;
- "Black propaganda"—propaganda activities carried out covertly. The U.S. Department of Defense, the Central Intelligence Agency and other agencies carrying out propaganda activities are mostly in this category, including secret control of domestic and foreign media, buying politicians and a large number of infiltration activities;
- "gray propaganda"—through bribes, inducements and other means to induce other countries that is, through bribes and inducements, to induce "opinion leaders" or media practitioners in other countries to act as their spokespersons, so as to achieve the purpose of promoting U.S. interests and influencing government decisions in the relevant countries. The targets of "gray propaganda" include not only U.S. opponents, but also U.S. allies.

The British author Francis Stoner Sanders wrote a book called *The Cultural Cold War and the CIA* about how the United States influenced Soviet leaders and intellectuals through "gray propaganda" during the Cold War. Readers will be surprised to learn that many very famous people were on the CIA list, and they all received favors from the United States, including many prominent Western European intellectuals. Many of the stories and details are evocative. Among these three types of national strategic communications activities, "black propaganda" and "gray propaganda" are largely carried out by the U.S. Department of Defense, the CIA, and other secretive agencies, receiving very large budgets, often in the tens of billions of dollars.

It is important to understand that none of these events happened by chance. Chinese scholar Wang Shaoguang (王绍光) has written a book review of Sanders' book. He believes that after reading this book, one can conclude that the CIA is actually the hidden "propaganda department" of the United States. George Kennan, who proposed the containment strategy, once said, "This country has no ministry of culture, and the CIA was obliged to do what it could to fill the gap." There are many media and publishing houses around the world funded by the U.S. government, and their positions will be influenced by the entry of U.S. capital.

The public opinion environment in China is also more complex now, with more diverse views. Therefore, when we read the content published by the media, we need to have the ability to think and judge independently. Lippmann was a major figure in American communications and one of the key figures in charge of propaganda in the U.S. government. During the World War II era, Lippmann conducted extensive research on social psychology, and these findings profoundly influenced American journalists. Journalists would incorporate values into news stories to achieve the propaganda they wanted. The public was then influenced to passively accept their logic when reading or listening to the news. In Sanders's book *The Cultural Cold War and the CIA*, general impression is that the targets of the U.S. government's propaganda are liberals who are better grasped and more likely to elicit a response. However, by examining the available records, this is not necessarily the case. In post-World War II Europe, the real targets of U.S. propaganda were non-Communist left-wing intellectuals with a sense of disillusionment and frustration, not liberals. For example, the United States tried to influence some people who had participated in the communist movement, such as the French writer André Malraux and the British writer George Orwell.

In addition to these overt strategies, Sanders describes in his book how the CIA implemented strategic objectives. The CIA developed a cadre of agents in allied and hostile countries who were able to constantly speak for the United States, and they also shaped a value system, such as the United States being an integral part of the global system and U.S. leadership being conducive to global development.

Joseph Nye, former U.S. Assistant Secretary of Defense and professor at the Kennedy School of Government at Harvard University, is the originator of the concept of *soft power*. In his theory, soft power is naturally occurring. Nye believes that any culture that has a certain appeal has a certain amount of soft power. He gives many examples from the United States and Britain, and also talks about how Westerners were particularly envious of the Chinese when China was strong. In the 18th century, Europe's economy was not as strong as China's, and there was a gap in the living standards of the people. At that time, the Chinese way of life was the object of Westerners' imitation, for example, the Westerners' habit of drinking afternoon tea came from China.

Nye deliberately ignores the role of the massive covert activities of the U.S. military and intelligence agencies, easily dismissing them by saying, "it does not mean that the CIA plays no role in generating soft power."[1] In fact, the

U.S. government places great importance on the development of U.S. soft power, and Nye, who served as assistant secretary of defense, is one of the central figures in building U.S. soft power. We need to be clear that our perceptions of many things are not natural but are guided by public opinion.

How China Builds Its International Discourse

On various social media in China, we can see a lot of information deliberately spread by Western media (especially American media), and many of these messages are deliberately fabricated. What should we do facing such disinformation? How should China establish its international discourse?

China still has some difficulties in building an international discourse. First, China does not have an independent discourse system that is recognized by the world. In the process of China's development, there are many things we are still exploring. In China, we say "crossing the river by feeling the stones" as there is no concrete reference. Whether it is the peaceful rise, peaceful development or other concepts, we still lack a complete theoretical system to support our discourse. The Canadian sociologist Daniel A. Bell has proposed a theoretical system, namely "Neo-Confucianism + Socialism", but the Chinese need a more systematic study on their own term.

Second, Western countries, led by the United States, still hold the hegemony of international discourse, still spread prejudices about China, and hijack the discourse on international issues related to China. For example, in terms of the exchange rate issue, the foreign exchange reserve issue, and the trade issue mentioned earlier, Western countries are always trying to create public opinion and make everyone think that only their explanations are just. But in reality, the nature of the problem may have little to do with their explanations, they just want to control public opinion and guide people's perceptions of China. No one may listen to China's explanations, or no one may understand them, because discourse is a preconceived thing. Once the Western media have introduced public opinion into a certain way of thinking, the public will only think in accordance with that stereotype. Such stereotypes built up under the hegemony of discourse are very difficult to break.

Again, compared to Western media, Chinese media is still underdeveloped, and Chinese media is still basically "fetishistic" in its analysis of many issues, with little independent thinking and judgment. When Chinese media take foreign information to form their own analytical framework, they will be influenced by the Western discourse, because this analytical framework is exactly the kind of values that Westerners want to export.

Finally, China's approach to managing the media and its skill in mastering the discourse lags far behind that of Western countries. In the United States, for example, although there is no dedicated propaganda department, the CIA and the Department of Defense are all engaged in foreign propaganda work. They develop communication strategies, construct international discourse, and exert influence on other countries. Although China has a department dedicated to propaganda, its propaganda skills significantly lag behind the United States in terms of technique.

We all know that propaganda is important, and that "the barrel of guns" (force) and "the pen"(writings) are the two pillars of the Chinese Communist Party's success. However, propaganda work in China today has become somewhat limited. China has a socialist market economy system where the government does not order but directs behavior in the market. In fact, the same thing is true for propaganda. The U.S. government does a very stealthy job when it comes to guiding the media. Americans place great emphasis on freedom of the press, but anyone who has worked in the American media knows that there is no such thing as freedom of the press in the United States. The U.S. is concerned with "controlled dissemination of information" in its foreign propaganda work, which means that the government has control over the dissemination of information. In today's world, the U.S. government's decisions are so important that all media workers in the U.S. want preferential treatment from the government and priority access to certain information. In this way, they can earn more eyeballs and gain more revenue. Therefore, media workers in the United States want to maintain a better relationship with government officials, otherwise they will not get any information. The U.S. government uses this method to control public opinion.

The U.S. government's strategic planning requires the cooperation of many parties, including the media, NGOs, foundations, and others, and requires many skills to communicate and coordinate with various groups and organizations. Chinese institutions responsible for overseeing advocacy work also need to learn these skills to facilitate the dissemination of ideas and build China's discourse.

U.S. foreign propaganda will also be achieved through a large number of government-funded and government-supported NGOs that foster proxies and pro-U.S. forces around the world. If U.S. foreign propaganda relied exclusively on government agencies to preach, the effect would be completely different. In China, the government is accustomed to sending many preaching missions around the country to preach the spirit of the Party Congress, but this method is hardly acceptable to foreign populations. Westerners often have stereotypes about government propaganda, so government missions often cause resentment among people, who believe that what the government says is unreliable.

We need to learn to do a better job of propaganda in a market economy, which involves a discourse that needs to be more skillfully guided by the government. One of the tasks China now faces is to build a persuasive and internally consistent discourse that allows other countries to understand why it is right for China to follow its own path and is conducive to its development.

The root cause of many of China's problems is that we do not have a complete discourse system. Therefore, even though China is doing better than other countries, there are still many people on the Internet who cannot make an objective analysis and evaluation of China's development, and there are always people who think that the moon is rounder in foreign countries. In fact, few countries in the world have developed better than China in recent years. This is a strange gap (between China's magnificent development and the international evaluation on China), and the current evaluation is abnormal.

There are some people who like to fragment Chinese history. In 2009, as we celebrated the 60th anniversary of the founding of the People's Republic of China, some media liked to compare first 30 years earlier with the 30 years later, a rather absurd way of looking at history. After the founding of China, the 60 years of modernization and industrialization in China would not have been possible without the foundation laid in the first 30 years. Without the foundation of the development of heavy industry in the first 30 years, the development of light industry in the second 30 years would have been a castle in the sand. To explain clearly why China has succeeded, we need to explain clearly the rugged journey of development during these 60 years, which also requires a discourse system. During the past 60 years, China has completed the 200 years development of Western countries. How did China manage to achieve it so quickly? How can we understand the logic behind this? China has developed so fast that it is impossible to say the Chinese system has no superiority. In Western discourse, the system in Western countries is democratic, while China is not, and Westerners do not approve of the Chinese system. But China has achieved more than what the West did in recent decades, both in terms of social and economic development. So can we still say that the Western system is superior? Social scientists need to study and account for these phenomena.

The rise of China is a miracle in human history, and no other similar example can be found in the last 200 years of world history. Many researchers have tried to explain it, and the Chinese themselves are exploring it, but no convincing discourse has yet emerged. Joshua Cooper Reimer, a leading expert on China, has proposed the Beijing Consensus, an attempt to systematically articulate China's unique development path, but it has not been clear either.

John Naisbitt was a global sensation in the 1980s, and his book, *Megatrends: Ten New Directions Transforming Our Lives*, was translated into more than two dozen languages and was a global bestseller. In the 1990s, he came to China, built an institute in Tianjin, observed and studied China for more than a decade, and wrote a book called *China's Megatrends: The 8 Pillars of a New Society*, which attempted to explain the miracle of China's rapid development and summarized the eight pillars that support the development of Chinese society. But Naisbitt, after all, is a Westerner, and he does not fundamentally challenge the Western system, except to say that democracy in China is different from the West: The West is a horizontal democracy while China is a vertical democracy. Horizontal democracy means that everyone has equal rights, and everyone is the same when voting, but the decisions made by the vote are not necessarily implemented in the end. The advantage of vertical democracy is that people's demands can be fed back directly to the top, and then fed back down from the top to be implemented. He cited many events since China's reform and opening up, including a kind of up-and-down interaction for key reforms such as the land contract responsibility system. It is all about foreigners helping the Chinese sort out their experience, while we ourselves still lack a discourse system, making it difficult to tell the Chinese story.

In dialogues with other countries, China tries to use its own words to explain problems, but in the current situation, it is difficult for China's own explanation to be accepted by other countries. In international dialogues, we need to be good at convincing Westerners with their words. Discourse can be inherited and transferred, and although we can borrow the Western discourse, we need to add a new interpretation. If we create a discourse that is completely unrelated to or not inherited from the Western discourse, it will be difficult for them to accept it.

Only by constructing a proper discourse can Westerners accept Chinese logic. For example, there is a dispute between the Chinese and the Westerners on the issue of democracy. Westerners cannot accept our discourse; they think that only the Western system is democratic, and that other countries must be authoritarian if they are different from them. This dichotomy is a trap, and it is a big discursive misunderstanding. There are never only two types of human political systems, democracy and autocracy. Since Westerners believe that their culture is inherited from the ancient Greek and Roman times, we can start with ancient Greece. Aristotle was one of the first thinkers to classify political systems into six categories, of which the current political system (democracy) of Western countries is only one of them. Aristotle talked about the legitimacy of each type of political system, its foundation, mass support, and the rise and fall of the system. Since thousands of years ago, the Greeks already recognized that there are so many categories of political systems, how can Westerners today think that there are only two categories of political systems?

Moreover, democracy in Western countries is actually degenerating. According to American political scientist Fukuyama, the American style of "vetocracy" will ruin American democracy. Aristotle also pointed out that any political system has a period of rise and a period of decline, and he also analyzed the manifestations of various political systems in the period of decline.

When our knowledge system is more well-rounded, we will not easily fall into the discourse system of others. When we step out of the discourse system of others, we can find the logic of our own discourse. We need to explain "the Chinese road" (*中国道路*) in terms that Westerners can understand, so that they can ask one more question about why. Only in this way can we make Westerners look at China more objectively and understand China's behavior.

The Rise of China's National Power and China's International Status

In recent years, China has developed rapidly, with a rapidly growing economic output and great progress in building a government-led social welfare system and modernizing its national defense. Against the backdrop of the global economic crisis, China has managed to maintain rapid economic growth, which has attracted worldwide attention and many comments on China's national power and its international status. There is great concern about when China will surpass the United States and become the world's largest economy. Some researchers in the United States are more concerned about how China will use that power in the international arena if it surpasses the United States economically. Radicals argue that China's rise will challenge U.S. hegemony and that the United States must unite all forces in Asia to contain China's rise, while moderates argue that China has benefited greatly from the current international system and will not undermine it, and that developed countries in Europe and the United States can benefit from China's rapid development.

China's power is indeed rising rapidly, but it is a challenge to calculate it. Goldman Sachs has published a series of studies on the development of China,

Russia, India and Brazil since 2003 (Goldman Sachs chief economist, Jim O'Neill, first introduced the BRIC concept in 2001). According to the report, if the current development trend continues, the world economic map will change dramatically in the next few decades; among them, China's economy will expand rapidly, with China's GDP surpassing that of the United Kingdom in 2005, Germany in 2007, Japan in 2016, and finally the United States in 2041.

While this conclusion by Goldman Sachs is based on different rates of economic growth in each country, it does not take into account the appreciation of exchange rates. If the currencies of some of the world's strongest economies were to depreciate significantly, or if the RMB were to appreciate significantly, Goldman Sachs' forecast of GDP growth would be far from reality. In fact, it is not very appropriate to calculate economic strength by exchange rate, because the structure of each country's economy is different, and some economic sectors are not competitive areas, and these sectors may be underestimated or overestimated because of different exchange rates. Take the United States as an example: In the U.S. economic structure, the service sector accounts for a large proportion, and the service sector is largely free from the threat of external competition, so these sectors have high wages and high benefits. The prices of public transportation, cabs, restaurants, and barber stores in many U.S. cities are comparable to those in China (except that you have to convert dollars to RMB), and the exchange rate difference between the dollar and the RMB is not reflected here at all. So, it seems that either the US service industry is grossly over-valued, or our service industry is grossly undervalued.

Angus Maddison, an economic historian for the Organization for Economic Cooperation and Development, disagrees with the use of current exchange rates to measure the size of countries' economies, preferring to use purchasing power parity (PPP) to measure the strength of the world's economies across years. According to Maddison's PPP method, China surpassed Japan in 1992 to become the world's second largest economy. Madison has repeatedly emphasized that his projections are "conservative estimates," predicting that China's economy will be 1.07 times larger than that of the United States in 2015 and 1.5 times larger by 2030. According to Madison's calculations, the U.S. economy is not as large as announced, while the Chinese economy is larger than the official figures.

An increasing number of international economic organizations use the purchasing power parity method to calculate economic aggregates for each country. For example, the World Bank published a report in 1997 entitled "China in 2020," which assumed that the average annual growth rate of China's GDP would gradually slow from 8.4 % to 5 % after 1997. In 1997, the Asian Development

Bank published the report "Rising Asia," which made three possible estimates of China's economic trends: First, an optimistic scenario in which China's GDP per capita grows at 6.6 % from 1995 to 2025; The second is the pessimistic scenario, with a per capita GDP growth rate of 4.4 % from 1995 to 2025; the third is the basic scenario, with a per capita GDP growth rate of 6.05 % from 1995 to 2025. Under the third scenario, by 2025, China's GDP per capita will be equivalent to 38.2 % of the U.S. GDP per capita, while China's population will be more than four times larger than the U.S. population. That is, China's GDP would be 1.5 times that of the United States in 2025. These projections are based on the purchasing power parity (PPP) method.

While the PPP method of calculating GDP makes more sense than the exchange rate method, it also has many unsatisfactory features. For example, the PPP method counts similar consumption as the same price, but in reality, there are differences in similar consumption. For example, the quality of different brands of cars varies greatly in price; similarly, the quality and price of housing also vary greatly. But in the PPP calculation, these differences are ignored. This creates a gap between its results and reality. Before the fall of the Berlin Wall, the GDP of the GDR was high by the PPP method. However, after the reunification of Germany, the GDP of the regions that were formerly part of the GDR fell by the wayside. There are political reasons for this, but it is true that the quality of GDR products is not as good as that of the Federal Republic.

Therefore, we must guard against both arrogance and presumption when calculating China's economic aggregates. Whether calculated by the purchasing power parity method or by the exchange rate, it is entirely possible for China's total economic output to exceed that of the United States in the next decade or so. This is because China's economy is growing faster than that of the United States, and its population is several times larger than that of the United States, and the RMB will continue to appreciate in the future.

Goldman Sachs still seems to have underestimated China's growth potential. China's economy grew rapidly during the Eleventh and Twelfth Five-Year Plans (2006–2015), and China's GDP surpassed that of several world powers to become the world's second largest economy. In 2015, China's GDP was more than twice that of Japan, and more than the combined GDP of Germany, France, and the United Kingdom.

Although China's economic strength is likely to surpass that of the United States in the next few years, the road of China's development may not smooth. We can only predict the future now based on known information, but many factors may emerge in the future that we did not anticipate, including changes in economic structure, changes in the external environment, and changes in policy. In the future, it is difficult to predict what factors will play a role during what time and in which way.

In the 1950s, the Soviet Union grew rapidly and was the first to launch artificial satellites into space. It was thought that the Soviet Union would soon become the largest economy in the world. However, a series of international political and economic events disrupted the trajectory of the Soviet Union, which eventually collapsed instead. But after the signing of "the Plaza Accord[2]", the yen appreciated sharply, and the Bank of Japan's monetary policy aimed at the exchange rate, trying to prevent the yen from continuing to appreciate by all means. As a result, the excessively loose monetary policy created a huge economic bubble, with the size of the Japanese real estate market and stock market expanding rapidly, and Japan's GDP also grew rapidly. At one time, international public opinion was talking about when Japan would overtake the United States. Japanese companies invested heavily in the U.S., blowing up the bubble in the U.S. real estate market, but when the U.S. economic bubble burst, Japanese companies also became the biggest victims. The Japanese economy has been in ruins ever since.

There are many similar examples. For example, until the international financial crisis in 2008, Iceland had one of the highest GDP per capita in the world and was considered an economic miracle in the developed world. But after the outbreak of the financial crisis, Iceland fell into bankruptcy. In the next decade or so, China's development will also encounter many difficulties. Can we learn from history and avoid repeating the same mistakes?

First, China's economy has a high degree of external dependence, and its rapid development in recent years has been closely related to the rapid growth of export trade. However, the international financial crisis may prevent demand in external markets from returning to pre-crisis levels soon, and China's economic structure will face the threat of overcapacity if it fails to make adjustments. China needs to find new external markets or stimulate domestic demand to cope with overcapacity.

Second, China's development is not balanced enough, and the regional gap, the urban-rural gap, and the gap between rich and poor among different social groups are large, constituting a destabilizing factor within the society. The international economic crisis has affected China differently at all levels of the economy, and some industries and social groups have been greatly affected. The Chinese government is actively building a unified social security system for urban and rural areas to provide basic protection for all people. This plays an important role in alleviating social conflicts, maintaining social stability and ensuring future development.

Thirdly, China's rapid development is still a kind of extensive development, with serious consumption of resources and energy, and industrial production has also caused serious environmental pollution problems. Diseases caused by environmental pollution affect people's health and aggravate social costs. In addition, China's carbon dioxide emissions have become a problem of international relations. Developed countries in Europe and the United States have threatened to impose "carbon tariffs" on China's exports on the grounds that carbon emissions are responsible for climate change. If China is sidelined by developed countries because of emission reduction, its future development will also be affected.

Fourth, China's demographic dividend is gradually disappearing. 2012 saw the first decline in China's working-age population, followed by a wave of population aging. If China does not actively prepare for the aging process and rapidly improve the quality of its workforce, its economic development will slow down considerably when it becomes "old before it gets rich".

Fifth, there are factors of instability in China's neighboring regions. For example, the U.S. is fighting a "war on terror" in Afghanistan and Pakistan, and the U.S. is constantly conducting military exercises with India. If there is major unrest in China's neighbors, China will also be disturbed. Thus, China's development depends on internal stability as well as on the international landscape.

If China can properly deal with the above issues and resolve these conflicts, the Chinese economy can continue to maintain its growth momentum, moving to a higher level and embarking on a healthier development path. As the size of China's economy increases and China's comprehensive national power grows, international public opinion has a different assessment of China's international status.

The contribution of China's economic growth to the global economy is easy to be recognized, and the role of the Chinese economy in future global economic development will grow more and more important. From this perspective, China is certainly a responsible power that plays an important role not only in East Asia, but also globally.

Some U.S. conservatives believe that although China's national strength has increased significantly, it is still difficult to call China a responsible power for a single reason: many of its "friends" are the "enemies" of the United States, which are perceived by Americans as "failed" states. They believe that in the case of the Iranian nuclear issue and the North Korea nuclear issue, China's "friends" are the "enemies" of the United States. They argue that China failed to cooperate with U.S. sanctions against Iran and North Korea, and its unconditional aid to African countries undermines Western efforts to democratize Africa.

But the point is, should Americans evaluate China's contribution to the international community? Should Americans set the standards for China on its responsibility for the international community?

China has provided substantial aid and direct investment to developing countries in Asia, Africa and Latin America, making an important contribution to the development of these countries. Since the 1990s, European and American countries have tied aid to African countries to democratization, resulting in ongoing civil wars and stagnant development in these countries. The democratization that began in the 1990s accelerated the polarization of these African countries, intensified the conflicts and contradictions between ethnic groups, and even caused ethnic hatred and killings. Is this indiscriminate democratization in the interest of the African people? Are the European and American countries acting responsibly? Some analysts point out that European countries promoted democratization in their former colonies in order to better control these countries. During the colonial period, European countries deliberately mixed many religious, cultural, and racial contradictions and oppositions when drawing the boundaries of their colonies in order to facilitate strategy of "divide and rule". After these colonies left colonial rule, these religious and racial contradictions again became the tools of European countries. Many African countries are rich in resources, so European countries use democratization to divide the political elites of African countries. And if political groups dare to prevent them from dividing Africa's natural resources, they will be subverted by "color revolutions". China does not support such democratization by Europe and the United States, and China has been vilified for actively helping African countries develop their economies.

In East Asia, China is also an active promoter of regional cooperation. The Chinese government actively participates in the "10+1" and "10+3"[3] cooperation in East Asia, promotes the establishment of a free trade area between ASEAN member countries and China, and promotes monetary and financial cooperation between ASEAN and China, Japan and South Korea. The Chinese government actively promotes cooperation among SCO member states in opposing international terrorism, separatism and religious extremism, and actively promotes economic cooperation and development among member states in order to eradicate the social roots of these three forces.

China has also made great contributions to the denuclearization of the Korean peninsula, actively organizing the Six-Party Talks on the Korean nuclear issue and providing a platform for negotiations to resolve the issue. China is actively improving its environment and pursuing a sustainable development path. In the face of the economic crisis, China's stimulus package plan includes many programs to support new technologies and new sources of energy, which provide a solid foundation for sustainable development. However, China's sustainable development depends not only on the transformation of its economy, but also on a stable external environment. China hopes that developed countries will be united in their cooperation against international terrorism and will not engage in double standards; China hopes that in the face of the economic crisis, countries will be sincere in their stance against the return of protectionism and that no country will use environmental standards to erect invisible barriers; China hopes that in the face of international disputes, all parties will resolve their problems through negotiations rather than threats, sanctions, or even military action.

The Chinese government emphasizes peaceful and harmonious development and the coordination of various interests. China is willing to maintain the existing international system, but international relations are an interactive relationship. And if some countries insist that China's development is a challenge to them and want to use the existing international system to contain and isolate China, it will inevitably cause conflicts. As China's national power grows, it is capable of creating a more stable neighborhood through greater regional cooperation. The future relationship between China and other countries will be mutually beneficial and symbiotic.

Notes

1 Joseph S. Nye, "Soft Power: The Means to Success in World Politics," https://www.belfercenter.org/sites/default/files/legacy/files/joe_nye_wielding_soft_power.pdf (Belfer Center, Harvard University, n.d.), Page 15.

2 On September 22, 1985, the finance ministers and central bank governors of the United States, the Federal Republic of Germany, France, the United Kingdom, Italy, and Canada had a meeting at the Plaza Hotel in New York. The meeting reached some consensus over the goal of jointly intervening in the foreign exchange market and bring down the dollar's value. Then the yen appreciated sharply, and Japan's domestic economic bubble grew sharply. Finally, the bubble burst caused the long-term stagnation of Japan's economic development.

3 "10+1" means ASEAN plus China, and "10+3" means ASEAN plus Japan, South Korea and China.

6 China's Institutional Advantage

*Once I had an interesting conversation with a member of Bundestag, he talked a lot about the "end of history" and the triumph of liberal democracy in the world probably in 2008. His analysis was so obviously encrusted into a very fashionable American school of thought that I cannot help to remind him that the dichotomy between democracy and autocracy is an artificial invention to serve the current political purposes, while it cannot reflect the reality either of the ancient Greece where democracy has been invented, or of today's world, because there are many other political regimes. Plato at lest described 3 political regimes, according to the number of rulers in question, and 3 other perverted regimes, so that makes 6 political regimes in total in his analysis. Why should we become more simplistic than our ancestors while today's reality is much more complex and complicated? That's why I decided to write a series of papers that analyse China's puzzle about political regimes and evolution of Chinese political system. Some of those papers have been written only around 2017, before the holding of Chinese communist party's 19*th *congress. Chinese political system may not be a perfect one, but we are ready to improve it instantly by pushing forward the reform process. That's a dialectic vision to which Chinese people is familiar and that might be the origin of China's recent success.*

Since its reform and opening up, China has experienced rapid economic development, social harmony and stability, and has made tremendous progress not only in terms of economic scale but also in terms of per capita income and social welfare. However, there are still questions about the direction and methods of

China's progress. Many argue that China does not have Western-style democracy and free elections, nor does it have multi-party rotating rule. Our future development will encounter many more problems, which some have attributed to institutional problems.

But if we take a closer look at Western democracy, we will find that the democracy—that the West is so proud of—actually has many flaws.

The Myth of Democracy—A Few Stereotypes about Democracy

Democracy Is Always a Good Thing

"Democracy is always a good thing"—this statement may seem fashionable, but in saying it, we fall into a trap of stereotypical thinking. People divide the world polity into two types based on the difference of political systems, which are democracy and autocracy. In this dichotomy, democracy becomes a "good thing" because no one agrees with autocracy. But if democracy and autocracy are not diametrically opposed to each other, does it make sense to say that "democracy is a good thing"?

In 2016, the emergence of two "black swan" political events, the British referendum to leave the European Union and the election of Donald Trump, a real estate tycoon with no political experience, made people doubt whether the democratic system would fail. From the UK referendum to leave the EU to Donald Trump's rise in the US presidential election, people are interested now in the failure of "democratic system". In fact, a few years ago, we already witnessed somehow the decline of "democracy" in the US. The congress dominated by Republican majority refused to approve anything that the Democrat administration might request, even to let the administration shut the door, for lack of budget. Political science pundits like Francis Fukuyama, also began to question whether democracy is supreme, as he suspected that "vetocracy" would bury American democracy.

However, whether in the West or in China, people are faced with a "democratic paradox": on the one hand, democracy is a sacrosanct goal people are looking for, but on the other hand, democracy is the ideal which is most likely to leave people dissatisfied. When we say that democracy is good, we are trapped by a dichotomy, a confrontation between democracy and dictatorship. People will choose democracy, because no one will stand for dictatorship. But if you are told that those two things are not in contradiction, what will you think about? For centuries, democracy has been synomymous with tyranny of the majority, so a sort of majority dictatorship.

Even in ancient Greek politics, political regimes were classified according to the number of people in power, but not according to the dichotomy between dictatorship and democracy. If the power is exercised by one person, it could be monarchy or tyranny; if the power is exercised by a few people, it could be either aristocracy or oligarchy; if the power is exercised by the majority of people, it could also be either republic or democracy. In other words, no matter how many people are in power, a political regime could be good or bad. In a monarchy, if the king takes care of his subjects, people may feel very comfortable; but if the power is taken by a tyrant, and he cares only about his own personal interests, the one person's power might be turned into tyranny, a very bad regime. In an aristocracy, if those patricians in power are characterized by glory and commitments, people may enjoy their lives and like the regime; if the patricians only take advantage of their positions for personal profit, then the regime will become an oligarchy. If the majority of the population sets rules and laws, and people abide by those laws, a republic is a good governance, but if the majority change its opinions very often, and laws and rules are shelved, and people are chasing personal interests as they like, then the regime fails and becomes a democracy. In the eyes of Plato, democracy is a little bit like anarchy. Anyway, bad regimes are all more or less autocratic, no matter if power is in the hands of one person, a few people or the majority.

So, what is democracy? Democracy today is only a form of decision-making, a voting system. People make decisions according to the opinion of the majority. However, is the majority always right? Talking about democracy, Westerners would trace it back to ancient Greece. But in the ancient Greek city-state politics, for quite a long time, democracy was not considered to be a very rational form of decision-making. Think of Socrates, the greatest ancient Greek philosopher. How did he die? Isn't it because he was condemned by the majority and sentenced to the death penalty? Moreover, the reasons for that verdict were purely "unwarranted," because he was supposed to have "confused young people".

In Democratic Countries, There Must Be Liberal Democracy

In countries where democracy is practiced, people enjoy a certain amount of freedom, and therefore, some people put a label on democracy that in a democratic country there must be a liberal democracy.

From a philosophical point of view, freedom and democracy are contradictory to each other. Zakaria, a leading American political commentator, has written that he is worried that the American political tradition of liberal democracy will split and eventually exclude the value dimension of freedom from the political system, leaving only democracy. In fact, the founders of the United States were so concerned about the tyranny of the majority, an aspect of democracy, that they put in place a series of mechanisms to counteract the tyranny of the majority, such as lifetime tenure for Supreme Court justices. Since the Iraq War, the United States has not only preached democracy internationally, but has also presented itself as a democracy and acted with democracy and majority opinion at home. What is the end result? The U.S. Congress passed the Patriot Act, which is used to monitor the activities of U.S. citizens at all times in the name of the Patriot Act, severely violating their right to privacy and freedom. When Snowden discovered the secret, he was simply unable to resist the strong pressure as an individual, had to flee the country, and revealed the matter to the public, bringing further awareness to the U.S. government's trampling of freedom in the name of democracy.

Fundamentally, democracy requires equality, and freedom requires unrestricted freedom. According to this logic, if unfettered freedom is allowed to develop at will, it will definitely lead to some degree of inequality, which in turn will undermine the foundation of democracy. Social movements such as "Occupy Wall Street" have shown that in recent years there has been a serious inequality in social distribution in the developed countries of the West, which also shows the contradiction between freedom and democracy. At this time, the public began to question freedom on the basis of democratic principles, and a serious division in society emerged.

Many Western researchers believe that social movements in Arab countries such as the Arab Spring are "offshore revolutions" orchestrated by the United States. The result of democratization in Arab countries has been an increase in the power of extremism. In the Arab countries where the so-called democratic revolutions succeeded, most of those who came to power were Islamist parties. They called for the rule of the state by Islamic law and plunged society into a state of severe illiberalism. From the Islamic revolution to the Arab Spring, theorists in Europe and the United States began to doubt whether a social revolution in the name of democracy could really achieve the goal of freedom and democracy. Now, more and more Westerners are beginning to doubt the validity of the liberal democracy argument.

"Separation of Powers" Is the Only Form of Democracy

Others argue that democracy is about checks and balances of power, and that the "separation of powers" is therefore the quintessential form of democracy. In fact, if we look back to the founding of the United States, we see that the separation of powers was created largely to limit democracy and the tyranny of the majority.

The political elites who wrote the Constitution for the United States were not subject to any electoral process, nor did anyone prove their legitimacy as representatives. They were very concerned about the future of America being controlled by the tyranny of the majority. So, they crafted a political system that would provide checks and balances between powers. So, the "separation of powers" was not a typical form of democracy, but a special aristocratic political framework set up to limit the tyranny of the majority in the United States. It can be said that the political elites who set up the "separation of powers" political framework were somehow "anti-democratic".

Democracy Does Not Make Big Mistakes

It is often said that although a democracy has its flaws, the greatest advantage of a democracy is that no big mistakes are made, because in a democracy, very small mistakes can be detected and corrected. This is actually a false statement. Because there is no shortage of examples in history of democracies making big mistakes. For example, the decision to launch the Iraq war was made by the United States in a democratic form.

When the Bush Jr. administration decided to go to war in Iraq, a majority of members of the U.S. Congress voted for it, including Hillary Clinton, who was a Democratic senator at the time. The Bush Jr. administration was a Republican administration, and most members of Congress voted for the Iraq war, but this ultimately proved to be a serious mistake. On the one hand, after the war was launched, the world discovered that Iraq did not have weapons of mass destruction. On the other hand, the young military officers represented by Saddam Hussein who used to control the development of extreme Islamic forces in Arab countries were engaged in nation- and state-building in the name of modernization, and they saw religion as a sign of backwardness. After the overthrow of Saddam's regime, the extremist Islamic forces expanded rapidly and evolved into a major factor that threatens the stability of European and American societies today. Is this not a huge mistake made by the democratic system?

In addition, one of the major reasons for the outbreak of the financial crisis in 2008 was the deregulation of the financial sector by the U.S. Congress. The deregulation of the financial sector by the U.S. Congress was the result of lobbying by various interest groups in the democratic mechanism, especially financial groups. Through vigorous lobbying, these financial groups pushed the U.S. Congress to change some of the laws that oversaw the financial markets by a majority. After these laws were discarded, financial activities went out of control and eventually evolved into a huge crisis.

These are the consequences of imperfect democratic decision- making mechanisms, and it is clear that the assumption of a democratic system making no big mistakes is also an untenable mindset.

The Paradox of Free Elections

Some people believe that democracy means free elections, that is, giving people the right to vote freely. A great paradox is implied in this view.

When comparing the political systems of China and the West, some people always think that the fact—that people in the West can freely elect their leaders—means that the Western democratic system is more advanced. They do not realize that free elections in the West also have flaws.

The 2016 U.S. presidential election can reveal an important issue: although the election gives people the freedom to choose a candidate, there were so few options to choose from. The American voters deserve sympathy because they had to choose between a "crook" and a "madman". This reflects a great dilemma facing free elections in the West today. In the process of free elections, there are several problems that are very difficult to control.

In the paradox of free elections, on the one hand, it is believed that the democratic tradition goes back to the ancient Greek period, and on the other hand, it is believed that the greatest principle of a democratic system is free elections. This contains a great paradox, because in the ancient Greek period, leaders were not elected, but were chosen by lottery. The ancient Greeks realized that elections were an unreliable affair because the process could be manipulated. Therefore, they believed that only the drawing of lots was the will of God, and that if everyone was to have an equal opportunity to hold power, the best way to decide who would hold what office was by sortition.

The premise of democracy is that all candidates are equal, so drawing lots is the fairest. In ancient Athens, there were public offices that were not considered "fat" but rather a burden. But all citizens had to take responsibility, and if the lottery decided that the position would be held by someone, he would probably have to accept his own fate. In a way, sortition is a fairer method than elections, because the process removes all human factors.

In Europe, the practice of sortition to determine public offices lasted for a long time and was still used until the time of the medieval Venetian Republic.

Later, the European city-states were unified into nation-states, and the size and population increased dramatically, making it difficult to implement sortition. As a result, various localities needed to send representatives to participate in national decision-making, and later these representatives became elected and eventually developed into a representative system. However, the number of people eligible to vote was extremely small at first, representing only a few percent of the entire population, which is called aristocracy. It was not until later, when all male citizens over a certain age could participate in universal suffrage, that the representative system became known as a representative democracy. In a representative state, ordinary citizens do not start out with the right to vote. European countries entered the period of representative government at the end of the 18th century, but members of parliament were not very representative of the population for a reason: the government had so many restrictions on citizens who could vote that most citizens were not entitled to vote.

In the early days of the United States, the members of Congress were also not very representative, since the number of citizens who participated in elections was very limited. At that time, representative government did not equal democracy.

The British state defined its system as an aristocracy. Although there was a monarch, the monarch was a head of state with no real power, and the power of the state was mainly in the hands of Parliament, whose members were mainly representatives of the aristocracy. By 1832, the British electorate had only increased to 4 % of the population.

Against this background, people in Western countries continued to organize social movements to demand universal suffrage. In 1860, the United States became the only country in the Western world where all white males had the right to universal suffrage.

German men gained universal suffrage in 1871, after the victory in the Franco-Prussian War and the establishment of the German Empire. France did not abolish the high property qualifications for voters until after the February Revolution in 1848, after which ordinary citizens gained universal suffrage. The Nordic countries did not achieve universal suffrage for men until the late 19th and early 20th centuries. Women's democratic movements for universal suffrage in these countries lasted for many years, and women did not gain the right to vote and the right to be elected at the same time. Usually, the right to vote was granted first, and the right to be elected many years later.

The timing of women's suffrage varied from state to state in the United States. It was not until 1920 that the U.S. Congress passed a law officially recognizing the right of white women to vote on the same basis as white men. Black Americans gained the right to vote much later: the Civil War ended in 1865, but it was not until the 15th Amendment to the U.S. Constitution was enacted in 1870 that black Americans were nominally given the right to vote, and some states achieved mixed governments of white and black.

In 1877, disagreement over the outcome of the presidential election led to a political deal between the Republicans and Democrats: the Democrats supported Republican Hayes for president, but the federal government had to withdraw its troops from the South and turn the South over to white Southerners to govern. This gave Southern blacks the right to vote in name only. And although Northern blacks had the right to vote, they were rarely given the same opportunities as whites in practice and were treated as second-class citizens.

It was not until the 1950s, under the leadership of Martin Luther King, Jr. that black Americans began mass non-violent protests. Representatives of the Black American movement also came to China for support, and in the 1960s, Mao Zedong made a public statement supporting the democratic struggle of Black Americans and received representatives of the Black American movement at Tiananmen Gate[1]. It was not until 1964, when the U.S. Congress passed the Civil Rights Act, that the voting rights of black Americans were officially recognized.

However, the civil rights movement of black Americans continued for many years, and the long-standing segregation made it difficult to implement the Civil Rights Act of 1964. Later, the U.S. Supreme Court facilitated the implementation of the Civil Rights Act, and several significant decisions were made in favor of blacks to assert their rights. In 2008, Barack Obama was elected president of the United States, the first black president in American history.

Although the American people have struggled to gain universal suffrage, the political elite can still exclude them from the power game through mechanisms such as primaries, superdelegates, and campaign financing. In the 2016 U.S. presidential election, Democratic nominee Hillary Clinton referred to voters who supported Trump as "deplorables" in her campaign. Although public opinion also accused her of being politically incorrect, she did inadvertently reveal the American political elite's view of the population.

In any case, the representative system is considered today to be a typical feature of a democratic system. That is, when the country is big and the population is large, it is impossible for the people to vote on any issue, so it is necessary to elect representatives who will govern instead of the people. How to elect representatives? In fact, there are many theorists who have long argued that in the actual election process, people cannot elect the best representatives. This is because there are several problems in the process of election.

First, random elections can get into a self-perpetuating cycle. If different representatives are elected, there will be a situation where some people think A is better than B and C, while others think B is better than C and A. No optimal result can be selected after selection.

In the 18th century, the French Enlightenment thinker Condorcet proposed the "voting paradox"[2] to illustrate the potential problems of democratic elections. Ultimately, like a dog chasing its own tail, the electoral process is circular, with no end result in sight.

Second, in the election process, candidates need to be elected in campaigns, but voters do not know what these candidates are really like. In such a situation of serious information asymmetry, often the final result is not what voters want to see. In Europe and the United States, we can often see a phenomenon that after a highly elected leader takes office, public support begins to decline rapidly, in sharp contrast to the campaign. One of the major reasons for this is information asymmetry. When voters cast their votes, they do not know how these candidates will govern in the future. Candidates reveal friendly and well-intentioned messages during the campaign, but once they take office, voters are disappointed when they implement policies that are different from what they were promised, creating a huge contrast in public opinion. Therefore, the political election is the same as investing in the capital market, where ordinary voters and stockholders can only vote or invest based on some one-sided and fragmented information, and they are often disappointed in the end.

Third, as evidenced by the election campaigns in Western countries in recent years, elections are directly related to wealth. The more money you spend, the more likely you are to be elected. Former U.S. Vice President Al Gore once wrote a book revealing some facts about the U.S. presidential election process. At the time, members of his campaign team had suggested to him that by dropping money in certain areas and certain parts of the country, the votes in that area would appear different. Gore didn't believe it at first, but later found that doing what the campaign team said worked very well. He was amazed at how the election had become like this. What's the point of elections, if smashing money is all it takes to gain an advantage?

Fourth, the premise of free elections is that each candidate should present his or her governing platform and let voters vote based on their own judgment of these platforms. However, in fact, candidates often smear each other in order to win elections and use various means to get voters involved in the political atmosphere they create, which affects voters' rational judgment. To what extent can such candidates implement policies that are beneficial to the people?

Fifth, if people only pay attention to the issue of elections, but ignore the issue of decision-making in a democracy, society may also fall into the trap of "democratic tyranny". The term "democratic tyranny" was coined by French political sociologist Alexis de Tocqueville. He was the first person to analyze the American political system from the perspective of democracy. Tocqueville did not limit his analysis to ideology, but analyzed the deeper problems of American democracy in detail. For example, he found that the American people of that era were only concerned with some immediate issues of profit distribution and lacked a long-term vision. He believed that in the long run, the American people would fall into the trap of "democratic tyranny", that is, they did not care about politics except for the election process, and left everything to the elected rulers to decide. The people become the sheep, and the rulers are the shepherds. Although the rulers are not as brutal as despots, it is still a degree of tyranny.

Tocqueville's fear is that if democracy is only a formality, then people will become "docile slaves" outside the process of electing their leaders. For a long time, it has been difficult for the American people to express their opinions on government policies, except during the election process, and the government no longer considers the will of the people. This confirms Tocqueville's fears.

A Plausible Lie: A One-Party System Cannot Guarantee Political Integrity

Another specious lie about democracy is that a one-party system cannot guarantee political incorruptibility and that only a multi-party system can supervise each other. For example, some Westerners believe that the multi-party cooperation and political consultation system led by the Communist Party of China, which is practiced in China, is imperfect, and they think that only a multi-party system can supervise each other and ensure political cleanliness. This understanding is lopsided.

From a historical point of view, this argument simply does not hold water. Whether it is the two-party system in Britain and the United States, or the multi-party system in continental European countries, these political systems are the products of specific historical circumstances.

Originally there were no parties in the British Parliament, but in the 17th century, the issue of the king's succession divided into two factions, the Whig and the Tory, and later two parties were formed.

In the 17th century, King Charles II of the Stuart dynasty of England had no children, and his brother, the Duke of York, became the heir to the throne. However, a group of parliamentarians thought that the Duke of York might be Catholic and opposed his succession to the throne. In the 19th century, the Whigs became the Liberals and the Tories became the Conservatives.

The emergence of a two-party system in the United States was also an accident of history. In the War of Independence, the American founders abhorred party politics. They saw it as a source of corruption and decadence in Europe. Therefore, in the Constitutional Convention, the delegates from each state were all enthusiastic, thinking and working in the same direction, a typical "one-party system".

Later, because both Hamilton and Jefferson were particularly strongmen, their views on many issues diverged so sharply that the state delegates eventually split into two camps, forming two competing political parties around Hamilton and Jefferson, respectively.

By the time the first U.S. President Washington left office, he already felt the dangers of bipartisanship to American politics. In a famous speech delivered at the end of his term, Washington warned representatives of the American political class that if American politics were caught in a whirlwind of partisan bickering, it would divide American society and provide an opportunity for foreign intervention in American politics.

Today, we can see the strange phenomenon of candidates framing each other in the U.S. presidential election process, while the three major U.S. intelligence agencies blame foreign interference for all the scandals in the U.S. elections.

The multi-party system is a product of the French Revolution, where representatives from all over France formed different parties by region after the revolution. The Jacobins, as we are familiar with, are representatives of the Brittany region. The more conservative Girondins, on the other hand, came from the southwestern part of France known as the Gironde. A multi-party system is more unstable than a two-party system, because the parties in the middle are prone to change their minds and change sides. In a parliamentary system, the majority of the parliament forms the government. If the middle parties keep changing sides, it will be very unstable who is in the majority, and it will cause the government to fall down frequently.

To change this situation, European countries such as France changed their election laws in the 1950s to introduce a two-round majority voting system. In the first round, voters could vote for as many parties as they wanted according to their political preferences; in the second round, voters could only vote for one of the candidates of the two parties that won in the first round.

But according to this practice, the voter's choice is actually very limited, because in the second round of voting, if neither of the two candidates who won in the first round is their favored candidate, they can only choose a candidate he considers less bad. Moreover, this electoral procedure forces multiple parties to move closer to the poles, forming two camps, left-wing and right-wing, with the middle party having to look to the largest party on either the left or the right in the election.

Over time, parties in multi-party countries have also become largely polarized. While polarization solved the problem of political instability, it did not solve the problems of popular concern. As a result, popular discontent with traditional political parties increased rapidly due to the unequal distribution of wealth and increased social polarization. At this time, some parties that were originally suppressed by this majority two- round voting system rose to the top and did well in the elections.

This was the case, for example, with the National Front, a far-right party in France. Unlike in the United States, France has limits on the amount of money that can be spent on campaign sponsorship, but the government does provide a financial subsidy to parties that receive more than 5 % of the vote. In the past, the National Front had little room to survive in both the left and right-wing camps in France, sometimes receiving just enough votes to meet the 5 % threshold set by the electoral law to receive a small government subsidy. But more often, the National Front does not receive enough votes to meet the 5 % threshold and is forced to pay for its own massive campaign expenses.

In the 2014 European Parliament elections, however, the National Front, contrary to the norm, emerged as the biggest winner in France, with the largest number of seats in the European Parliament. The victory of the National Front, a typical anti-European integration party, is a great irony, as it shows that the French public is already extremely distrustful of the cause of European integration.

This phenomenon also occurred in the 2016 U.S. presidential election. Trump was a dark horse who fought through the opposition of Republican bigwigs to win the primary and become the Republican nominee. Trump is not a typical Republican, and he has supported the Democratic Party in the past. He is a "political animal" who smells the "blood" in the political campaign and is inspired by the enthusiasm. To some extent, Trump fought and won the election against the two traditional party machines on his own. This result shows that the American public has lost trust in the two traditional political parties.

The political rebellions that have occurred in Europe and the United States in recent years have shown that multi-party and two-party systems do not necessarily reflect the wishes of the people. That is, they are not always perceived as "democratic". The effectiveness of multi-party or bipartisan alternate rule is now being questioned by the public.

Multi-party systems can curb corruption, but they also have their limitations. Both historically and realistically, multi-party systems in the West have not eliminated corruption. Instead, Western countries have seen some institutional designs that allow for open corruption.

Since the 19th century, representative government has been common in Europe and the United States, and for a long time thereafter, public governance in Europe and the United States was also known as the patronage system (also known as the spoils system). This means that the party that wins the election can distribute government resources to those who contributed to the election victory, and everyone can "share the spoils" as they please. This system has a pernicious effect on public governance, and no one is held accountable for the effectiveness of the country's governance. Therefore, the multi-party system at that time was very corrupted. In 1883, the U.S. Congress passed the Pendleton Act, which regulated the management of the U.S. public service and limited the patronage system, ensuring the normal functioning of the state apparatus and gradually stabilizing public governance.

Rotating parties are prone to the problem of irresponsible public finance. On this issue, James Buchanan, an American economist and Nobel laureate in economics, has an opinion that the reason why public finance policies in democracies are in disarray and why debts are escalating: multiple parties are in power in rotation. In order to be able to gain the support of voters and stay in power longer, the ruling party uses expanded public finance spending to benefit the voters who support them. However, if every government does this, it will make the government spend a lot on public finance, causing the debt to keep growing and eventually leading to inflation. In this regard, there is an ancient Chinese saying that "the government should be constant and the rule must be regular" (政贵有恒、治须有常). In other words, political governance is a long-term matter, so public policy should have a certain stability, to give the public a kind of expectation. Political governance cannot be changed at will. Multi-party rotational rule breaks this order. The traditional Chinese political concept is that the public needs to have a reliable expectation of public order, so that the people can carry out other social activities according to the expectation. From this perspective, rotating rule affects the stable social and economic development and the implementation of policies.

In addition, a multi-party system may affect political stability. In a multi-party system, party representatives can change positions and exchange interests at any time. So, in a multi-party country, it is common for the government to be overthrown. Even if a party is already in power, its representatives sometimes have interests with other parties, and if the opposition party gives them better promises than the current one, these party representatives may change sides. And the parliamentary coalition of non-ruling parties may overthrow the existing government and reshuffle the cabinet.

The French Fourth Republic was a typical period of multi-party politics. During this period of multi-party politics, party alliances changed very quickly, and governments were particularly unstable. The French government at that time was called "quarterly government," which means that almost every quarter there was a reversal of party alliances and a change of government. How could public policy remain stable if each government did not stay in power for more than one quarter? Later, when France faced a serious political crisis, politicians had to elect General de Gaulle, a hero of World War II, and ask him to straighten out French politics. De Gaulle accepted the appointment on the condition that he had the power to amend the constitution. He then implemented a majority two-round voting system in the election process, which is the current electoral system in France. In the first round, all parties were allowed to participate, but only the two parties that received the most votes in the first round were eligible for the second round, and the other smaller parties were naturally eliminated. By amending the electoral law, France gradually transitioned from a multi-party system to a bipolar party system, culminating in the creation of the French Fifth Republic. The current system in France has changed the severe instability of government caused by the multi-party system. The French practice shows that it is not the case that the more political parties there are, the better the government will express the will of the voters.

Lobby groups have an important role in Western multi-party systems, but there are many that represent the interests of their funders. Who funds lobby groups? The wealthy, of course. Lobby groups do not provide campaign support to politicians and members of Congress without conditions. Those politicians who rely on lobbying groups to get into Congress, of course, have to return the favor by supporting the lobby's positions at the polls. Even Professor Schattschneider, who was president of the American Political Science Association, once joked, "The flow in the pluralist heaven is that the heavenly chorus sings with a strong upper-class accent."

Political scientists in the United States keep peddling the idea that only a multi-party (two-party) system can curb corruption because, institutionally, there is an opposition overseeing the ruling party. However, this specious view does not stand the test of reality and history. in 2015, a best-selling book in the United States, "Clinton Cash," pointed the finger at the Clinton Foundation, exposing its various irrational activities. The book's author, Peter Schweitzer, is an in-depth investigation journalist and one of the founders of the U.S. Government Accountability Institute. He points out that when Bill Clinton was in office, he spent a lot of money on lawsuits because of the scandals, and he had little money when he left office. But from 2001–2012, Clinton's fortune quickly grew to $136.5 million. In addition to Clinton's payments from lecture events everywhere, much of this had to do with foreign donations to the Clinton Foundation. Of course, such donations would not be unrequited, and there is something fishy about many of the foreign-related cases that Hillary was involved in lobbying, both as a senator and later as secretary of state.

WikiLeaks revealed that the Clinton Foundation was involved in bribes to business companies that helped certain U.S. companies start educational companies abroad, and that those companies returned the favor by giving Clinton an honorary directorship that would have given him an easy $16.5 million annual salary. Those companies would regularly donate millions of dollars to the Clinton Foundation. At the same time, many of USAID's donation programs have also proven to involve the Clinton Foundation, meaning that Hillary, as Secretary of State, sometimes approved the taking of government money and putting it in her own pockets.

There are also U.S. companies that have overseas resources, but transactions for these resources require U.S. government approval. Hillary also pushed for approval of many related projects during her tenure as secretary of state. Therefore, Wikileaks said that Hillary could only use her private email address for certain email correspondence and did not dare to use the official email address of the State Department, probably because she was afraid that the mysteries in the emails would be discovered.

In fact, it is not uncommon for American politicians to use their power to establish improper relationships with money, thereby enriching themselves. But the rhythm with which Clinton Foundation found the way of enriching itself was so fast that it is uncommon in the history of the United States. Still, the Democratic Party is by no means alone in doing such things. Schweitzer, author of *Clinton Cash*, notes that members of Congress from both parties "extort" businessmen and corporations. Money flowing into politics is also used to "buy" certain political positions. For example, a member of Congress must pay money to his or her party in order to get a spot on certain congressional committees. Certain committees can approve projects and have more power, and it costs more money to get on those committees. Politicians treat these deals as investments, and when they get a position, they can get more money from companies or businessmen when they approve projects.

In recent years, the U.S. Republican Party and the Democratic Party have been entangled, with members of the government and Congress belonging to different parties. Each side often arguing its own case, and corruption has continued to occur. The Clinton Foundation and the money relationship between U.S. politicians and forces outside the country show that the U.S. multi-party system has failed to curb corruption, and that the so-called democratic politics in the West is to some extent synonymous with money politics.

China's political system is completely different from that of Western countries. Although there were political parties in China after the Revolution of 1911, party politics was soon replaced by warlordism, followed by the Japanese invasion, which led to a national war of resistance. From the latter part of Sun Yat-sen's reign, the KMT worked to establish a party- state system in China that unified party and state. Later, the KMT formed a united front with the Communist Party during the War of Resistance against Japan, but after the war was won, it sought to destroy the Communist Party.

After gaining victory in the Liberation War, the Chinese Communist Party truly established a political system suited to China's national conditions. Unlike the political parties in the West and not quite the same as those in the Soviet Union and Eastern European countries, the purpose of the Chinese Communist Party's political activities was not to run for office, but to mobilize the people. First, it mobilized the people to work for the establishment of a new China, and later to work for socialist modernization. China's modernization still has a long way to go, and the historical mission of the Chinese Communist Party needs continuous efforts to be accomplished.

Throughout the world history, multi-party system does not guarantee clean politics, since most multi-party countries do not have clean politics. Instead, the one-party system of Singapore provides us with an alternative political model for reference.

On the issue of multi-party system, Washington, the first president of the United States, in his famous farewell address, warned the American political elite to be wary of the tendency of party politics in American politics. He argued that if party politics were allowed to develop, it would not only cause serious divisions among the American people, but would also provide a ground for foreign interference in American politics. But U.S. politics eventually evolved into a pattern of two parties ruling in turn. With the 2016 U.S. presidential election, Washington's fears back then were not unreasonable, and this gives us another perspective to think about multi-party politics.

Thomas Friedman, a *New York Times* columnist who came to China in 2008, argues that China's ability to develop rapidly is no accident, and that there is a deep political institutional context behind it. He believes that China's political system today has some kind of inheritance and continuation of the historical Confucian tradition of ruling groups, which is completely different from Western political parties that represent different interest groups and compete with each other. Many people in the West only agree with the idea of a regime produced by multi-party competition, which is a very shallow political concept.

Why People Fall into the "Myth of Democracy"

Why, then, do many people fall into the "myth of democracy"? Envy of developed Western countries may be the psychological basis of this situation, and this mentality has become an important lever for Western countries to use democratic movements to interfere in the politics of other countries.

Since the overthrow of the Qing Dynasty, the concept of democracy has been widely spread in China. To most Chinese, democracy means that the people are in charge, that is, that politics is in order: those in power listen to different opinions and consider the interests and positions of the people. Such orderly system is not directly related to a multi-party system. But westerners believe that democracy means multi-party competition, free elections, and free public opinion, and that the absence of any elements is tyranny.

Under the influence of Western public opinion, the Western concept of democracy has a strong penetrating power, and many people believe that the Western political system is more "developed" and that only by democratizing according to Western standards can China enter the ranks of modern countries and become a developed country.

There are even people who self-righteously disparage China and the Chinese people, looking down on China's political system and traditional culture, which is a typical colonial mentality. As China continues to develop, fewer and fewer people will endorse such views in the future. Of course, those who hold this view also include many foreigners, and even some leaders of socialist groups of countries have such a bias. They believe that success is only possible if they follow the Western path of development.

Others argue that developed countries are democracies, that this is the international trend, and that China should follow the trend. Is this really the case? To a large extent, this argument comes from a political propaganda. The so-called League of Democracies in the West is in fact a political movement, and we should be wary of unconsciously falling into the political propaganda of the West. If we follow the mindset set by others, we risk falling into a state of serious division.

Let's think about Yugoslavia. Before the dramatic changes in Eastern Europe, Yugoslavia was, by Western standards, the most suitable of the Eastern European countries for democratization, in terms of political tolerance and otherwise. However, immediately after the introduction of free elections, Yugoslavia was deeply divided and eventually led to the dissolution of the federation. Until now, it has not escaped the shadow of civil war. Only by recognizing the nature of the so-called democracy in Western political discourse can we help improve and develop the political system of socialism with Chinese characteristics and make the world "look east" and agree with China's development model.

Socialist Democracy and China's Institutional Strengths

China's economic development and social progress over the years is evident to all. Why has China achieved so much? Some attribute it to the socialist system with Chinese characteristics. But this is not accepted by those Western countries that hold the power of international discourse. Chinese political scientist Tianjian Shi (史天健), a former associate professor of political science at Duke University, has been doing research on the stages of democracy in China since the 1980s, and he has found that every 10 years, Chinese people believe that democracy in China has improved significantly. Although his research was conducted in accordance with the scientific standards of American political science, the article was rejected by the journal and his findings were not accepted by the American political science community.

The democracy that the Chinese speak of, i.e. socialist democracy, is a consultative democracy. In other words, the government should fully listen to the views of the masses and reflect the interests of the people in the decision-making process. In this regard, we need to further strengthen and take more into account the interests and ideas of grass-root people.

In addition, the multi-party cooperation and political consultation system led by the Communist Party of China is also a major innovation in Chinese democracy. Western public opinion always likes to speculate about China's one-party system, not knowing that there are many democratic parties actively advising the Chinese government on public policies. The multi-party cooperation and political consultation system under the leadership of the CPC is a great political creation of the CPC, other democratic parties, and people without party affiliation, and it has grown out of the soil of Chinese society.

The political consultation system has been practiced in the government of the Republic of China since the overthrow of the Qing Dynasty, and political consultation was also engaged in during the reign of the Kuomintang, but other democratic parties did not actually have the power to participate in politics. After the founding of New China, the multi-party cooperation and political consultation system under the leadership of the Communist Party of China (CPC) allowed democratic parties to truly participate in the political life of the country and in governmental decision-making. The multi-party cooperation and political consultation system under the leadership of the CPC is able to truly, extensively and permanently represent and realize the fundamental interests of the broadest number of people, as well as the fundamental interests of all ethnic groups in the country, and also effectively avoid the drawbacks of the old-style political party system of representing a few people and a few interest groups. Its innovation lies in its ability to unite all political parties and non-partisan people closely to strive for common goals, which can avoid the drawbacks of lack of supervision in one-party rule as well as the drawbacks of multi-party rotational rule and vicious competition. The institutionalized, procedural and standardized political consultation system can pool all kinds of opinions and suggestions, promote rational decision-making, avoid social tearing caused by party interests, class interests, regional and group interests, and therefore avoid deadlock in decision-making.

This system is not only in line with the actual situation of contemporary Chinese society, but also in line with the excellent traditional culture of the Chinese nation, which has always advocated that the world is for the common good, tolerance and inclusion, and seeking common ground while reserving differences. The Chinese system is a major contribution to human political civilization.

At the same time, China has a more systematic system of training and selection of officials. According to the current cadre selection system, China's national leaders have been trained in grass-root society and have accumulated a great deal of experience in public administration, and at the same time, these leaders have to firstly study political, economic and management theories systematically in party schools. They have both a theoretical foundation and practical experience. This is completely different from the bureaucratic system in Western countries. Take these two American administrations for example, one of them is a freshman senator and the other is a real estate tycoon who has never been involved in politics, neither of them has sufficient experience in social governance.

In addition, the Chinese believe that reform is a process, and that the political system needs to be constantly adjusted to new situations, and that only by keeping up with the times can we not fall behind. Successive Chinese leaders have emphasized the need for China to learn from the successful experiences of other countries. In the process of building China's institutions, we have borrowed from the social management experience of many developed Western countries. If Western countries become enamored with the superiority of their democratic systems and do not keep up with the times, the political system may become an obstacle to social progress or an excuse for interest groups to block reforms.

Extensive consultation of public opinion is an important part of socialist democracy. But if we only attach importance to listening to public opinion but fail to form a unified decision, we may fall into the dilemma of deliberation without decision and inefficiency. Therefore, democratic centralism embodies its superiority. Steve Jobs famously said that consumers do not know what they want, the subtext of which is that consumers' penchants need to be guided by entrepreneurs. This statement also applies in the political sphere, where people sometimes do not know in which direction they want society to go, and need leaders to show the way and lead society in the right direction. That's why democratic centralism is so important.

Finally, there are two Chinese idioms that apply very well when it comes to building political systems. First, we must not be presumptuous. China has a long history and culture and rich traditional political experience. British economist Angus Maddison once wrote a book titled "The Performance of the Chinese

Economy in the long run", which proves with a lot of data that for almost 900 years of history China has been a country with social stability and the highest per capita income in the world, and its total economic volume in some periods accounted for more than 1/3 of the world economy. Such a development requires the support of a social system that can never be summarized in terms of feudal autocracy. Therefore, China must take stock of its historical experiences if it is to achieve a rejuvenation of its civilization. These lessons have made a huge difference in the world and are bound to continue to have a huge impact in the future.

Secondly, we cannot afford to be arrogant; after 1949, China went from being a poor country to a modern industrial power in a very short period of time. According to the United Nations classification standards, China has one of the most complete industrial systems in the world. And, China's economy is still growing and is on its way to becoming the world's number one economy. Despite all the progress China has made, there are still many problems that need to be solved on the road to development, such as environmental pollution, uneven distribution of medical and educational resources, disparities in regional development, inadequate supervision mechanisms for officials, and corruption still occurring from time to time. Therefore, we still need to humbly study and learn from the experiences and lessons of other countries, and constantly reform the factors in the system that hinder economic development and social progress, so that we can make our people happier and our society more harmonious.

From Ideological Fanatic to the Return of Professional Civilian Officials

From the founding of the People's Republic of China to the reform and opening up, China has tried many models of governance, including learning from the Soviet model. After accumulating much experience, China has moved from the dogmatic model of ideological dominance, where everything had to be done according to "Marxist and socialist principles," to a modified traditional model of governance.

After the reform and opening up, China's governance model began to emphasize the role of professional civil officials, and great importance was attached to the cultivation of government civil servants' ability to govern. The traditional Confucian spirit of " Be the first to bear the world's hardship, and the last to enjoy its comfort" (先天下之忧而忧， 后天下之乐而乐) was brought up again, requiring civil servants to be both efficient and ethical. The promotion of

Chinese civil servants depends on their performance, and the evaluation of officials' performance, which was originally based on GDP growth, has now been supplemented by social development criteria (e.g., poverty reduction) and environmental protection criteria. This has created an atmosphere of healthy competition among officials at all levels and departments of government. China's public governance depends on this group of professional civil officials.

In fact, the system of professional civil officials based on the imperial examinations has been the basis of the public governance system in ancient China, a system that has also inspired Europeans.

Since the days of ancient Greece, Westerners have been searching for a cure for governance. Plato thought that letting philosophical kings rule society was the best way. But the ancient Greeks never practiced this method. The Italian missionary Matteo Ricci came to China in the late 16th century and observed the political system of the late Ming Dynasty. He argued that one of the major differences between China and Europe was that China was governed by literati (who Ricci considered to be the equivalent of what Plato called philosophers). In Ricci's writing, China during the Ming Dynasty was managed in an orderly manner, and the state was administered entirely through professional civil officials.

Later, European countries also reformed their bureaucratic systems in the course of their development, constructing systematic bureaucratic systems with professional state administrators and mechanisms to achieve modernization. In contrast, both the civil official selection system in ancient China and the cadre selection system in modern China, although not entirely dependent on free elections, have mechanisms that are closer to Plato's proposition that officials are selected from among professional public governing talent. Modern Chinese leaders are selected on the basis of a system of meritocracy, which requires not only managerial ability but also a broad-mindedness. As the saying goes, "Those who do not plan for decades are not good enough to plan for the moment; those who do not plan for the whole picture are not good enough to plan for a sector"(不谋万世者不足谋一时，不谋全局者不足谋一域), which is the highest level of selection of officials in China.

Former Federal Chancellor Helmut Schmidt has visited China several times and met with many Chinese leaders, including Mao Zedong. He disagreed with the notion that China's one-party system was a dictatorship. He believes that the Communist Party's one-party system has a role model in Chinese history, which is the imperial examination system. Officials selected through the imperial examinations had something in common with Communist officials in that they were not elected from the aristocratic class or other closed ruling class. They had to pass tests, prove their ability through their political performance, and slowly move up the ladder. It is possible for anyone of any origin to become the leader of a country through this system. When Schmidt spoke of the capabilities of China's leaders, he said with admiration, "I am impressed by the degree to which some of them have mastered economic policy. There are few government leaders in the world who can match them in that regard."

Looking around the world, the system of professional civil officials is undoubtedly China's greatest contribution to the public governance of human society. But too much civil power can go wrong. Thus, the rule of officials has always been an important issue in the traditional Chinese political system.

Matteo Ricci has documented the Ming government's practice of periodically purging officials. In his records, the Ming government conducted a critical review of all local senior officials every three years. After the 1607 review, the court tried more than 4,000 officials. Among them were those who were corrupt and bribed, those who neglected their duties, those who sentenced prisoners too harshly, and those who ruled too hastily and thoughtlessly, and so on. These officials could receive punishments such as removals from their public positions, removal of aristocratic titles, demotion, and exiles to other provincial areas as an idle officer. The central officials of the Ming dynasty were also reviewed every five years, and the procedures were equally strict, and the punishments were equally serious.

Since the founding of the People's Republic of China, there has also been a review and purge of public officials every few years to maintain the purity of the civil service. It is an official management system with Chinese characteristics that eliminates incompetent and misbehaving officials through regular reorganization and purging. It can both train officials to become the backbone of China's public governance and prevent some officials from becoming too powerful and difficult to restrain.

Pragmatism and the Chinese Political and Cultural Tradition

The Successful Governing Experience of the Chinese Communist Party

The Communist Party of China has also made mistakes since it came to power, but the Communists have always been able to reflect upon their experiences and correct their mistakes. There was never a shortage of people in the Communist Party who spoke out impartially, and this was a common demand of the Confucian scholar and scholarly class in China. Mencius once said, "The people are the most important, the community is second, and the ruler is the least." This emphasizes the relationship between the primary and the secondary in Chinese society, and the rulers of ancient China had to learn from this famous quote of Mencius.

The Chinese Communist Party takes Marxism as its guiding ideology, but in the process of concrete practice, it by no means holds Marxism as its only principle. Chen Yun (陈云) once proposed: "One has to be respectful to the reality, not blindly to the superiors, nor to the books ." In other words, Marxism is not a dogma that is set in stone.

Marx and Engels, who experienced only the early stage of industrial revolution, envisioned the stages of development of the future society, but did not specify how it would work. Lenin pursued development models such as the New Economic Policy, but later the Soviet model had many problems. China imitated the Soviet model in its early years, with some success and some failure, but eventually abandoned it. The older leaders of the Chinese Communist Party did not practice the socialist development model either. They had made some attempts and had some experience but did not develop a systematic theory and development model.

China is still in the primary stage of socialism, and it is necessary to break through some ideological shackles. In the 1992 Southern Talks, Deng Xiaoping made the assertion that "planned economy is not equal to socialism, but capitalism also has economic plans; market economy is not equal to capitalism, but socialism also has markets", breaking through the misconception that a socialist country cannot develop a market economy, and that the socialist market economy system is the basis for China's rapid development. The socialist market economy system is the basis for China's rapid development.

The market mechanism facilitates competition and greatly promotes China's economic development, but the market does not automatically correct supply imbalances in the economy, which can lead to economic crises. Therefore, China does not treat the theory of market-determined resource allocation as a dogma. When China's development encountered external shocks, the government intervened decisively in the economy each time, effectively reducing the impact of the international economic crisis on China's economic development. The Chinese government has also played an integral role in supporting industrial development, and China is now a world leader in quantum communications, wireless Internet, high-speed rail, and infrastructure development.

It can be said that during a few decades, China has completed the development path of Western countries for over 200 years. But our system is still imperfect and needs constant adjustment. There are still many institutional obstacles to China's development. For example, corruption still exists among officials, and these issues need to be addressed through reforms to improve the monitoring system and prevent corruption.

China will persist in reform and opening up, and constantly reform and improve the socialist system. The original purpose of reform and opening up is to break the shackles of the system and achieve development. The purpose of reform is to sweep away those elements in the old system that do not adapt to the changing times and replace them with new ones.

In the reform process, we must be wary of temptation and prevent going astray. We must remain modest and prudent, adhere to the spirit of seeking truth from facts, and prevent adventurism and "leapfrogging" reforms.

In an exclusive interview with Russian television, Xi Jinping said, "It is no easy task to deepen reforms in a country like China with a population of more than 1.3 billion people. China has been reformed itself for more than 30 years, and the reforming process has entered uncharted water. It can be said that the easy, all happy reform has been completed, delicious meat are eaten, the rest is to gnaw the hard bones. This requires us to be bold, take steady steps. To be bold, , that means, we have to move forward in our refom, no matter how difficult it might be. We will take all responsibilities, overcome hard difficulties, even if we have to wade through dangerous beaches. Taking steady steps, that means, the direction must be accurate, driving must be stable, especially we cannot affort to make subversive errors."

China's reforms must take care of Chinese traditions, take into account Chinese realities, and proceed in a gradual and orderly manner. When the government tries to reform a specific issue, it must be done in one go, without leaving any residue problems.

Chinese Political and Cultural Beliefs

Beginning with the Soviet Union and Eastern European nations' dramatic change, the Eastern Bloc's belief in communism seemed to collapse. The Eastern Bloc's firm belief in the ideal of realizing communism through the socialist road encountered a great challenge, and the international communist movement suffered a major setback. So that after the reform and opening up, the Chinese government put more emphasis on the development concept of the primary stage of socialism. In this background, the situation of the ideological struggle in the international community also gradually eased.

At that time, Christianity, Buddhism, Islam and other religious forces began to spread rapidly in Chinese society, which had a great impact on grassroot society. After the opening of China's market, there were a lot of behaviors that violated the moral rules in the society, and some people attempt to generalize this phenomenon, and attribute all unruly and profit-oriented behaviors to "Chinese people's lack of faith".

In fact, the claim that "Chinese people have no faith" is largely a public opinion campaign created by certain religious forces to expand in China. In reality, this argument does not hold water. China is one of the four ancient civilizations, the only one that has survived history without interruption. Its unique hieroglyphic script allows us to communicate with thinkers from 2,000 to 3,000 years ago, to read their philosophies, and to draw from them a wealth of intellectual resources. In addition to the unbroken lineage of writing and cultural systems, another characteristic of Chinese civilization is the deep-rooted national sentiment of the Chinese people. In a way, this national sentiment is the faith of the Chinese people.

When we talk about faith, there are always people who think that only the practice of monotheistic religions such as Christianity and Islam is considered faithful. In fact, almost all monotheism developed from Judaism. If you carefully read the story of the Bible, especially the Old Testament, you will find that it is a history of the suffering of the Jews. The ancient kingdom of Judea was at a crossroads in the Middle East, and whatever people came through, there almost always preyed on the Jews and sold them into slavery and hard labor in other countries. The story of Moses leading the Jews out of Egypt tells how he brought a group of Jews who had been sold into Egypt back to Palestine. The Old Testament believes that the Jews suffered because they were not strong in their faith, and that the Jews were ravaged by the other nations because there was a division within them, and some were tempted by foreign religions to stop believing in the God of the Jews. As long as there were divisions within the Jewish people, other nations would take advantage of this division to harass the Jews, occupy Palestine, and turn the Jews into slaves. But as long as the Jews are united, God will bless the Jews and there will be wise leaders like King David who will make the nation prosperous.

The Chinese do not have a Bible, nor is there a classic that concentrates on the suffering of the Chinese people, nor do the Chinese simply blame all of their historical misfortunes on some foreign religion. However, the sufferings and misfortunes of the Chinese people throughout history have strengthened their patriotic sentiments. Whenever the Chinese nation was invaded by foreigners, there were always heroic figures who stood up to the persistent enemy and saved the people. These heroes are the saints and role models in the hearts of the Chinese people. Such memory has many similarities with the experience of the Jews, that is, once the nation is divided, foreigners will invade and the Chinese nation will be poisoned. Therefore, it is the belief of the Chinese people to be loyal to the motherland, to defend the country, and to contribute to the unification of the country. Only when the country is not divided can the Chinese nation be free from the bullying of foreigners. National unity and national solidarity are the prerequisites for a prosperous society and individuals. Therefore, after modern China was invaded by the Western powers, many benevolent people, many scientists and entrepreneurs emerged in China to fight for the victory of China. The Chinese have the spirit and determination to win. Chinese people worship their ancestors, but are not too believing in ghosts and gods, from Nüwa (女娲补天) mending the sky to Dayu taming the floods (大禹治水) and Yugong moving mountains (愚公移山), Chinese legends and stories all reflect the spirit of Chinese people's struggle against nature. To change the natural environment, solidarity among people is essential. Chinese esteem the power of the collective, and Chinese civilization is based on this unity and harmony, which is the Chinese people's sense of family.

The Chinese believe that home and country are unified, and that home and the world are unified. That is why the Chinese literati and scholars have always had the ambition of cultivating the body, bringing the family together, ruling the country and pacifying the world. The classic moral codes that Chinese respect are those related to the love of family and country, such as Yue Fei's story to serve the country, and Wen Tianxiang's poem, "As death befalls all men alike, I'll keep a loyal heart to make a name in history." (人生自古谁无死，留取丹心照汗青) Another very famous example is the story of Lin Zexu's destruction of opium at Humen (虎门销烟) in the late Qing Dynasty. Lin Zexu destroyed in public more than 2.37 million pounds of opium, giving a heavy strike at the British who were plundering in China. After the defeat of the Qing Dynasty, Lin Zexu was falsely accused by the surrenderists, dismissed by the Daoguang Emperor, and exiled to Xinjiang. Even so, he wrote the poem "I'm always ready to sacrifice myself in the interests of our nation, how can I evade this duty only because in the face of disasters?"(苟利国家生与死，岂因祸福避趋之)

In the Chinese loyalty to family and the country, family and country are one and the same. Without this loyalty to family and country, how could a group of scientists such as Qian Xuesen, Guo Yonghuai and Deng Jiaxian, who had already achieved fame and fortune abroad, have come back to build the motherland in the early days of the founding of the new China? They all made great contributions to China's nuclear and space project named "two bombs and one star". Nan Rendong, the father of China's "celestial eye", returned to China with a low annual salary equivalent to only one day's salary that he got abroad. But even so, he was determined to return to his homeland, and to find a site for the radio telescope with great efforts, and finally realized his wish of making China the country with the largest radio telescope in the world.

Xi Jinping stressed at the first national civilized family commendation conference: "The family is the cell of society; family harmony is social stability; family happiness is social peace; and family civilization is social civilization. We have to realize that only when thousands of families are good can the country be good, and the nation be good." This is precisely a modern interpretation of the family feeling in Chinese culture.

After the Cold War, Russia's economy withered and people's living standards fell to the ground; after the disintegration of Yugoslavia, ethnic conflicts intensified and war broke out; the Arab Spring, like a prairie fire, destroyed Libya and Syria and caused a huge wave of refugees. All this reminds Chinese people of the century of humiliation in China's modern history. "When the nest is overturned, there is no egg intact" (覆巢之下，安有完卵). These international events have reinforced the Chinese belief that only when the country is strong can the people live and work in peace and happiness.

Only the Sinicized Marxism Will Be Useful for Chinese

China follows the path of socialism with Chinese characteristics and follows the basic principles of Marxism. After Marxism was introduced into China, some people demanded the absolute implementation of Marx's ideas and claimed to be true Marxists. However, the actual situation in Europe, where Marx lived, was very different from that in China. And historical experience showed that a revolution based on European proletarian urban uprisings would not work in China until Mao Zedong proposed the revolutionary path of "encircling the cities by the countryside", which put the Chinese revolution on the right track. Mao Zedong's Theory of Contradiction and Theory of Practice are important theoretical foundations of the Chinese revolution, an important achievement of Marxism's Sinicization and a product of the combination of Marxism and

Chinese practice. Only by following this path can Marxism truly become the ideological basis for guiding Chinese practice.

Chinese culture is not an exclusive culture. From Buddhism to Marxism, foreign cultures have had a tremendous impact on China, but they have all eventually undergone a process of sinicization. After Buddhism was introduced to China from India, it had been merged with Chinese culture to develop a branch named Zen Buddhism. Zen Buddhism later spread to Japan and Korea, influencing the culture of the entire East Asian region. After Islam was introduced to China, it also went through the process of "interpreting the scriptures with Confucianism", and many Islamic classics and teachings were only accepted by Chinese believers after they were sinicized.

We made the mistake of criticizing traditional Chinese culture as "feudal dregs" during the cultural revolution period. Later on, we found that if we discarded traditional culture, China would lose its development direction. Without traditional culture, China will lose its roots, making it difficult to achieve long-term development. With regard to cultural traditions, we must commit to removing the falsehoods and preserving the truth, and then we can carry it forward and interpret Marxism in the context of Chinese culture. In this way, the Chinese people can better understand and accept Marxism. By guiding the Chinese people with sinicized Marxism, we will surely achieve the great rejuvenation of Chinese civilization.

Notes

1 In 1963, Mao Zedong issued the "*Statement of Supporting the Just Struggle of American Black People against U.S. Imperialist Racial Discrimination*"; in 1968, Mao Zedong issued "*Statement of Comrade Mao Zedong, Chairman of the Central Committee of the Communist Party of China, Supporting the Struggle of American Black People Against Violence*"; Mao received on the Tiananmen Gate Robert William, the leader of the American Black People's movement.

2 Under the majority rule, everyone votes according to his preference. Most people prefer x to y, and most people prefer y to z. According to logical consistency, this preference should be transitive, that is, most people prefer x to z. But in practice, most people prefer z to x. Thus, a majority rule of voting to determine social or collective choice would have circular outcomes, like a dog chasing its own tail, in an endless loop. As a result, none of these alternatives can obtain a majority of votes to pass. This is called "the voting paradox", and it is a kind of difficulty inherent in all public choice problems.

Part II

The Crisis of Globalization and China's Solutions

7 The Globalization Crisis and the New Globalization

As the international financial crisis in 2008 triggered a big wave of anti-globalization, Chinese scholars held several conferences to discuss the origin of the crisis and the future of globalization. I have been invited to many of these discussions in 2008 and 2009, so tried to scrutinize not only the immediate reasons that led to financial crisis, but also deeper reasons that make the original globalization unsustainable. Here I put these analyses together with other papers written in 2017 and try to give somehow an orientation to China's future development in global economy.

In the aftermath of the global financial crisis in 2008, various protests took place in Europe and the United States. Social movements such as "Occupy Wall Street" began to target globalization, criticizing financial liberalization at its core as the culprit of the financial crisis. At the same time, some voices critical of China began to appear in Western public opinion, claiming that China was the only beneficiary of globalization, attempting to redefine globalization and taking measures against China.

The way we regard the crisis of the Western system triggered by the economic crisis and the way we view the next step of globalization will profoundly affect China's future development strategy, and we must take these issues seriously.

Deregulation and Globalization

It is the nature of capital to chase profits. If countries do not set barriers to capital and implement a completely free market economy, capital can flow freely around the world in pursuit of profits, so that it will promote the development of globalization. However, historical experience shows that a country always puts certain obstacles to the flow of capital, either out of geopolitical concerns or out of fear of capital outflow from the country.

After World War II, the United States implemented the Marshall Plan to help Western European countries recover their economies, and U.S. companies were able to enter Western European markets. The two oil crises of the 1970s triggered a "stagflation" in Western economies, characterized by stagnant economic growth and inflation. The two phenomena, which are almost impossible to occur simultaneously in Keynesian economics, emerged simultaneously. The inflation rate in the United States was 1.4 % in 1960 and reached 13.3 % in 1979, and the unemployment rate in the United States reached 10.8 % by the end of 1982. Economic stagflation made Keynesianism unpopular in the Western world, and several theories against Keynesianism became the theoretical basis for the economic policies of European and American governments, including neoliberalism represented by Austrian economist Friedrich August Von Hayek, monetarism represented by University of Chicago professor Milton Friedman, and the school of supply side economics represented by Stanford University professor Arthur Laffer. In the early 1980s, Reagan was elected president of the United States, and Margaret Thatcher became the prime minister of the United Kingdom. These two landmark events announced the dominance of neoliberalism in the Western world and started the process of globalization.

This globalization, which began in the 1980s, has gone through several stages with several distinctive features.

The Governments of Developed Countries in Europe and America Began to Deregulate and Let the Market dictate the rules of Economic Development

Financial deregulation is an important step in the neoliberal movement. Neoliberalism wants the nation-state to be subservient to the economic subject, which is an entrepreneurial demand for economic freedom; they oppose any government regulation of the market, advocate privatization of public services, and reduce public spending and social spending. The rights of the market were sanctified in the name of economic efficiency, and Western governments that believed in neoliberalism began to remove all kinds of administrative or political barriers from the market to facilitate capitalists who sought to maximize their personal profits. The pursuit of maximizing personal profit became a rational mode of behavior.

Neoliberalism was on the rise and the Western schools of economics were lopsided. The monetarist and schools of supply side economics were predominant in economics, attributing the boom of financial industry and its high profits to the role of four policies: (1) continued economic deregulation; (2) debt-dependent mergers, acquisitions, and leveraged buyouts; (3) the economic effects of speculation; and (4) the beneficial market-enhancing effects of derivatives. Wall Street began to hire a large number of graduates in mathematics, physics, and chemistry, and used a large number of mathematical models to deal with financial derivatives that even financial professionals could not quite understand, with the fancy claim that these models could be a reliable and fundamental risk management tool for financial derivatives.

In this background, the U.S. and European stock markets were affected by a large number of mergers, acquisitions, restructurings and leveraged buyouts, and market conditions were constantly updated, attracting more and more private investors. At the same time, governments began to reduce corporate taxes and encourage investment and financial innovation. This government-initiated movement soon became a movement driven by large multinational corporations.

Under the Influence of Developed Countries, Developing Countries Have Begun to Shift Their Development Strategies

From the 1950s to the 1970s, Western development doctrine argued that in order for developing countries to truly embark on the path of development, they must break the monopoly of developed countries in manufacturing industries and change the economic model in which developing countries have been providing cheap raw materials to developed countries. As a result, "import substitution" became the development strategy of most late-developing countries. Specifically, the government supported a number of state-owned enterprises to produce most-needed manufactured goods, and gradually get rid of the dependence on imported manufactured goods. However, after the 1980s, with the criticism of Keynesianism in Europe and the United States, the "import substitution" strategy was no longer encouraged. On the contrary, Western countries began to criticize the "import substitution" strategy of developing countries, arguing that such a strategy required governments to use high tariffs to foster "infant industries." It has also led to corrupt practices such as "rent-seeking", wasted public expenditure, and supported a number of inefficient state-owned enterprises. At the same time, Europe and the United States also persuaded developing countries to adopt the growth model of importing foreign enterprises to encourage exports. The "Four Asian Tigers" are typical examples of export-led growth to upgrade industries and improve economic competitiveness.

In the late 1970s, China implemented reform and opening up and joined the international division of labor system. China's participation in international markets has contributed to the rapid development of globalization.

International Economic Organizations Promote Liberalization Around the World

In the late 1980s and early 1990s, a group of economists from the U.S. Treasury Department, the World Bank, and the International Monetary Fund began to advocate neoliberal policies, full liberalization of financial markets and privatization in developing countries, especially in countries that need technology imports. These measures were later summarized as the "Washington Consensus". The liberalization of finance led to an acceleration of capital flows, and many countries in Asia and Latin America attracted large amounts of foreign capital because of the opening of their markets. But they were unable to control the use of capital, and the foreign capital created large economic bubbles, which burst and led to financial crises in these countries in the 1990s. In order to provide rescue loans to these countries in crisis, the International Monetary Fund (IMF), representing the interests of European and American countries, put forward many conditionalities, requiring these countries to further open their markets, privatize some national assets, and sell them to European and American enterprises. In the early 1990s, with the collapse of the Soviet Union and the dramatic changes in Eastern Europe, many countries adopted "shock therapy" by privatizing large numbers of state-owned enterprises and introducing Western capital, which also accelerated the development of globalization.

The Macroeconomic Policies of European and American Countries Have Objectively Promoted Globalization

In the 1980s, the U.S. increased interest rates to curb inflation, and the banking sector's earnings increased significantly, which attracted a large amount of foreign capital to the U.S. and drove the dollar's appreciation. President Reagan was very pleased with this trend and declared in his State of the Union address that the United States would become "a global capital investment paradise". But all this was accompanied by a serious blow to the manufacturing industry: the U.S. manufacturing industry is gradually declining.

In 1985, the Reagan administration had to discuss countermeasures with Western European countries and Japan, and finally reached the "Plaza Accord" at the Plaza Hotel in New York, after which the G7 countries intervened in the market to bring down dollar value, and the yen appreciated. With the depreciation of the dollar, it was supposed that the US export would benefit from this tendency. But the US still had a huge trade deficit. For many American companies, the deregulation allows them to invest more easily elsewhere, and they transferred part of the production process to Asian countries. Corporate outsourcing (that is, they are only responsible for assembly or sales) has become a major trend.

After the signing of the Plaza Accord, the long-term depreciation of the U.S. dollar boosted the recovery of the U.S. manufacturing industry, and other countries and regions in East Asia indirectly benefited from the currency peg to the U.S. dollar. The appreciation of the yen caused the decline of Japanese manufacturing industry, so Japanese manufacturing industry turned to produce high value-added products and expand overseas investment, and some countries in Southeast Asia absorbed the investment of Japanese enterprises. Asian economies grew at a faster pace.

The process of transferring low value-added production to developing countries made Western companies much more profitable, and financial liberalization made it easier for companies to raise funds in the capital market, lowering financing costs and making business expansion faster. In this process, multinational companies became the biggest winners.

The Superfacial Prosperity of the U.S. Economy

As the production process of American companies shifted, American society changed significantly and the gap between rich and poor widened, and the policies of the U.S. government widened this gap even more.

The Ability of U.S. Labor to Negotiate Has Declined

The process of shifting production from U.S. firms to developing countries has tilted labor negotiations within the United States heavily in favor of the employers. When labor made demands for higher wages, the management would always threaten to move production lines elsewhere. Labor has lost its bargaining leverage and the average wage of the U.S. workforce has not increased for years.

In fact, the average American's wages have not increased, apart from inflationary terms, from the 1970s, and in some industries have even decreased. In December 2000, the average hourly wage for U.S. businesses was comparable to its level in September 1968, and was 5 % lower than its peak in 1979. The income of middle-class families in the United States also declined slightly from 1989 to 1995. In 1998, the income level of the U.S. middle class was only 4 % higher than in 1989 and only 8 % higher than in 1979. The distribution of wealth in the United States in the 1990s was even more dramatic, with the share of wealth owned by the upper 20 % of the population rising from 59.6 % to 62.9 % in 1990–1992, while the share of wealth owned by the remaining 80 % of the population declined accordingly. In 1999, the U.S. poverty rate was higher than it was in 1979.

The Policies of the U.S. Government Have Widened the Gap between the Rich and the Poor in Society

Starting from the Reagan administration, the U.S. government has been cutting tax for the rich in its policies based on the assumption of supply side economic school view. According to this theory, the rich will be more inclined to consume and invest after the tax cut, which can stimulate production, create jobs, and eventually the government can get more tax revenue due to economic growth.

However, in order to keep the budget balanced, starting from the Reagan administration, the U.S. kept cutting spending on social welfare programs to reduce the government deficit. When protests arose in society, the Reagan administration went out of its way to use the military against workers in order to crack down and dismantle the unions. As a result, with the shrinking of the manufacturing industry, the power of unions continued to be weakened and the gap between the rich and the poor in the United States rapidly widened.

As it became increasingly difficult to invest profitably in manufacturing, U.S. capital began to shift massively to the service sector from the 1980s onward. The non-manufacturing sector began to expand rapidly as the service sector became less unionized and more accessible to capital. Wholesale and retail trade were the most dynamic sector in the United States in the 1990s. The U.S. media explained this by the fact that this industry made extensive use of new technologies such as computers and the Internet, which increased labor productivity.

However, the U.S. media rarely mentions that labor costs in these two industries have remained extremely low for a long time. In 1993, real wages (excluding benefits) for front-line production and non-management workers were 17 % lower than the real wages of workers in 1973 (the highest level since World War II). The U.S. wholesale and retail industries peaked in tax rate increases from 1993 to 1999 on the back of high investment growth and correspondingly higher profit levels (50 % for wholesale and 33 % for retail).

U.S. Monetary Policy Leads to Financial Expanding and Bubble Burst

Low prices of imports from developing countries depress the inflation rate. Central banks in Europe and the United States lowered interest rates, further stimulating financial markets. The boom in financial markets drove consumption growth, and this boom masked rapid debt growth.

The U.S. tax code requires that capital gains be taxed at a lower rate than dividends and allows companies to write off interest payments entirely. U.S. corporations have taken full advantage of this provision. From 1994 to 1998, the annual value of stock repurchases by U.S. nonfinancial corporations tripled; from 1997 to 2000, the total annual value of stock repurchases by U.S. nonfinancial corporations amounted to $220.2 billion, $299.5 billion, $261.3 billion, and $246.4 billion, respectively. Corporate stock purchases are in the interest of corporate executives because as stock prices rise, their holdings of corporate preferred stock increase in value as well. Some senior employees in technology companies were also pleased because they also received a share of preferred stock.

As the Federal Reserve provided an accommodative credit supply environment, financial activity by nonfinancial firms also began to grow. These companies not only bought back their own stock, but also bought the stock of other companies. The increasing value of the stock increased the book equity of the companies, which in turn increased their ability to lend. This gave the financial bubble the power to inflate itself.

When the financial bubble rose, a variety of investment institutions have promised a higher rate of return on investment, and people are prone to ignore the risk of investment. Moreover, the investment institutions often make a complex portfolio that is hard to understand. A variety of financial fraud can hide in this "irrational mania." After the outbreak of the financial crisis, the United States revealed a variety of financial fraud cases, including the huge fraud case of the famous former president of NASDAQ, Madoff.

As the stock market continued to rise in face value, the U.S. government's tax revenues from the stock market grew, and in 1998, the Clinton administration even achieved a government budget surplus. At the same time, however, the private sector deficit increased even more (a figure that illustrates the extent to which households and companies used loans to pay for consumption). In the early 1990s, the U.S. private sector had a surplus of about 5 % of GDP, but by 2000, the sector's balance reversed and its deficit accounted for 6 % of GDP, which means that consumer borrowing in this sector rose by 11 % in 10 years. Since then, it can be said that the U.S. economy has grown increasingly dependent on the size of private indebtedness for growth.

After the Internet bubble burst in 2001, the U.S. economy was in recession. But after Federal Reserve Chairman Alan Greenspan slashed interest rates several times, the U.S. housing bubble took off again. Banks began offering loans to people who could not afford to buy a home. These poorly insured loans were called "subprime loans" and were packaged into financial assets and sold into the market because of their high risk. Greenspan was a big proponent of subprime lending at the time, calling it an important financial innovation.

French economist Piketty's studies prove that in the past three or four decades, the purchasing power of the lower and middle classes in the United States has not increased significantly, and household indebtedness has risen sharply. Yet those bankers and securities dealers continue to take advantage of the wind of financial liberalization to promote all kinds of loans to low-income households, because these financiers always need to find a way to lend out the large savings of the very wealthy to them for profit. In other words, the distribution of wealth in the United States is grossly unequal, with the rich saving large sums of money in the banks, and the banks lending these savings to low-income people in various forms in order to make a profit. This created a perverse form of lending and a perverse financial system. Eventually, because the incomes of low-income people grew so slowly, they were unable to pay off their debts on time, and debt defaults led to a crisis in the entire financial system.

The Crisis of Legitimacy of U.S. Politics

After entering the second half of the 1990s, the U.S. economy appeared to be booming on the surface, but the grossly uneven distribution of U.S. society sowed a crisis in this prosperity. After the bursting of the housing bubble, the U.S. government faced a double crisis of policy failure and political legitimacy.

The Burst of the U.S. Real Estate Bubble Is the Last Straw That Broke the Camel's Back

In the late 1990s, U.S. banks and financial institutions staked their profit expectations on growing private debt, using a variety of methods to get individuals to borrow and spend money, and then packaging the individual debt and selling it to other institutions through the market. Such debt transactions constituted the main transactions in the U.S. debt market in the late 1990s and were crowned as "financial innovations".

The banks' innovation was to expand their debt, which they did in new ways, increasing in size relative to the cash that they had at their disposal. The innovation of holding companies was to find ways to issue more bonds and preferred stock, and then they use the cash back to buy the stock of other companies. The trend of corporate mergers that emerged in the 1980s was a typical financial innovation. When some companies have bad earnings and their stocks don't sell, financial companies package them as high-risk, high-return junk bonds and unintentionally let people know that some big companies are going to buy them, and investors get wind of it, start buying those financial products, betting that these companies will be bought at a higher price in the future.

However, in 2006–2007, when the Federal Reserve raised interest rates to prevent inflation, those who had taken out "subprime" loans to buy homes fell into an instant debt trap. After the Fed raised the prime rate, the interest rates on these loans rose rapidly, so many home buyers with low incomes could not afford to repay their loans. As a result of the defaults, the banks repossessed the collateral, and the properties changed hands between the banks and their customers, which leaded to the bursting of the real estate bubble, with the value of the properties then shrinking dramatically. The banks and other credit institutions made bad loans repeatedly, and the company's share price plummeted, so liquidity was short. There was no longer a market in which to borrow working capital. Thus, the credit crunch leads to a full-blown recession.

The Government's Debt Crisis Has Triggered a Political and Economic Crisis

The large number of bad loans of financial institutions required government money to make up for them. On the one hand, the U.S. Treasury took out hundreds of billions of dollars to put out the fire; on the other hand, the Federal Reserve implemented quantitative easing and issued trillions of dollars of new money to replace the bad debts in the banking system into its own hands. These measures saved the U.S. banking system, but made the government debt increasing. At the same time, this approach has also caused a great backlash in American society.

Since the 1990s, both 80 % of the gains in financial assets made by U.S. households, and almost all of the "private deficits", have occurred within the wealthiest sectors, mainly within the financial sector. As a result, after the crisis, public opinion in the United States blamed the financial sector. However, because of the government's relief, not only did the financial sector not lose anything, some institutions even took advantage of the opportunity to get rich. In mid-September 2011, the "Occupy Wall Street" movement expanded from New York to Washington, D.C., with many American cities responding, fully demonstrating the American people's dissatisfaction with government policies. It is against this background that the Republican Party and the Democratic Party began to go to extremes, with the Congress firmly opposing the government's proposals. The government's efficiency in implementing policies declined, since the two parties were deadlocked, so the U.S. seemed to have a long road out of the economic crisis due to political battles.

The Economic Recovery in the United States Is Weak; the Financial Burden Is Getting Heavier; The Debt Then Becomes a Time Bomb

The U.S. is still not out of the shadow of recession, with high unemployment rate but no growth in investment rate. Against this backdrop, U.S. government public spending, which plays an indispensable role in sustaining economic growth, has been forced to cut public spending drastically under a bipartisan agreement, so the U.S. economy will not recover quickly in the foreseeable future. Stiglitz, a professor of economics at Columbia University and Nobel laureate in economics, pointed out that it is no longer meaningful to discuss whether the U.S. economy meets the economic definition of recession (i.e., two consecutive quarters of negative growth); the U.S. economy has fallen into a kind of high unemployment, low growth dilemma, and the resulting reduction in fiscal revenue and debt growth will become the norm.

Although Cuts in Government Spending Also Involve Less Military Spending, the Cuts affect More Social Welfare Spending

This satisfies the demands of some right-wing Republicans, but increases social injustice. 2011 negotiations between the Obama administration and Congress to raise the debt ceiling were premised on reducing the future level of social benefits enjoyed by the poor, especially the curtailment of pensions and other benefits for the elderly. In an economic crisis, cutting social benefits can exacerbate people's sense of injustice and trigger social unrest. What happened in the UK is likely to be repeated in the US, which will likely lead to economic losses, lower investment and recession.

Statistics Prove that the Largest Consumer in a Society Group Is Actually Not the Upper Class, But the Middle Class

The U.S. middle class has already suffered a major blow in the financial crisis, and if their social benefits are repeatedly reduced in the future, the spending power of the middle class will further decline. The U.S. economy is mainly driven by consumption, and if consumption continues to be weak, it will be difficult for the U.S. economy to find new growth points. Due to the slow economic growth, inflationary pressure will gradually increase, the U.S. government's fiscal revenue will continue to decline, and ultimately the US government can only expand the debt to maintain government operations. But if the debt continues to increase, this approach will arouse suspicion from foreign investors.

The Federal Reserve Implemented Three Quantitative Easing Policy, But the Second and Third Effect Is Significantly Weaker Than the First

Moreover, from the perspective of U.S. investment, the massive increase in liquidity has not prompted a major increase in investment, which is similar to the liquidity trap hypothesis proposed by John Maynard Keynes back then. Since the nominal interest rate cannot be negative, it would not be functional to stimulate the economy when the interest rate has been reduced to the lowest possible level. Due to liquidity preference, people still prefer to hold cash in hand during recessions and do not invest immediately, so monetary policy is ineffective when the economy is caught in a liquidity trap. In the context of globalization, there is a new explanation for the liquidity trap: when the economic growth prospects of developed countries, like the European countries and the United States, are not good, the large amount of liquidity released by the central banks of these countries does not flow to the investment market in their own countries, because companies in these countries are not optimistic about their own markets. Statistics prove that direct investment flows to developed countries did not increase with the easing of monetary policy, but more investment flows went to the markets of emerging countries, increasing the inflationary pressure in emerging markets.

The Bumpy Prospects of Globalization

Western Public Opinion Blaming China for the Global Economic Crisis

As the economic crisis has evolved, U.S. public opinion has begun to blame China, arguing that China-centered globalization has caused the institutional crisis in the West. For example, Thomas Paley, chief economist of China Economic and Security Review Commission in the U.S. Congress, wrote that China-centered globalization poses a comprehensive challenge to U.S. economic and geopolitical security, putting the United States at an extreme international disadvantage.

Paley acknowledges that globalization was initiated by developed countries in the United States and Europe, and has attracted the participation of some developing countries. However, he argues that China's participation has diverted globalization from the trajectory designed by the West. According to Paley's studies, from 2001–2007, the U.S. trade deficit with China led to the displacement of a large number of jobs and the loss of 2.3 million American jobs. This phenomenon is manifested in different ways in all 50 U.S. states. Across all industries, the average American worker loses $8,146 in income each year. Paley argues that involving China in globalization has accelerated China's industrialization and strengthened its military and industrial strength. However, the United States has long been dependent on manufactured goods imported from China, and none of its factory equipment is in working order. If a large-scale, prolonged war were to break out, U.S. industry would not be able to cope with the situation. In addition, Paley argues that China's participation in globalization has yielded large trade surpluses, access to large foreign exchange reserves, and the purchase of many U.S. Treasury bills. In 2014, China owned an estimated $1.27 trillion in U.S. Treasury bills, about 11.8 % of the public's holdings, which constitutes a soft spot for U.S. finance. Of course, Paley acknowledges that the U.S. has taken precautions to monitor the sale of U.S. Treasury securities in the market and, if necessary, to "freeze" Chinese assets, as the U.S. did with Iraq, Libya or Iran. Paley also reminded U.S. politicians that the more U.S. government assets China holds, the more influence it will have on U.S. government decisions. He cited the example of the 1956 British-French intervention in the Suez Canal, in which

President Dwight D. Eisenhower used the large amount of British bonds held by the United States to pressure the British government to withdraw British troops from the Suez Canal and return its operation to Egypt.

Traditional Western economists have analyzed globalization as a win-win game, arguing that globalization benefits both developed countries (investors) and emerging countries (labor providers). Paley, on the other hand, analyzes China's participation in globalization as a zero- sum game, arguing that China's rise has potentially or substantially harmed the geopolitical and economic interests of the United States. He argues that China's rapid rise on the winds of globalization, its substantial growth in manufacturing power, and its rapidly strengthening fiscal capacity have enhanced its attractiveness in three ways.

For one thing, China's geo-economic power is strengthened when its manufacturing strength increases its attractiveness to other countries. For example, China imports large amounts of energy and raw materials from overseas, making some raw material-producing countries much more dependent on China. In turn, these countries import large quantities of manufactured goods from China and therefore become China's export markets.

Second, globalization has made China the world's factory, an assembly base for manufactured goods, and an indispensable link in the world's industrial chain. The result of this pattern is that if China's interests are damaged, it will lead to damage to the interests of upstream component supplying countries and also to the interests of downstream consuming countries.

Third, as China's processing capacity strengthens, so does its financial capacity, which allows China to aid some countries at critical times, gaining support from some countries and creating financial dependencies.

On the contrary, Paley argues that globalization has weakened the U.S. position in the global, and especially in the Asian geopolitical landscape in two ways. On the one hand, Chinese companies have become the sole producers of many products, reducing the possibility of U.S. imports from other regions and making the United States more dependent on China, which would be vulnerable to any disruption in Chinese supplies. On the other hand, globalization has created a production chain in East Asia: components produced in Southeast Asian countries are shipped to China for assembly and then shipped to European and American markets. This makes Southeast Asian countries more economically dependent on China and strengthens China's geo-economic power. Due to the special geopolitical position of Southeast Asia, these economic activities will certainly weaken the influence of the United States in Southeast Asia.

Although there are many mistakes in Paley's analysis, the judgment of Europe and the United States, blaming China for the crisis caused by globalization is a trend for the future, may lead to various consequences, about which we should be precautious.

The Bumpy Future of Globalization

Globalization has brought about a redistribution of wealth, and enterprises in developed countries in Europe and the United States have been the biggest beneficiaries of globalization. They have gained the largest profits, and executives of large enterprises have accumulated much wealth. However, while European and American enterprises are expanding overseas, there are trends such as industrial hollowing and deindustrialization within European and American countries, and the employment situation there is severe. As the financial crisis deepens, European and American governments are more and more impotent to regulate sovereign debt, and it is very possible to have future social and political crises in Europe and the United States.

The Profits and Operations of European and American Multinational Enterprises Are Increasingly Decoupled from Their Home Economies

Although Europe and the United States are in a debt crisis, while the prospects for economic recovery are bleak, large multinational corporations in Europe and the United States are not having a hard time. In fact, since the outbreak of the economic crisis in 2008, U.S. corporate profits have been growing rapidly. In 2011 first quarter, U.S. corporate overall annualized net profits were $1.45 trillion, which is the most profitable quarter in history. In 2010, U.S. corporate net profits have increased from a record low of $1.05 trillion in 2008 to $1.41 trillion, which is a 34.29 % increase.

The fact that U.S. companies are earning so well is due in large part to U.S. companies' investments overseas, especially in emerging markets. Take U.S. investment in China as an example: in 2008, the average rate of return of U.S. companies' investment in China was 33 %, much higher than their investments in other markets. Some European companies have also seen their profits grow from emerging markets, especially China. For example, Audi derives 1/3 of its profits from the Chinese market, and Audi earns 50 % more profit in China than in Germany.

With the development of globalization, the profits of European and American companies in overseas markets have exceeded those in their domestic markets.

For example, in 2007, U.S. companies earned $884 billion overseas and $714 billion domestically. In 2008, U.S. companies earned $956.3 billion overseas and $532 billion domestically. That is, the companies earned 1.8 times of profits from overseas than those from domestic. From 1999 to 2008, U.S. companies' overseas earnings grew at an annual rate of 18 %, and in 2008, U.S. companies earned $956.3 billion overseas, up more than four times as the $181.9 billion earned in 1999.

Many large European and American multinationals make their investments and profits in overseas markets, and because of their origin, taxes are skewed toward overseas governments. This creates a further decoupling of national capital markets from the national economy. The stock market reflects the business performance of companies, and the stock price of companies with good performance goes up. If rising stocks are in the majority, the market environment will result in an overall upward movement in stock prices. However, since the performance of many large enterprises in Europe and the United States mainly comes from overseas markets, when the economy of Europe and the United States is in recession, the performance of enterprises is not too much affected, so the performance of the stock market in Europe and the United States is better than the performance of the overall economy of Europe and the United States.

Europe and the United States Lack the Will for International Cooperation, and Excessive Money Printing Seems to Be the Mainstream Trend, So Inflation and the Resulting Political and Social Unrest Will Become the Theme of the Next Phase in Europe and the United States

When the financial crisis broke out in 2008, G20 members had coordinated policies to prevent economic recession together. However, in the face of the future debt crisis, the G20 may encounter increasing difficulties in coordinating the macroeconomic policies of its members.

Many countries are aware that because of the hegemonic position of the U.S. dollar in the international monetary system, the United States can shift some of the burden to other creditor countries in its response to the crisis. These countries want the U.S. to take responsibility and implement a more responsible monetary policy. But the U.S. believes that the fundamental cause of the crisis is the global economic imbalance, and that in order to restore balance, emerging economies must take greater responsibility, especially China, a major trade surplus country, which should not only allow the yuan to appreciate faster but also expand imports. In fact, China has expanded its imports since the financial crisis began in 2008, and the increasing imports have been an important engine for the rebound of many countries. But China is unlikely to handle the yuan's exchange rate and open its capital markets as quickly as the U.S. would like to see, and China and the U.S. are unlikely to agree quickly on these issues.

Continental European countries have called for a tax on cross-border financial activities, a hypothesis put forward long ago by the American economist Tobin, who argued that it would curb short-term financial speculation but would not affect long-term investment. But countries such as the United Kingdom and the United States would not agree to such a measure, because cross-border financial activities are a major part of their economies and a major source of their profits and tax revenues. If the implementation of the "Tobin tax" scares off international investors, London and New York, two international financial centers will be the biggest victims.

If the world's major economies cannot reach international cooperation in the future, it is likely that the world's major economies will go their own way. In fact, many governments throughout history have resorted to inflation to solve their sovereign debt problems, especially the hegemonic currency holders in the international system who can easily get out of debt distress. This was true for Britain in both world wars, and it was true for the United States in the 1970s. When Western European countries complained about the problems caused to them by the devaluation of the dollar, this was the response of the Nixon administration's Treasury Secretary John Connally: " The dollar is our currency, but it is your problem." Therefore, it is inevitable that in the future the U.S. will devalue the dollar and use it to get out of its debt mess. The debts of some EU member states are subject to financial speculation and the probability of default increases. As a result, yields on these bonds in the market will climb up, increasing the cost to finance economies, and recession seems to be a foregone conclusion. To relieve the recession pressure, the ECB began buying bonds of troubled countries. Although the market temporarily maintained stability under the intervention of the European Central Bank, such rescue method is the same as that of the Federal Reserve, which in fact, is also called "money printing."

The appreciation of the yen pressure is huge, and the Japanese government has said to take all means to prevent the appreciation of the yen. But the Japanese Ministry of Finance cannot solve the appreciation problem by selling yen with borrowed money. Japan will eventually ask the Bank of Japan to "print money" in order to lower the yen exchange rate.

If all developed countries respond to the crisis by "printing money", a return to the high inflation and low growth of the 1970s in the global economy will become more likely. In this context, the future world will become increasingly uncertain: the legitimacy of the leadership in the developed countries will be questioned; people will become confused about their ideology of democracy and market logic; the opposition to the governments will arise, and at the same time the opposition will be so divided that it will not be able to form a mainstream force to lead the future world's development. Low growth, high inflation, high unemployment, inefficient political systems, and restless social groups are all likely to be the future trends of the world.

Emerging Economies Such as China Are Developing Rapidly in the Process of Globalization, But They Also Face Many Challenges

To avoid falling into the "middle-income" trap, China must pay attention to the following issues in its future development.

1. Continue to maintain overall economic growth and reduce dependence on the markets of developed countries. The debt situation in Europe and the United States will not improve in the short term, the developed countries are destined to live a period of "hard times". Only through fiscal tightening, increasing savings, and improving competitiveness, can they get out of the crisis. The rapid development of emerging countries over the years is related to their increasing exports to developed countries. The shrinkage of export markets will inevitably affect the future development of emerging countries. Therefore, the only way to maintain sustainable economic development is to expand domestic demand and therefore to change development mode. In the past, many countries have become middle-income countries, but because of their dependence on external markets, they were unable to adjust their economic structure quickly when they were hit by external shocks. As a result, they fell into crisis and could not save themselves, losing the opportunity of development.

China is rapidly industrializing and urbanizing at a faster pace. As the "factory of the world," China will certainly experience more imported inflationary pressures than developed countries for one reason: since the non- industrialized economy of developed country is dominated by the service sector, rising raw material and energy prices affect developed countries less than manufacturing-based countries. Economists in the United States and some international economic organizations have publicly advocated that the Federal Reserve relax its inflation target and set the annual average core inflation index between 4 % and 6 %, instead of the current 2 %. The inflation targets for emerging economies, such as China, should be changed accordingly, and the government should put more effort into addressing the social consequences of inflation, helping the disadvantaged, subsidizing supply in certain areas, etc.

2. China should continue to promote trade and investment liberalization and build international discourse. We should encourage large multinational companies to move more R&D projects to China as well, further expanding their share of the Chinese market, which will also strengthen China's economic power. The Chinese market is now the largest or fastest growing market for many large multinational companies and will become even more attractive to them as the Chinese economy transforms. We should turn these "stakeholders" into our "lobbying groups" and encourage them to spread the word on the international stage about China's success and China's contribution to world economic growth. In short, these companies are making a lot of money in the Chinese market, so they can make a small contribution to the development of China's soft power.

3. China should steadily reform its financial system and gradually open up its capital market, and must not allow international speculative capital to enter and leave the Chinese market at will. The internationalization of the RMB should be carried out in a step-by-step manner, and the firewall to shield speculative capital should not be abandoned for the sake of internationalization.

Putting pressure on RMB appreciation seems to be a card used by the US to force China to open up its capital account, while historical experience proves that premature opening of the capital account will lead to large capital in and out, destabilizing the exchange rate and affecting the smooth development of the real economy. Developed countries in Europe and the US are currently maintaining loose monetary policies to solve their debt problems caused by the financial crisis. If China opens its capital account too early, a large amount of speculative capital will take advantage of the situation and create a huge asset bubble in China. The speculative capital then quickly withdraws, leaving the economic problems caused by the bursting of the bubble behind.

4. It is important to handle well the relationship between expanding domestic demand and maintaining the competitiveness of China's economy. Expanding domestic demand requires readjusting the ratio of labor to capital distribution, in order to make the distribution appropriately tilted toward workers. But it is also very important to grasp the degree of adjustment. China has entered the ranks of middle-income countries where production costs are rising rapidly in comparison with the shrinking labor. The coastal provinces where contract manufacturing industry is concentrated have already experienced difficulties in recruiting workers. European countries have learned a lesson from the debt crisis and decided to "cut back" on social welfare spending and nominal wages in order to improve their export competitiveness. In the past, people could not understand why the countries with lower wage costs than China

could not attract as much foreign direct investment as China does. Although these countries have low wage costs, they lack skilled workers and engineers, and they also have poor infrastructure. But European countries have skilled workers and engineers, as well as good infrastructure, and if they can improve their efficiency and lower their wage costs, it will be a huge challenge for China. For China to remain competitive and attractive, it must improve the ability to work together across sectors and continuously improve the skills and efficiency of its workforce. Only by keeping labor productivity in China increasing, can China remain competitive in the world economy.

5. Chinese enterprises are investing rapidly overseas. In the process of encouraging Chinese enterprises to "go abroad", they should also pay attention to preventing political risks in the investing countries and price risks in the international market, establishing their own sales networks, creating their own brands, and expanding the value-added part of the profit chain. Chinese companies' direct investments abroad are mainly in developing resources, energy, or some important raw materials. These investments have both political and price risks, and some Chinese companies fail to fully consider these risks. For example, some Chinese companies may not take into account local laws and regulations and sign cooperation projects in the form of "investment for resources". In fact, the constitutions of some countries clearly state that resources cannot be used as collateral. Other "investment-for-resources" contracts are theorictically valid for decades, but may not be recognized in the event of a regime change. In recent years, international markets have seen high prices for resources, which are often priced in U.S. dollars, and there is a negative correlation between the dollar exchange rate and resource prices. When the dollar weakened, resource prices were high, but if the U.S. changed its monetary policy in the future and the dollar became strong again, the price of resources on the international market would plummet. Those countries that borrowed dollars for oil development were plunged into debt crisis. We should learn from history.

At present, globalization has put developed countries in a dilemma: if they do not support globalization, they cannot benefit from the rapid development of emerging economies, but further participation in globalization will make it more difficult to change the pattern of "poor governments + rich companies". China has benefited from globalization, but it must also avoid falling into new traps, such as being dragged down by excessive investment in the sovereign debt of developed countries, losing both monetary sovereignty and wealth. As long as China sticks to and improves its own system and does not blindly follow it, its economy will be able to grow better after the crisis is over.

The Trend of Counter-Globalization

What do the Brexit and the election of Trump, the "black swan events" mean? Beneath the surface of the "political crisis" lies a wave of "anti- globalization" grievances in developed countries. These grievances have begun to spread to the political sphere and will quickly spread to the economic and trade spheres. Globalization is facing a great threat. China is considered to be the biggest beneficiary of globalization, and its rapid economic development over the years has been closely linked to the development of globalization. How likely is the reversal of globalization? How much impact will it have on China? How should China lead the new round of globalization?

In recent years, globalization has regressed, both in terms of international trade development indicators and in terms of cross-border investment indicators. From 1990 to 2007, total global trade in goods grew from $3.45 trillion to $14.24 trillion, and global GDP grew from $22.6 trillion to $57.97 trillion. Global trade grew more than twice as fast as economic growth. However, since the economic crisis, global trade growth has lagged behind economic growth for a long time. Similarly, cross-border private investment, which grew rapidly before the economic crisis, has been declining in recent years.

In this situation, globalization has become the target of all. The political newcomers in Europe and the United States like to take globalization as a scapegoat for the economic recession.

Donald Trump, who was elected president of the United States in 2016, constantly made trade liberalization an object of attack during his campaign, claiming that the root cause of the stagnant U.S. economy lies in international trade liberalization.

The United States, Japan and developed European countries have not been able to find new growth points since the economic crisis. Economic growth has been sluggish, and governments have continued to use fiscal and monetary policies to stimulate the economy with little success, while the diminishing benefits of macroeconomic policies are evident.

The Federal Reserve has implemented several rounds of quantitative easing, and interest rates have been maintained at around zero. The European Central Bank and the central banks of European countries that are not part of the Eurozone, such as the United Kingdom, Switzerland, and Denmark, are all pursuing negative interest rates. The Bank of Japan has also started to implement negative interest rates after implementing several rounds of quantitative easing. With the debt of developed countries climbing rapidly after the economic crisis, there is little room for these countries to continue using fiscal policy to stimulate their economies, and monetary policy has become the only tool available. However, in the case of Europe and Japan, the use of negative interest rates to stimulate the economic rebound is not very useful. Monetary policy has run out of tricks.

In this context, the governments of Europe and the United States are increasingly looking to protectionism and revitalization of manufacturing, hoping to seize the last straw. For example, the Obama administration wanted to use the stimulus package to revive the manufacturing industry and change the status quo of the declining U.S. manufacturing industry. The U.S. joined the Trans-Pacific Partnership Agreement and the Transatlantic Trade and Investment Partnership Agreement, in an attempt to reestablish U.S. leadership in the world economy and to exclude emerging economies from the new international trading system. This exclusionary system is clearly against the trend of globalization.

In 2017, Trump announced his withdrawal from the Trans-Pacific Partnership after his inauguration as president, and his campaign ideas of withdrawing from NAFTA and the World Trade Organization were even more radical. It remains to be seen whether the withdrawal from the Trans-Pacific Partnership Agreement represents a return to protectionism in the United States.

Why the Developed Countries Are Now "Against" Globalization?

In 2016, two events, the British referendum on leaving the European Union and the election of Donald Trump as the president of the United States, highlighted the rise of extremist sentiments in European and American societies. This extremist sentiment, also referred to as the rise of populism by the mainstream media in Europe and the United States, reflects some of the changes that have taken place in European and American societies in recent years.

In the 1950s and 1960s, the struggle between the two camps, led by the United States and the Soviet Union respectively, was intense, and blue-collar workers in the United States gradually joined the middle class during this period. Labor pay and social welfare were important areas of competition between the two camps over the superiority of the system, and neither dared to slow down. But after the two oil crises of the 1970s, the Western economies entered a prolonged period of "stagflation," when inflation remained high and growth stagnated simultaneously, leaving policymakers familiar with Western macroeconomics at a loss. In the 1980s, Reagan and Margaret Thatcher launched the "neoconservative revolution", which broke down the labor unions in the United States and Britain and promoted financial liberalization. Starting from the 1980s, European and American companies began to make massive investments overseas, especially in East Asian countries, where foreign investments could lower production costs and increase competitiveness. Financial liberalization and trade liberalization greatly facilitated this process, and globalization became popular for a while.

While globalization has made many European and American companies profitable, there has been a trend toward de-industrialization in these countries. Along with de-industrialization, large corporations have more of an advantage in wage negotiations, while labor has lost its bargaining leverage. U.S. companies went the furthest and fastest in the process of deindustrialization, with the result that after the economic crisis, the average pay for blue-collar workers in the United States was less than it was in the 1970s. De-industrialization has exacerbated the unequal distribution of wealth in Europe and the United States, and those who work in financial conglomerates are a small group, but they are the biggest beneficiaries of globalization. The consumption of the middle class is the driving force of economic development in Europe and the United States. However, with the shrinking size of the middle class and the decline of consumption power, the economic growth in Europe and the United States has lost its momentum. With the shift of production processes, a large number of people in Europe and the United States are surrounded by uncertainty in their lives. They are unable to adapt to the new changes brought about by globalization, and their labor skills are aging, while they cannot keep up with the new development situation. In Europe, these unemployed people became a social burden, social assistance became an important part of government spending, and the debt burden prevented the governments of these countries from using fiscal spending to stimulate economic growth.

At the same time, the development of communication technology has made technology transfer much easier than the past, lowering the threshold for emerging countries to master new technologies and shortening the time to catch up with developed countries. After the economic crisis, emerging countries have developed rapidly, and their contribution to world economic growth once exceeded that of developed countries. Some analysts believe that developed countries are plagued by social problems such as an aging population, and their future contribution to the world economy will continue to be lower than that of emerging countries. These predictions have made developed countries feel threatened.

In developed countries, the development of the Internet and wireless communication technology has enabled the self-media to break through the control of traditional media on public opinion. Over time, public opinion in developed countries began to accuse globalization of benefiting only those groups in control of capital in developed countries while hurting other groups. Social movements such as "Occupy Wall Street" represent these voices, and it is by inciting the discontent of these people that Donald Trump was elected president of the United States.

The gradual fermentation of popular discontent in Europe is mainly reflected in the emergence of extreme political ideas and the rise of political figures with extreme views. In recent years, with the outbreak of the refugee crisis, the flow of migrants to Europe from all over the world has galvanized European enthusiasm for nationalism and national sovereignty. Various public opinion polls show that the group supporting European integration is rapidly shrinking, and according to this development trend, it is still possible for far-right politicians in European countries to come to power by election in the future.

The Impact of Deglobalization

Deglobalization has had a huge impact on both developed and developing countries. In developed countries, the polarization of the political ecology makes it impossible to implement any effective policies to restructure the economy. On the contrary, the more politicians advocate extremist policies, the more attention they get from the public, but extremism does not help, it can only put government officials under enormous constraints. In such background, it is not surprising that economic growth in developed countries has stagnated, and many prominent economists have referred to the stagnation of economic growth in developed countries in recent years as the "Great Stagnation".

The U.S. economy seems to be gradually coming out of stagnation and is a leader in the Western world. However, the recovery of the U.S. economy relies mainly on the rebound of the stock market, which is still a bubble economy to some extent. In terms of corporate earnings, most U.S. companies are not growing their profits. The rebound in U.S. employment relies mainly on service industries such as retail trade, while the number of jobs in the U.S. manufacturing sector has not increased significantly, which indicates that the plan to revive the U.S. manufacturing sector has not been successful. The U.S. stock market has improved in large part because long-term low interest rates and quantitative easing policies have stimulated investment enthusiasm in financial market. Some years ago, the dollar exchange rate was low, and resource prices were high. Many U.S. companies were scrambling to develop shale gas and shale oil. Fueled by quantitative easing, the development of shale gas was sought after by the market, and there was a proliferation of shale gas-related corporate bonds and stocks.

However, the business of investing in energy is soon to come to an end as energy supply rises, and market demand appears to be lacking due to weak global economic growth. The Fed's ultra-loose monetary policy has been in place for nearly 10 years, and it is time to enter a rate hike cycle anyway. If further delay may lead to uncontrollable inflation, many pension funds and other social welfare funds rely on "fixed interest income" will not last, because they invest in Treasury bonds and other stable investments—with an annual return of only about 1 %—simply cannot pay their expenses. If the Fed raises interest rates, investment costs rise. Subsequently, capital will leave the resource markets; energy prices will decline; the stock market bubble will burst on shale gas and other junk bonds; and the United States may enter a new recession.

Developed countries issue hard currency. Since the economic crisis, almost all central banks in developed countries have implemented quantitative easing and later negative interest rates. The super-easy monetary policy released a huge amount of liquidity, and due to the rapid economic growth of emerging countries, they became a destination for corporate investment in developed countries. Companies in emerging countries also engaged in borrowing cheap foreign currency and returning to their home countries to invest in arbitrage. Large amounts of hot money began to flow into emerging country markets, stimulating the formation of asset bubbles in these markets and creating an atmosphere of frantic chasing of asset investments.

However, after the Federal Reserve withdrew from quantitative easing in 2014, a large amount of capital flowed back to the U.S., chasing portfolio assets, and resource prices plummeted. Emerging countries, many of which are resource exporters, became the biggest casualties. Brazil, South Africa, and Russia all experienced major exchange rate devaluations that could almost be described as currency crises, resulting in high inflation and rapidly slowing economic growth, with Brazil's economic difficulties even evolving into a political crisis.

The Future of Globalization and China's Strategic Choice

The reversal of globalization will continue for some time, and with the election of Donald Trump as president of the United States, the possibility of extreme political figures coming to power in European countries is on the rise. These figures are opposed to trade liberalization and to globalization.

Globalization was driven by developed countries, and now they are turning to promote reverse globalization, which will surely affect the future development trend of the world economy. Against this background, it is necessary for China to become a leading force in leading the new round of globalization in order to maintain its strong economic development and fill the vacuum left by the developed countries.

To this end, China should grasp the following development trends:

Attract More Technical Talents to China, Make China a Happy Land for Technology Development, and Make the Chinese Market a Fertile Ground for New Technology Growth

In fact, the era when developed countries held the core technology of industrial manufacturing is long gone, and counter-globalization will not help them to revive the manufacturing industry or improve their situation in the global economy. According to different criteria of manufacturing, the United Nations has divided industrial manufacturing into 39 major categories, 191 medium categories and 525 small categories. China is the first country in the world to have a complete industrial system according to the UN standards. The complete system allows manufacturing companies in China to easily realize a wide range of complementary work and find a variety of complementary products and components, saving a lot of time and effort. This advantage will allow China to attract more innovative companies to invest in the coming period.

The Trump administration has encouraged the return of traditional industries, for which he has taken the risk of withdrawing the United States from the Paris Agreement. The withdrawal has discouraged many entrepreneurs in emerging industries in the U.S. They are dissatisfied with the current situation in the U.S. and are eager to look for new investment opportunities outside the country. This is an opportunity for China to attract emerging companies to invest in China. China should adopt a more flexible strategy in attracting foreign technical talents and foreign technology companies to start businesses in China, and encourage foreign talents to come to China to develop new products, new business models, and to lead the world's new trend of technological innovation.

China Should Grasp the Firewall of Capital Control and Gradually Open Up Its Financial Market

In the coming period, the differences in the monetary policies of the United States, Japan and developed European countries will become more obvious, and the impact on international financial markets should not be underestimated. Specifically, developed countries have been implementing extremely accommodative monetary policies for nearly 10 years, but now their monetary policies are beginning to diverge. The Federal Reserve has entered the interest rate hike cycle, while the European Central Bank and the Bank of Japan are still implementing negative interest rate policies. Differences in monetary policy can cause volatility in capital markets.

During his campaign, Trump promised to increase government spending and improve infrastructure after his election, while also reducing taxes on the middle class to stimulate their spending. These promises, coupled with the expectation of a Fed rate hike, have pushed the dollar upward. But the U.S. has nearly $ 20 trillion in government debt, and every 0.25 %age point increase in interest rates by the Federal Reserve will cost $ 50 billion of the U.S. government's debt interest payments. If the U.S. government increases the fiscal deficit, the double deficit will soon lead to a new debt crisis. The reason why the Federal Reserve is dragging its feet on raising interest rates is a reflection of its concerns. In the dollar exchange rate market, the change in the long-term exchange rate of the dollar is not an appreciation but a depreciation, which also reflects the concerns of international investors.

China should be prepared to grasp the pace of financial opening and not remove the firewall of capital controls too quickly, and we should be wary of the impact of a new debt crisis on China's capital markets.

Rationalize the Suspicion of Developed Countries and Reduce the Expectation of Technology Transfer from Large Western Enterprises to China

As China's power grows, suspicion of China in the developed world is rapidly increasing. The U.S. Congress has increased scrutiny of investment from China, and Americans are concerned about the outflow of new U.S. technology, which they believe will further imbalance the power of the West versus China. The European Union has also begun to discuss increased scrutiny of foreign investment, with a clear target on China, and the EU is concerned that Chinese investment in Europe will lead to an outflow of European technology.

In the past, in the process of globalization, China has mainly received technology transfers from developed countries. For this reason, we had applied preferential policies to many large multinational companies in the hope that they would transfer some technology to China. But in the future, technology transfer will not be the dominant form of cooperation between China and developed countries, because the technological capabilities of Chinese companies are rapidly emerging, and China will be able to achieve self-sufficiency in the future.

Protectionism is on the rise in developed countries, and while they remain China's largest export markets, export growth in these traditional markets is very limited. China's future technological innovation will have to rely more on Chinese companies than on technological cooperation with developed countries.

Further Promote the Cooperation between China and Emerging Countries

Emerging countries still have huge room for infrastructure development and huge room for improvement in consumption and services, which makes them interested in cooperating with China. Emerging countries have a better demographic structure and a more open mind, and are more willing to participate in new international cooperation and establish a more reasonable coordination mechanism. All in all, emerging countries are the main force in promoting a new type of globalization. China needs to develop new markets and build international discourse, and the BRICS summit in Xiamen in 2017 created a model of mutually beneficial cooperation, a model of "South-South cooperation" that is bound to stimulate more interest in mutually beneficial cooperation among emerging countries. Cooperation between China and these developing countries will certainly change the future pattern of world economic growth and the structure of the world economy.

U.S. investment firms have already predicted this trend. Goldman Sachs predicts that by 2050, the top 5 countries in the world economy will be the 4 BRIC countries (China, India, Brazil, Russia) and the United States. Goldman Sachs also predicts that by 2050, the "New Diamond 11" (Mexico, South Korea, Indonesia, Turkey, Iran, Egypt, Nigeria, Bangladesh, Pakistan, the Philippines, Vietnam) will have more GDP than the United States and twice the GDP of the European Union.

PwC also suggests in The World in 2050 that the total GDP of the seven largest emerging economies (Brazil, China, India, Indonesia, Mexico, Russia, and Turkey) is already comparable to the G7 (Group of Seven) in 2015 in terms of purchasing power parity, and that by 2040, the total GDP of the seven largest emerging economies will be twice that of the G7. By 2050, the EU's GDP share of global GDP will drop to less than 10 % and the US GDP share will drop to 12 %.

China should take advantage of the current historical opportunity to further open up the markets of developing countries and take advantage of the market opportunities presented by the industrialization of these countries and the expansion of the middle class to promote Chinese investment and trade facilitation to these regions. China can work closely with a wide range of developing countries to change the global cooperation framework and save the global multilateral free trade.

On the basis of controlling China's domestic economic development, China can take advantage of the wave of reverse globalization in developed countries to expand China's international discourse, use investment and trade to expand its influence among developing countries, and reshape the international system in favor of China's development.

8

Global Governance and the New Globalization

Since the financial crisis of 2008, I have been invited to talk about the crisis management and global governance, as a financial crisis is somehow contagious, and becomes quickly an international crisis. On the approch of a G20 summit in Hengzhou, I wrote down a few papers in 2016 to analyse the global governance and the importance of global governance in promoting somehow a more balanced globalization.

In September 2016, the G20 summit was held in China for the first time. Since the outbreak of the international financial crisis in 2008, the global economy has been in a continuous downturn. Although the G20 has made some progress in coordinating macroeconomic policies, jointly responding to the crisis and reforming the international monetary system, international public opinion has begun to question how useful the G20 is and whether it can still play a role in leading the development of the world economy.

G20 members are located on five continents, with 2/3 of the world's population, and the total economic volume of G20 members accounts for 85 % of the world's economy and 80 % of the global trade volume. If G20 members can coordinate and implement a unified economic policy, its impact on the world economy is self-evident.

In 2016, China hosted the G20 Summit for the first time, and the G20 Hangzhou Summit helped build China's voice on issues of global governance and future global development.

In recent years, China has developed better than any other G20 member, but China's voice in world economic development is insufficient, and its development model is questioned by some countries. In international trade, cross-border investment and public governance, Western countries still hold the discourse, but their development concepts are not necessarily correct. We need to clarify our thinking and point out the problems in the Western discourse. China needs to make its voice heard and take control of the discourse on future development.

Mastering the discourse of development is not only about making China's voice heard in the international arena, but also about letting the Chinese people know what the Chinese government thinks about the world's development and giving them confidence in China's development model.

What Is the G20?

What kind of mechanism is the G20? What is its place in the global economy? The leaders of G20 members meet every year to discuss global economic issues, and the finance ministers and central bank governors of G20 members often meet to discuss macroeconomic policy coordination. It can be said that the G20 has become a forum that attracts much attention from international public opinion in terms of discussing and dealing with global affairs.

However, to date, the G20 is not a formal international organization, since it has no permanent body of its own, and G20 summits are chaired by its member states in turn, with the government of each country organizing that year's meeting. Therefore, the G20 is in fact a club, which is substantially different from an international organization such as the United Nations, and is based on the principle of coordination and coherence, with each member country voluntarily implementing its resolutions without any coercive power.

Historically, the G20 has evolved from the G7. After the oil crisis in the 1970s, the developed countries in the West fell into economic stagnation. In order to coordinate macroeconomic policies and prevent beggar-thy-neighbor behavior, the French President Valery Giscard d'Estaing proposed to convene a meeting of the leaders of the 5 most economically developed countries at that time (the United States, the United Kingdom, France, Germany and Japan) to jointly discuss a plan to coordinate macroeconomic policies. In October 1975, the preparatory group decided to invite Italy to the meeting, and in November of the same year, the first summit of the 6 nations was held at the Château de Rambouillet, on the outskirts of Paris. In 1976, when the second summit was held, the United States offered to invite the Prime Minister of Canada to the meeting. Since the second meeting, the framework of the G7 has been fixed.

The G7 summits played a role in responding to the oil crisis and stabilizing economic growth in developed countries. However, after the 1980s, Western leaders became less interested in this mechanism, as the new leaders of Western powers, such as U.S. President Reagan, French President Mitterrand, German Chancellor Kohl, and British Prime Minister Margaret Thatcher, did not like to discuss macroeconomic issues. In 1985, at the Plaza Hotel in New York, the United States, Japan, the Federal Republic of Germany, France, and the United Kingdom reached the Plaza Accord, in which the five countries decided to intervene in the market to devalue the dollar and appreciate the yen and the deutsche mark. In 1986, the five countries met again in France to consolidate the terms of the Plaza Accord and reached the Louvre Accord. These major international monetary and financial decisions were made at meetings of the finance ministers and central bank governors of these countries.

In the early 1990s, the world landscape changed dramatically with the collapse of the Soviet Union. After the collapse of the bipolar system, Russia was considered a loser, but as a reward for its "peaceful transition," the G7 invited Russia to participate in some of the G7 summits from 1991 onwards. After 1997, Russia was "officially" admitted to the G8 (Group of Eight) summits, which it attended every time. But this is just a political game of the West, which is trying to bring in Yeltsin to support Russia's "democratic transition".

The G7 was originally established to coordinate the macroeconomic policies of the most advanced industrial countries, and each year the G7 summits discuss important global economic issues. However, the G8 summits only symbolically analyze global economic issues and state the G8's position, without making actual decisions. This is because the leaders at the G8 summits are not well versed in economic issues, and the discussion of economic policy is transferred to the G7 meetings of finance ministers and central bank governors. After the crisis in Ukraine, Russia was "hung out to dry" by other countries, and the G8 reverted to the G7. Since the late 1990s, emerging countries have been rising rapidly, and the share of the G7 members in the world economy and their influence have been declining. Even the public opinion in the Western countries thinks that the G7 no longer represents the future direction of the world economy, and it seems that this mechanism can be put to an end. In this context, the G7 hosted the meeting for Finance Ministers and Central Bank Presidents in Cologne, Germany, in June 1999, and Canadian Finance Minister, Paul Martin, suggested that a forum covering 20 economies be established. In December of the same year, the first G20 Finance Ministers and Central Bank Governors meeting was held in Berlin, Germany. In 2003, Paul Martin was elected Prime Minister of Canada, and he advised U.S. President George W. Bush Jr. to elevate the G20 Finance Ministers and Central Bank Governors meeting to the level of a summit, but Bush Jr. did not follow this suggestion.

In 2008, the financial crisis broke out in the United States and subsequently swept through the entire Western world, plunging the global economy into recession. At this time, the developed countries again remembered the G20 mechanism.

The first G20 summit was held in Washington, D.C., and in 2008. In 2009 and 2010, the leaders of G20 members met twice a year until 2011. When the world economic situation was stabilized, the frequency of G20 summits returned to once a year. The eleventh G20 summit was held in Hangzhou in the fall of 2016.

What Are the Roles of the G20?

The G20 played a positive role in stabilizing the world economy in the aftermath of the international financial crisis, which was comparable to the Great Depression of the 1930s, according to many analysts after the outbreak of the financial crisis in 2008. During the Great Depression, countries lacked policy coordination mechanisms and all tried to transfer the effects of the crisis to other countries, which eventually made the economic crisis uncontrollable and intensified, and the world economy entered a long period of depression, and only after the end of World War II did it completely come out of the trough.

In the wake of the financial crisis, the leaders of G20 members agreed that all countries must take active measures to implement stimulus packages to prevent a further downturn in the global economy. Later, the leaders repeatedly said that all countries should actively deal with the consequences of the economic crisis and prevent a return of protectionism. It should be said that without the cooperation and efforts of G20 members, the world economy could not have been stabilized soon after the outbreak of the financial crisis, and there would not have been a situation where countries coordinated their macroeconomic policies to prevent a recession.

Leaders of G20 members also agreed on a financial and economic reform plan, expressing a concerted effort to improve transparency in financial markets, improve accountability, strengthen regulation of financial markets, promote financial market integrity, strengthen international cooperation, and reform international financial institutions. The plan sets short- and medium-term goals for reforms in each of these five areas. In terms of improving financial market transparency and accountability. The G20's short-term goals include strengthening the valuation of securities by the world's leading accounting institutions, increasing the disclosure of information on complex financial products by regulators and accounting institutions, strengthening the regulation of international accounting institutions, ensuring the transparency of information disclosure by accounting institutions, and strengthening the accountability of governments to regulators, etc. The medium-term goals of the G20 include strengthening cooperation among major global accounting institutions, establishing high standards of global accounting standards, and ensuring comprehensive, accurate and timely disclosure of financial risks by financial institutions.

At the G20 Summit, the reform of international financial institutions was on the agenda, the share of emerging economies in the international financial institutions (IMF and World Bank) and their voting rights were increased accordingly, and the issue of including RMB in the IMF SDR currency basket was first raised in the framework of the G20.

The G7 members are all developed countries, and it is easier for them to coordinate their economic policies, while the G20 members are both developed countries and fast-developing developing countries, which have different stages of economic development and different growth cycles, making it more difficult to coordinate macroeconomic policies. Over the years, developing countries have continuously raised some typical issues at the G20 summits, forcing developed countries to think about the needs and challenges encountered by developing countries in the development of the world economy.

However, in recent years, developed countries have increasingly relied on loose monetary policies in the process of coming out of economic stagnation. Because their additional currencies are hard currencies, which are important currencies in the international monetary system, the spillover effect of monetary policy in developed countries has been massive capital flows to emerging economies, prompting the creation of asset bubbles in these countries.

The G20 is also divided, as the different growth cycles and stages of economic development of its members have led to a divergence of interests in the process of global economic growth, making it increasingly difficult to coordinate macroeconomic policies. The developed countries are experiencing difficulties because financial institutions are in crisis, deflation and low price indices, so they tend to use extremely loose monetary policies. The Federal Reserve has implemented several rounds of quantitative easing to release liquidity, and the European Central Bank and the Bank of Japan have both used negative nominal interest rates to force financial institutions to lend their money. Emerging economies are experiencing completely different difficulties. While the financial crisis plunged developed countries into recession, growth in emerging economies remained strong. Emerging economies attracted a lot of liquidity released by the central banks of developed countries, and with high resource prices in international markets (many emerging economies are resource exporters), their economies grew fast, but inflationary pressures followed. So, in theory, these emerging economies should raise interest rates to curb inflation, but the difficulty is that the larger the interest rate differential between emerging economies and developed countries, the more money flows to emerging economies, and the more inflationary pressure emerging economies will face.

Leaders of emerging economies have said several times at the G20 summit that G20 members should enhance their coordination of monetary policies and that monetary policies of developed countries should pay attention to spillover effects. However, developed countries really do not pay much attention to these claims. For example, the Federal Reserve is the issuer of the U.S. dollar, which is the predominant currency in the international monetary system. And the Fed has never considered only the U.S. economy when formulating monetary policy. Because of the unique hegemony of the U.S. dollar, the Fed's policies have many spillover effects. The dollar is the sole pricing currency for oil and for most commodities. The movement of the dollar is negatively correlated with the movement of the prices of these commodities: when the dollar strengthens, the prices of these commodities fall; when the dollar depreciates, the prices of these commodities rise. After the financial crisis, the dollar depreciated and the prices of commodities such as oil skyrocketed. After the Federal Reserve decided to end quantitative easing and enter the interest rate hike cycle, the dollar appreciated and commodity prices fell. Brazil and Russia, emerging economies that are major resource exporters, have seen their economic growth cycles directly affected by the fluctuations in the dollar exchange rate.

The role and future of the G20 is in question due to the divergence of interests and the increased demand for macroeconomic policies. Against this backdrop, what can China do to re-energize the G20? This has received a lot of attention from international public opinion.

How to Revitalize the G20 Consultation Mechanism?

The G20 has played a positive role in preventing the spread of the economic crisis, a return of protectionism and a major global recession, but the G20 also faces new challenges.

The Macroeconomic Policies of Developed Countries Are Diverging

In 2008, following the international financial crisis, G20 members worked together to adopt accommodative monetary policies and proactive fiscal policies to stimulate the economic rebound. At that time, leaders pledged to refrain from trade protectionism and to cooperate with each other on macroeconomic policies, and the international cooperation averted a major recession in the world economy. However, after seven years, the economic situation of the developed countries within the G20 has changed, and their macroeconomic policies have begun to diverge. These differences in macroeconomic policies could lead to significant spillover effects that could have a major impact on the world economy.

For example, after several rounds of quantitative easing and seven years of ultra-low interest rates, the Federal Reserve began to change its monetary policy. in October 2014, the Fed ended quantitative easing, and in December 2015, the Fed raised interest rates for the first time. This means that the future of U.S. monetary policy will enter the era of "tightening the money", which will cause the dollar exchange rate reversal. The dollar has been appreciating since 2014, while the prices of resources and energy in the world market have plummeted, causing a huge impact on the world economy.

The European Central Bank has pursued a policy that is the opposite of that of the Federal Reserve. After years of reserve following the financial crisis, the ECB finally decided to implement quantitative easing in 2015, imposing negative nominal interest rates to hedge against the deflationary pressures experienced in the eurozone, in the form of additional monetary issuance, in order to stimulate investment and consumption.

The Central Bank of Japan has been implementing quantitative easing for some time, and although it has eased deflation in Japan, it has done little to stimulate the economy to rebound. Since Japan is facing the structural problems of aging population and insufficient labor supply, any macroeconomic policy is unlikely to have much effect in the short term.

The economic development cycles of the developed countries have produced significant differences, and their monetary policies have started to move in different directions. Monetary policy can have a direct impact on exchange rates, and the instability of the exchange rates of several major hard currencies in the international monetary system can produce strong external shocks to other economies.

The Reversal of Growth Trends in Developed Countries and Emerging Economies

Since 2008, the emerging economies represented by BRICS have maintained a strong growth momentum and become an important force driving world economic growth. From 2009 to 2013, BRICS became the main driver of world economic growth. However, from 2014, the economic growth of BRICS countries began to slow down. In 2015, Brazil and Russia have fallen into negative growth, showing the first signs of stagflation; China's economic growth also began to slow down; India's economic growth is not slow, but the rupee has depreciated significantly, and capital flight is serious.

These trends are related to the structural transformation of the economies of emerging economies. After the outbreak of the international financial crisis, emerging economies have faced the challenge of deleveraging and reducing their debt burden after maintaining economic growth with stimulus programs. The slowdown in economic growth is to some extent the result of government regulation. However, the recessions in Brazil and Russia were mainly caused by the plummeting prices of resources and energy in international commodity futures markets. Both Brazil and Russia are large exporters of resources and energy, and they are particularly sensitive to the prices of these commodities, especially when the government budgets are directly linked to resource exports. In addition, Russian recession could be also due to the economic sanctions from Europe and the United States because of the Ukraine crisis.

According to the Brazilian National Institute of Geography and Statistics (IBGE), the Brazilian economy grew by 0.1 % in 2014, while inflation was 6.41 %. Additionally, Brazil is experiencing a double deficit in the fiscal and current accounts. According to the Economist Intelligence Unit (EIU), the Brazilian government's fiscal deficit remained high at 6.3 % of GDP in 2014–2015; the current account deficit was 3.9 % and 4.2 % of GDP in 2014 and 2015, respectively. The twin deficits shook investors' confidence in Brazil's economic growth and accelerated the depreciation of the Brazilian currency (Real), which depreciated by more than 18 % in 2015. The currency devaluation triggered capital flight, causing a huge impact on Brazil's financial markets and the real economy. On June 3, 2015, in order to prevent capital flight, the Central Bank of Brazil announced another increase in the benchmark, and the interest rate was raised by 0.5 %age points to 13.75 %, and interest rates have been raised for the sixth time since November 2014. However, high interest rates are not conducive to investment and have also increased the debt burden of Brazilian companies. Popular support for the government in Brazil has been declining due to the economic downturn and high inflation.

Russia's economic situation has also been perilous in 2015. With revenues generated by oil and gas exports accounting for half of the Russian government's coffers, the Russian government's budget deficit continued to widen as oil and gas prices continued to fall on the international energy market, the ruble continued to depreciate, and capital flight became severe. In 2015, Russia's GDP declined by 3.7 %; in 2016, it declined by about 0.2 %.

The dollar is the pricing currency for resources and energy in the international market, so the plunge in resource and energy prices is mainly related to the dollar exchange rate, which Keynes' "monetary velocity" theory can fully explain. But because of the slowdown in China's economic growth, public opinion in Europe and the United States has made reduced demand of China the scapegoat for the world recession, creating divisions among emerging economies. In fact, the decline in China's imports is mainly due to price factors. For example, China is actually importing much more oil than before, but because the price of oil has fallen so much, the total price is still lower than before.

How to Promote the Development of the World Economy? All Parties Have Different Views

While G20 members share concerns about sluggish global growth, opinions vary widely on how to promote growth and what form it should take. The United Nations has launched a post-2015 development agenda with specific targets for world development, but governments are at odds over how to reach these goals.

Promoting world economic growth is the goal of the G20, but the G20 lacks a mechanism to track, review, and monitor implementation. In the post-crisis era, the role of the G20 in coordinating national policies and stabilizing world economic growth has diminished. In order for the G20 to continue to play its role, it must find new connotations of economic development, set new standards for measuring economic development, and continuously push G20 members to find new development goals.

Rebuilding the Discourse of International Trade

The Obama administration has attempted to establish new international trade rules through the Trans-Pacific Partnership Agreement and the Transatlantic Trade and Investment Partnership Agreement.

Why does the United States want new international trade rules? Many U.S. strategic experts acknowledge that it is because the U.S. wants to regain its competitive advantage, to compete strategically with emerging economies, including China, and to reduce the competitive advantage of the BRICS countries in the international economic arena. It is for this reason that none of the BRICS countries were invited to participate in the negotiations of these two new trade agreements.

The U.S. aims to use trade to restore economic power and seize the high ground in international trade negotiations by establishing new international trade rules. For example, the U.S. government has interpreted its attempt to renegotiate regional trade arrangements as an attempt to establish a higher standard free trade area, claiming to include environmental protection, intellectual property protection, human rights, and the degree of financial openness in the negotiations to establish new international trade standards.

According to international trade theory, the international trading system should be free and open, the lower the threshold, the better, allowing countries to give full play to their comparative advantages. An open international trading system will make the world a richer and more efficient place.

Therefore, from the perspective of traditional international trade theory, the high standard trade area advocated by the United States is actually a practice of raising the threshold from which many countries will be shut out. Historically, trade protection has taken various forms, such as technological threshold, environmental threshold, etc. Is the high standard trade area now proposed by the U.S. government a new type of protectionism? Chould the international trading system be better off with lower thresholds (more inclusive) or higher thresholds (more exclusionary)?

China does not need to compete with the U.S. on the details of specific trade negotiations, but we can revisit the theory of international trade and make the G20 a platform for promoting free and open international trade. In fact, if we return to the discussion of international trade theory, the U.S. approach may not be agreeable to most countries.

In addition, the U.S. government linked trade liberalization to financial liberalization in trade negotiations, arguing that financial liberalization is also a measure of the advanced nature of a free trade area. None of the major negotiators at the Bretton Woods Conference back then would have agreed with this argument. At that time, both Keynes, head of the British delegation, and White, head of the U.S. delegation, believed that financial liberalization would cause instability in the exchange rates and prices of national currencies, which would not be conducive to the development of international trade and cross-border investment. At their suggestion, the IMF gave the power to regulate capital flows to member governments. We need to learn from the experience and lessons of history to prevent repeating the same mistakes.

In discussing the future global development agenda and global governance objectives, we should emphasize that the regional trade framework must not conflict with the multilateral trade framework of the World Trade Organization (WTO) and must not hollow out the WTO. China has granted zero-tariff treatment to 97 % of the tariff lines of products from established LDCs (Least Developed Countries) in order to fulfill our obligation to help LDCs and promote their economic development.

In recent years, the world has reached a consensus on inclusive development, with countries agreeing that development must benefit all segments of society and that global development must benefit all countries in the world. From this perspective, international trade should also be inclusive, and exclusive trade rules are inconsistent with the consensus on inclusive development.

The Financial System Reform to Promote the Development of the Real Economy

Since the 1980s, financial liberalization has become the classic rhetoric of Western economics. Western public opinion advocates that financial liberalization can bring capital from rich countries to poor countries, therefore bringing development capital to poor areas, and at the same time, because the returns on investments in poor countries are often higher than in rich ones, these investments can also provide better payoffs for pension funds in rich countries. This is known as a "win-win game". However, the opening of capital accounts in Latin American countries and Southeast Asian countries in the 1980s allowed international capital to enter and exit these developing countries at will, creating great instability, with economic bubbles rising and bursting, causing the development of these countries to be constantly interrupted by financial crises. Some countries have fallen into the "middle-income trap". The financial institutions of developed countries have taken the opportunity to rob these developing countries and make a fortune.

The British economist Keynes went straight to the heart of the matter when he pointed out that the only place where investment and speculation are indistinguishable is in the financial markets. Therefore, the government must exercise some control over the financial markets.

Some people believe that financial liberalization is a trend of development and that many countries will choose to open their capital markets in the future. Indeed, many developing countries in Latin America, Africa and Asia have chosen to liberalize their finances and open their capital accounts despite experiencing multiple financial crises. However, if we study the details of the development of these countries, we will have a deeper understanding of the reasons why they opened their capital accounts. Generally speaking, one of the characteristics of developing countries is that their people are poor and do not have a habit of saving. Without domestic savings as a basis, a country's economy lacks capital for development, while the shortage of foreign exchange reserves prevents them from importing advanced machinery and equipment. In this case, in order to balance their balance of payments, they must choose to open their capital account and attract foreign capital at higher interest rates than in the international market. Thus, although some countries are often sacked by international capital, they still have to keep their capital accounts open to attract short-term foreign capital.

But this does not apply to China, which is not a typical developing country. China has a high savings rate, abundant domestic capital, and no shortage of foreign exchange reserves. It will not affect China's economic development by not fully opening the capital account. In the future, China should be selective in opening its capital account—only choosing those projects that are good for promoting China's economic growth—and prevent the negative impact on China's macroeconomy caused by the large entry and exit of short-term foreign capital. In 2015, China's capital market has experienced considerable volatility, which, in addition to regulatory issues, is largely related to excessive hot money entering and leaving the country. According to the Bank for International Settlements, hot money inflows into China have exceeded $1 trillion since 2010, 70 % of which were short-term loans of less than one year. In 2015, China's foreign exchange reserves fell by more than $500 billion. In addition to the growth of China's foreign direct investment with the implementation of the "Belt and Road" initiative, the decrease in foreign exchange was mainly due to the outflow of hot money from China as the Federal Reserve raised interest rates. With the outflow of capital, stock market prices lost support, and stock prices inevitably fell. By the same token, the capital outflow has increased the pressure of RMB devaluation to a certain extent.

In the future, the divergence of monetary policies in developed countries will become more obvious, which will create more opportunities for arbitrage activities of international capital. For emerging economies, the large capital outflow and entry will cause macroeconomic instability. In this regard, the G20 summit should discuss more on international arbitrage.

The BRICS New Development Bank (NDB) and the Asian Infrastructure Investment Bank (AIIB) have created a financing platform for infrastructure in developing countries. In the future, these banks will have to choose new currency "nominal anchors" for multilateral investments, such as using the IMF's Special Drawing Rights (SDRs) or a basket of currencies from AB members that includes multiple currencies. Using a basket of currencies would be more equitable and would avoid the disruptions caused by exchange rate fluctuations of hegemonic currencies in the current international system. Promoting global economic recovery through greater investment in infrastructure could lay a better foundation for future economic growth, which is the fundamental way to get the world economy out of long-term stagnation.

How to Improve Global Governance?

China's outbound investment is growing rapidly, and China's foreign bond holdings are increasing. In this context, the public management situation in other countries is directly related to the security of China's investments and the return on those investments.

How can international public management be upgraded and the quality of public management in each country be improved? Since the end of the Cold War, the United States has been promoting democratization internationally and creating public opinion that public administration can only be improved with a democratic system of government and greater political transparency. But it turns out that American-style democracy does not necessarily equate to good public administration. We need to build up the Chinese public's confidence in China's development model.

In fact, an exclusive emphasis on democracy will not solve either the internal problems of developed countries or the development problems of developing countries. For example, the U.S. democratic system has failed to curb political polarization. The polarization of bipartisan politics in the United States has pitted the Congress against the government. Democracy has failed to address this irresponsible behavior toward the public, and the American public is already expressing its discontent. In contrast, in developing countries, democratization has not improved public administration in many places, but has even created chaos. In developing countries, democratization may not be conducive to more effective government and better public administration without a sound bureaucratic system as a foundation, except for fostering political ambition. Western countries fund NGOs in developing countries in the name of promoting the development of democracy, but in fact they create social divisions in these developing countries.

The improvement of public management requires that the government can manage its finances well (to prevent rising debt, to have stable fiscal revenues, and not to cut taxes unprincipled) and can take responsibility for the social management system (health care and welfare system, education system, environmental protection and monitoring system, etc.). The G20 can negotiate specific standards and urge governments to make continuous improvements in this area. Developing countries should build bridges between civil society and government to help and monitor each other, rather than emphasizing confrontation and struggle. China can also help other developing countries improve their governance, such as by providing more scholarships and training opportunities for professional and technical staff. Developed countries should assist developing countries in training more skilled people. When developing countries have more skilled people, such as managers, doctors, lawyers, engineers, etc., the public management capacity of these countries will likely rise to a higher level, so that investments into these countries will be safe and the returns more secure.

In short, reorganizing the important development themes of trade, investment and public administration is crucial for China to establish a voice on the international stage. This will help improve China's influence and increase the self-confidence of the Chinese public.

A New Beginning for China to Lead Globalization

Although globalization is a highly controversial issue and "anti-globalization" forces have emerged in developed countries in recent years, we still need to look at globalization from both perspectives, promoting globalization in a more balanced and inclusive direction, actively managing the negative impacts and risks brought about by globalization. Therefore, the G20 is still an important global governance mechanism that can help us manage risks and promote global economic growth.

At the G20 Hangzhou Summit, Chinese President Xi Jinping's speech stated China's position on global governance, from which we can understand the

Chinese government's attitude toward the G20. Along these lines, the focus of future global governance should be on three points:

First, consolidate the role of the G20 as a global governance platform. The fundamental way to solve the world economic chaos and prevent the recurrence of crises lies in consolidating the role of the G20 as a global economic governance platform and promoting the transformation of the G20, from a crisis-response mechanism to a long-term governance mechanism. The biggest problem facing the world economy at present is weak growth. In response to this specific situation, the theme of the G20 Hangzhou Summit is "Toward an Innovative, Invigorated, Interconnected and Inclusive World Economy", which sets the goals of "Innovative Growth", "More Efficient Global Economic and Financial Governance", "Stronger International Trade and Development", and "More Effective Global Economy". The aim is to respond to the development needs of all countries, both to achieve stable short-term growth and to lay the foundation for long-term growth. Among these key issues, "innovative growth" focuses on promoting reform and innovation, developing new opportunities, and enhancing the long-term growth potential of the world economy; "more efficient global economic and financial governance" focuses on increasing the representation and voice of emerging market countries and developing countries and improving the world economy's ability to resist risks; "robust international trade and investment" focuses on building an open economy and stimulating the world economy's growth dynamics; "interconnected and inclusive development" focuses on implementing the United Nations 2030 Agenda for Sustainable Development and enhancing the world economy's competitiveness.

Second, the G20 governance model should be developed in the direction of sharing and linkage. Xi Jinping's keynote speech at the opening ceremony of the G20 Business Summit systematically elaborated on the concept of global economic governance based on equality, openness, cooperation and sharing, which clearly oppose protectionism, refrain from exclusive arrangements and dominance. G20 should strengthen policy coordination, foster communication for mutual understanding to ensure that the benefits are shared by all, and eventually, G20 can build an open and connected world economy. Since the international financial crisis, China's massive investment in infrastructure has stabilized China's economic growth and laid a more solid foundation for future growth. In recent years, China has also been actively promoting infrastructure connectivity on the international stage, expanding its infrastructure connections with other countries through the Belt and Road Initiative. Infrastructure investment is an important engine for economic recovery, helping to increase economic growth rates and promote economic growth in the medium to long term. At the G20 Summit, all parties reaffirmed their commitment to continue to promote infrastructure investment, encourage multilateral development banks to set quantitative targets for supporting high-quality projects, and take joint actions, including leveraging private sector funding, strengthening cooperation between old and new multilateral development banks, and promoting multi-party cooperation and co-financing, and the summit agreed to launch the Global Infrastructure Connectivity Alliance initiative to enhance cooperation and coordination among infrastructure programs.

Finally, global governance should make economic development more beneficial to more people, and economic growth should be more inclusive. The world cannot be a better place until all economies could benefit from it. In his speech, Xi Jinping used the phrase "the world is better when everyone is better" to express the meaning of inclusiveness in plain words. Economic growth is for the betterment of all. In this sense, the G20 belongs not only to the 20 member countries, but also to the whole world, and its development should benefit all countries and people. It is in this sense that the G20 Hangzhou Summit also invited leaders from some representative developing countries outside the G20 members, including Egypt, Senegal, Ghana, Kazakhstan and Laos.

To promote inclusive development, we must listen to the voices of more developing countries, so that all peoples can fairly share the benefits of world economic growth and achieve sustainable development of the world economy. At the G20 Hangzhou Summit, leaders made three "firsts" on development issues: for the first time, development issues were placed at the core of the global macro policy framework; for the first time, an action plan was formulated for the implementation of the 2030 Agenda for Sustainable Development; and for the first time, cooperation was launched to support the industrialization of African countries and LDCs.

Before the Hangzhou summit, the G20 summit was basically about matters among its members. But the Hangzhou Summit brought out the development issues of African countries and LDCs as well, truly demonstrating the global economic governance. Although these less developed economies do not account for much of the world economy, they are an integral part of global development. Moreover, solving the development problems of these less developed economies may open up new markets and find new ways for the development of the world economy.

The G20 Hangzhou Summit achieved important results in 5 areas: First, it maps out the path for the world economy. Leaders agreed to take further measures to promote structural reforms and economic growth. Second, the leaders of G20 members are determined to change the way of growth and inject new momentum into the world economy. The G20 leaders unanimously adopted the G20 blueprint for innovative growth. Third, G20 leaders are determined to improve the global economic and financial governance system. Specifically, China will establish an international tax policy research center to make a greater contribution to global governance, and G20 leaders pledged to strengthen international cooperation against corruption so that corrupt elements will have no place to hide within the G20 membership and beyond. Fourth, G20 leaders resolved to revitalize the two engines of international trade and international investment. Fifth, G20 leaders are determined to promote inclusive and connected development, strengthen global connectivity, and make the G20 summit agreements benefit the world.

After Hangzhou Summit, each G20 summit will review whether the goals set at the previous summit have been implemented, whether they need to be amended, and whether new elements need to be added. If the G20 platform is important for promoting inclusive development, it is no exaggeration to say that the Hangzhou Summit is a new milestone.

9

How China and the U.S. Can Achieve Mutual Benefits

In recent years, especially since Donald Trump came to power in the US, Sino-American relationship has become a hot topic of international media. Are those bilateral relations doomed to a confrontation and probably a war, as Graham Allison affirmed in his book "Destined for war: Can America and China escape Thucydides' Trap?" I try to give another angle of analysis based on the complementarity of US and Chinese economies. Here I put some of my analyses on the complicated relationship between China and the United States, written around 2018. If competition is an useful key element in a market economy, a somehow healthy competition between China and the US is not necessarily bad, because it will force both China and the US to better themselves in global arena. But that competition should not prevent two parties from cooperation on a number of global issues and challenges we are facing. People may not be accustomed to this sort of competitive cooperation relations, but it might be the characteristic that will mark the most important bilateral relationship in this world for a long time.

In early November 2017, U.S. President Donald Trump made a state visit to China. However, shortly after Trump's return to the United States, the White House released the U.S. National Security Strategy Report, which repeatedly addressed China and treated both China and Russia as strategic adversaries of the United States.

The relationship between China and the United States is quite complex, with the possibility of conflict and confrontation, but at the same time very stable.

According to the American political scientist John J. Mearsheimer's *The Tragedy of Great Power Politics*, there is bound to be conflict and confrontation in Sino-U.S. relations because China, having become the world's second largest economy, poses a threat to the U.S.-led international system, and the United States is bound to use various methods to contain China's development to prevent it from being overtaken. However, even so, U.S.-China relations are currently stable. It is safe to say that the close economic and trade ties between China and the U.S. are the ballast of Sino-U.S. relations, and that China and the U.S. are each other's most important markets and investors. This is a state of affairs that has never been seen in international relations in any past era, and no two countries are as dependent on each other as China and the United States are today.

U.S.-China Economic Cooperation and the U.S. Policy Turn

President Donald Trump signed an order in March 2018 to launch a Section 301 investigation into Chinese exports. Section 301 of the U.S. Trade Act is a very well-known legal provision that no other country has a similar legal provision. From time to time, the U.S. has used this provision to investigate trade with other countries, and then to negotiate with other countries on the basis of unreasonable and unfair trade transactions, and to retaliate when negotiations fail. Major U.S. trading partners, such as the European Union and Japan, have suffered from it.

The U.S. government launched an investigation into Chinese exports for two reasons: first, it accused China of forcing U.S. companies to transfer technology, linking the transfer of technology to the opening of the market; second, Chinese companies seriously violated the intellectual property rights of U.S. companies, and many of China's exports to the United States copied the patents of U.S. companies.

Both charges are "old". The "market for technology" did not exist after China's accession to the WTO, and China's practice is to give foreign companies "national treatment", i.e. foreign companies investing in China are equal to Chinese companies in all respects.

In the early stage of economic development, due to the lack of technological advantages, it was common to copy technology to produce products and then export them for foreign exchange. Japan was considered a "major player" in copying American and European technologies; Hong Kong, China, was a "paradise" for copying Western brand-name products; and Republic of Korea was criticized by Europe and the United States for counterfeiting Western brand-name products when it hosted the Olympic Games in 1988.

In recent years, China has increasingly emphasized independent innovation. The investment in R&D from Chinese companies sours, and cutting-edge technologies emerge rapidly in China. In 2016, China surpassed the United States in the number of patent applications. Against this backdrop, China is bound to pay more attention to protecting intellectual property rights and encouraging the development of innovative industries and will not shelter industries that copy Western technologies.

The huge U.S. trade deficit with China is partly caused by the calculation method of international trade, which no longer reflects the real trade transactions between China and the U.S. In addition, the U.S. government's restriction on exports to China has led to the inability of U.S. enterprises to take advantage of their industries and increase their exports to China, which also partly contributes to the U.S. trade deficit with China.

U.S.-China trade is a complementary and mutually beneficial relationship. U.S. companies transfer some of their production processes to China, which can reduce costs, improve efficiency and increase the competitiveness of U.S. companies in the international market. For example, Apple has only a design team in the U.S. The entire industrial production process is basically concentrated in China, and in recent years, although some production processes have been transferred to other countries, the main production process is still in China.

Apple's products are manufactured in China and then shipped to the United States and other countries. These products are also counted as China's exports when shipped to the U.S., therefore also "contributing" to China's trade surplus. In 2009, China's exports were so high that these processed goods accounted for about 60 % of China's total exports. In recent years, the share of processed goods has declined to about 38 %. In the era of globalization, it is difficult to say where the country of origin of a product is. Products assembled in China have many parts and components from other countries, but according to the current international trade calculation method, these products are counted as China's exports. In fact, the profits earned by Chinese enterprises in processing trade are not high, since most of the profits flow into the pockets of large multinational companies.

There are rumors on the Internet that China will suffer huge losses due to the trade friction between the U.S. and China, because many Chinese products use U.S. technology, such as personal computers that use Microsoft software. This argument simply does not hold water.

U.S. government officials in charge of international commerce seem to be stuck in their understanding of China from 20 years ago. If they don't get up to date and realistically understand China and her place in today's international trading system, I'm afraid they are making a big mistake.

When the U.S. strategically distrusts a country and treats it as an adversary, the U.S. habitually uses various "weapons," including international trade, to influence the bilateral relationship between the U.S. and that country. For example, after Trump took office, he asked China to make efforts to change the trade imbalance between China and the United States. Trump has also linked the trade issue to other international issues, such as Trump's demand that China "cooperate" with the United States on the North Korea nuclear issue. The U.S. gets used to "regulating" bilateral relations in this way, but such an approach reveals a huge bias of the U.S. on international relations that stems from the U.S. perception of its own economic status.

Since the 20th century, the United States has been the largest market in the world and, for a long time, the largest source of technology. Banning products from other countries from entering the U.S. market and prohibiting the export of U.S. technology to other countries is an important means for the United States to protect its leading position. It should be acknowledged that the United States opened its market to China and was once the largest export market for China. During the Cold War, the U.S. relaxed its technology export controls to China in order to gain an advantage (over the Soviet Union), which played a role in upgrading China's industrial technology.

However, since the 21st century, the weapon of technology embargo is no longer feasible to deal with the U.S.-China relationship, for two reasons. First, since global production chains have been formed, both the United States and China are in the same global production chain. The U.S. trade weapons have little effect, because many trade goods between China and the United States are intermediate products on this global chain, not final products. As a result, the U.S. trade sanctions against China will eventually be implemented on itself, ended up "killing a thousand enemies and damaging eight hundred of oneself" in old Chinese sayings. So the United States does not realize the seriousness of the consequences of trade sancions. Second, the formation of the Chinese market has significantly changed the position of the United States in the world economy. In fact, China has surpassed the United States as the largest market in the world. Whether it is automobiles or luxury goods, raw materials or industrial manufactures, the Chinese market has surpassed the United States in demand. As a result, U.S. companies will not answer their own government's call. Boeing, for example, decided to build an assembly plant in China when the Trump administration was trying to find ways to bring American companies' overseas investments back to the United States. Europe's Airbus, which has assembly plants in China, has not only expanded its share of the Chinese market, but has also made a significant contribution to Airbus' efforts to gain a larger share of the world market. Therefore, I am afraid that the U.S. government will have to pay a huge economic price if it regulates U.S.-China relations by preventing companies of other countries from entering the U.S. market.

The United States is accustomed to playing on technology export control to curb the development of its competitors, and the United States has imposed technology export controls on China for a long time. However, a study by McKinsey & Company shows that the U.S.-led Western technology embargo on China—has not only helped little in terms of hindering China's technological development—has instead facilitated it. For example, at the beginning of the 21st century, China tried to purchase supercomputers from the United States, but the United States refused China's offer. Three years later, China developed the Tianhe-1 supercomputer, the world's most advanced supercomputer at the time, and three years later, it developed the Tianhe-2 supercomputer, which remained the world's No. 1 supercomputer for three consecutive years. When the United States discovered that some parts of the Chinese supercomputer (such as chips) were made in the United States, it tightened controls on Chinese chip exports and banned Intel from selling XEON chips to China. In 2016, China developed the "Shenwei-Taizhou Light" supercomputer, which is not only nearly twice as fast as the Tianhe-2 supercomputer, but all components, including the chips, are made in China.

After the news broke out, some American netizens commented, "The chip ban is a dirty trick, and since the U.S. can't win through competition in a just way, it makes these dim tricks. Unfortunately, such ban by the U.S. government seriously damages the image of the U.S. technology industry which is supposed to be a reliable partner in the international market."

For many years, the United States was the world's largest market, so the U.S. threatened its trading partners with "Section 301" since it was so damaging that all countries were afraid of losing the U.S. market. Today, however, China has become the world's largest market, and Chinese demand determines the price of many products. The recovery of the U.S. economy relies heavily on export growth, and export to China is the fastest growing sector. If the U.S. loses this fastest growing market with the greatest potential, it is easy to foresee who will end up losing out.

In 2015, the Federal Reserve finally decided to raise interest rates eight years after the financial crisis. The speed of the Fed's rate hike is critical because the speed of the Fed's money recovery will determine the direction of the U.S. capital markets. However, the Fed was surprisingly cautious this time, raising interest rates very slowly, once at the end of 2015 and again at the end of 2016, and only 0.25 %age points each time. In 2017, the Fed raised interest rates for 3 times. After 5 rounds of rate hikes, the Fed's benchmark interest rate is only 1.25 %-1.5 %. Although the market was prepared for the Fed's rate hike, the U.S. dollar rose against other currencies, and the price of commodity futures fell under the influence of a stronger dollar. International investors were worried that the Fed's rate hike would get the stock market bubble burst too quickly, and a large amount of capital left the stock market, causing the dollar exchange rate to decline.

As the dollar exchange rate rises, some public opinion is again touting the U.S. economy, believing that the U.S. will start "shearing" again. Is the impact of the Fed's rate hike really that big?

It has been more than 10 years since the outbreak of the financial crisis in 2008, and the Fed's interest rates are still maintained at 1.25 %-1.5 %, which is not normal for such low interest rates, both from a historical and realistic point of view. In other words, the Fed is actually not too sure about the U.S. economic recovery, so they have to be cautious in raising interest rates.

In 2007, before the outbreak of the economic crisis, the effective federal funds rate in the U.S. was above 5 %. In 2008, when Lehman Brothers went bankrupt, the federal funds rate was still 2.64 %. Since then, the Federal Reserve has been cutting interest rates to 0 % and 0.25 %, while implementing quantitative easing. The extremely loose monetary policy saved the U.S. capital markets and to some extent curbed the U.S. economic recession. However, there are two sides of everything. The extremely loose monetary policy has also laid some hidden dangers.

The maintenance of zero or negative interest rates by the central bank for a long period of time can seriously affect the earnings of commercial banks and other financial institutions. The central bank interest rate is closely related to the return on fixed-income bonds such as treasury bonds, and many banks and social welfare funds (pension funds, etc.) benefit from investing in these bonds, which are then paid to the fund's beneficiaries. When the central bank interest rate is zero, the yield on fixed-income bonds such as treasury bills falls so low that at one point, the yield on 10-year U.S. Treasuries fell below 2 %. Many social welfare funds needed a 5 % to 8 % return on their investments to maintain their expenses, and such low yields made it impossible for them to continue with their traditional business model and had to convince regulators to let them invest in the stock market. However, the stock and futures markets are very risky, and if they lose money, it will cause a crisis in the social welfare system. Therefore, the U.S. Social Welfare Fund has been lobbying institutions such as the Federal Reserve and the European Central Bank to end their zero-interest rate policies as soon as possible. There are some commercial banks that are also traders of financial assets such as treasury bonds, and the ultra-low treasury bond yields have caused them to turn to the futures market, which has higher risks but higher returns, and some have fallen into the trap of futures prices and even face the crisis of collapse.

However, central bank interest rate increases are not without risk. Zero interest rates in previous years have led to a rapid recovery in leverage for many financial institutions and individuals, and their aggressive investments have led to a boom in the U.S. stock market. If the central bank raises interest rates, financial institutions and individuals will rush to repay their loans or switch to the bond market. Then, the stock market just regained its vitality may be turbulent again, because the financial bubble generated by the extremely loose policy may burst again. Another problem facing the U.S. is that as the Fed raises interest rates, the exchange rate of the dollar is also rising, and the U.S. economy's improvement is directly related to export growth, the dollar's appreciation will lead to a decline in the competitiveness of U.S. exports, affecting the next phase of U.S. economic recovery. In particular, the more the dollar appreciates, the more valuable the dollar assets held by foreign investors become, and the real value of the U.S. debt to foreign countries grows along with it. Can the U.S. accept this trend?

In the 1980s, when the dollar appreciated in tandem with rising U.S. interest rates, the Reagan administration had to intervene in the market through the G7 to keep the dollar down and the deutsche mark and **yen** up against the dollar. Perhaps the U.S. will soon have to negotiate with China on ways to stabilize the dollar and the yuan. Otherwise, as the dollar appreciates, the U.S. debt to China will become unsustainable.

The U.S. owes a lot of debt to China, and some members of Congress believe the U.S. government can no longer continue to borrow from China because the U.S. government has to pay China as much as $100 million in interest on its debt every day. China's central bank and financial institutions hold roughly $1 trillion in U.S. Treasuries, although they are still the most liquid and safest bonds in the international financial markets. The Federal Reserve's interest rate is directly related to the interest rate on U.S. Treasuries. In previous years, the Fed's monetary policy was so loose that the interest rate on U.S. Treasuries was very low, less than 3 % per year for 10-year Treasuries, but even so, there was more than $30 billion in interest on more than $1 trillion in Treasuries. In the future, when the Federal Reserve raises interest rates, the interest on U.S. Treasuries will rise. The U.S. government will have to pay China even more interest. China's holding of a large amount of U.S. Treasuries is tantamount to pinching the shortcomings of the U.S. For this reason, economist Lawrence Summers, who was U.S. Treasury Secretary and Harvard University president, has commented that there is a balance of financial terror between the U.S. and China, which is more stable than the balance of nuclear terror between the U.S. and the Soviet Union back then.

The U.S. does not want China to sell U.S. Treasuries because that would cause a crisis in the dollar and lead to a recession in the U.S.; China also does not want the dollar to depreciate significantly, which would cause huge losses to China's foreign exchange reserves. Therefore, China and the United States have a common interest in maintaining the creditworthiness of U.S. Treasuries and the exchange rate of the dollar.

Will Trump fulfill his promises in his campaigns? And if he translates his promises into economic policies, what will be the impact on China? The United States is the world's largest economy, and its policies will have a huge "spillover" effect.

Trump's promises on economic policy involve three areas, namely international trade, tax reform and infrastructure construction.

On the international trade front, Trump has fulfilled his promise to withdraw the United States from the Trans-Pacific Partnership after his election, although there has been little movement on the threat to withdraw from NAFTA and the WTO. In addition, Trump has threatened to increase tariffs on Chinese exports to the United States by 45 % and to define China as a manipulator of exchange rates. After Trump was elected president, those around him believe that trade issues involve many technical details and need to be carefully considered. As you can see, international trade is actually a double-edged sword, and if the U.S. completely returns to isolationism, not only will it have a huge impact on U.S. trading partners, but the U.S. economy could also fall into recession. At that time, Trump's support in the U.S. electorate must have plummeted. Of course, since he made a promise in the campaign, Trump will definitely implement some measures, even if they are only symbolic. For example, it is entirely possible that the Trump administration will impose "anti- dumping duties" on Chinese exports in certain areas. Of course, if the U.S. insists on isolationism, it would be tantamount to giving China the lead in setting the future rules of international trade. China can use this opportunity to promote regional and multilateral international trade negotiations.

In terms of tax reform, Trump's proposal was passed in Congress, and a new tax system for residents and businesses was introduced in 2018, reducing some of the taxes. Since the 21st century, the U.S. government has stimulated economic growth under the banner of tax cuts, but this policy has not been effective in stimulating economic growth, except for widening the gap between the rich and the poor in society. The direct consequence of tax cuts is the decline of government revenue. Considering the huge debt burden of the U.S. government and the Federal Reserve's entry into the interest rate hike cycle, it is not clear how the results of the Trump administration's tax cuts will be. Trump wants to make America great again, so also increase the military budget, and increase investment in infrastructure, both to stimulate the economy, but also to please voters.

Strengthening infrastructure is indeed necessary for the United States, the world's largest economy. *New York Times* columnist Thomas Friedman, who visited China on the eve of the 2008 Olympics, wrote an essay upon his return to the U.S. comparing the infrastructure situation in the U.S. with that of China, making a great satire of U.S. infrastructure and asking rhetorically: Who lives in a third-world country anyway? What the U.S. government needs to consider, though, is where they can find the money to build infrastructure in the U.S. Increasing the fiscal deficit is one way, but the U.S. government's deficit is already large, and any further increase could cause a backlash in the capital markets and could also trigger a debt crisis. This is not an unfounded concern, because once the Fed raises interest rates, the interest rate on U.S. Treasuries will rise, and the U.S. government will need more money to pay interest on its debt.

The situation facing the Trump administration is very similar to that of the Reagan administration. After Reagan came to power, he implemented the "theory of supply side economics" and "tightening " monetary policy. Although the combination of these policies brought inflation down and the economy began to be stabilized, the Reagan administration implemented the "Star Wars program" and engaged in a space weapons race with the Soviet Union, which led to a sharp increase in U.S. government spending and deficits, and therefore a rapid rise in public debt. The increase in government spending and capital demand caused the dollar to flow back to the United States, and the dollar appreciated significantly, eventually causing a serious imbalance in the U.S. international trade balance. After a few years, the U.S. could not hold out any longer and signed the Plaza Accord, forcing the dollar to depreciate.

Reagan relied on debt to stimulate economic growth, since he could still rest on the old balance, because when Reagan took office in 1981, the U.S. government's debt was less than 1 trillion dollars. But by 1988 when Reagan left office, the U.S. government's debt had reached 2.6 trillion dollars. Later, although Clinton controlled the size of the debt, Bush and Obama are "borrowing masters." Bush Jr. spent huge amount of money to fight the war in Afghanistan and the Gulf War, and Obama bailed out the financial crisis for the U.S. financial institutions, so the U.S. national debt quickly increased to $ 20 trillion.

Thus, there are probably many difficulties for Trump to emulate Reagan, and the policy effects will not be as pronounced as they were under Reagan. For example, when Reagan took office, the U.S. government debt as a percent age of GDP was just over 30 %. When Bush Sr. took office, it was 57 %, and now it is about 106 %, nearly twice as high as when Reagan took office. Under Reagan, the top marginal income tax rate was 70 %, and that number dropped to 28 % during his term. Today, the top marginal tax rate in the U.S. is 39.6 %, so Trump has much less room to cut taxes. The structure of the U.S. labor force was also very different under Reagan than it is today, largely reflected in the aging of the population. Under Reagan, the U.S. workforce grew much faster than it does today, and the labor force participation rate was significantly higher than it is today.

The Trump administration wants to strengthen U.S. infrastructure, and China can help, because Chinese equipment manufacturers are very competitive in the international market and can provide the necessary support to the United States. If the U.S. opens up the market for infrastructure construction, such as high-speed rail, Chinese companies can quickly make better services available to the American people. Considering Trump's campaign comments about the RMB exchange rate, we can also talk to the Trump administration about how to work together to stabilize the dollar exchange rate and reduce the speed and magnitude of the dollar's appreciation. In fact, the exchange rate of RMB going downis not due to a unilateral depreciation of the RMB, as the RMB has depreciated less compared to the Euro, the British Pound and the Japanese Yen. Instead, the RMB exchange rate going down is due to the significant appreciation of the US dollar. If the dollar continues to appreciate in the future, the U.S. international trade balance will deteriorate again, which may even affect the U.S. economic growth. Therefore, a significant appreciation of the dollar is not in the interest of the U.S. The Trump administration should cooperate with China to curb the significant appreciation of the dollar and jointly maintain the stability of the exchange rate between the dollar and the RMB.

The Variable-Sum Game between the United States and China

The U.S. National Security Strategy report treats China as a strategic adversary of the United States, reflecting a doctrinal concern that U.S.- China relations could fall into a "Thucydides trap".

However, the use of the Thucydides Trap to explain today's U.S.- China relations is itself a misreading of history. Thucydides was an ancient Greek historian whose work "History of the Peloponnesian War" between Greek city-states (the Athenian-led Tyrolean League and the Spartan-led Peloponnesian League) from 431–404 BCE. Although Thucydides used the word "fear" to describe the state of mind of the Peloponnesian League in the face of the rise of the Tyrolean League, the real trigger for the war was profit, not just psychological fear. Between 492 and 449 B.C., the Persian Empire launched three attacks on Greek city-states, several of which nearly brought Athens and other city-states to their knees, but the Greek city-states eventually repelled the Persians and won the Greeco-Persian War. During the war, Athens was the leader of the Greec coalition forces and all other Greek city-states had to pay taxes to Athens. For the sake of the war, the other city-states had nothing to say. After the end of the war, Athens had taken a liking to this and continued to tax the other city-states, which constituted an imperial act and caused resistance from the other city-states. The small city of Syracuse refused to pay taxes to Athens, and Athens attacked it. Sparta led the other city-states of the Peloponnesian League to fight a great war against Athens, which ended in Athens' defeat. There was a zero-sum game between Athens and Sparta. If Athens continued to tax other city-states, Sparta would suffer losses. Therefore, Sparta did not hesitate to fight Athens to the death.

International relations scholars have cited this story to explain the relationship between modern Germany and Great Britain. They argue that the rapid rise of the German Empire after reunification in 1871 aroused British fears, and that Britain put obstacles in the way of Germany's efforts, which eventually led to the First World War. Theorists believe that this is a modern version of the "Thucydides Trap". In fact, when the German Empire rose, it was already the late stage of European empire conquering the world, and the whole world had been basically divided by Britain and France and reduced to colonies or semi-colonies. Germany felt that there was not enough room for development, so it had to compete with Britain and France for "living space". Germany and Britain and France started a zero-sum game, Germany could only get new development space by fighting for those colonies that had been occupied by Britain and France, while

Britain and France were certainly not willing to lose their vested interests, so both sides had to fight each other.

During the Cold War, the relationship between the United States and the Soviet Union was also labeled as the "Thucydides Trap". Although the Cold War began early, the U.S. joined other Western countries in a massive siege of the Soviet Union after the launch of the first artificial satellite. The rise of the Soviet Union aroused the fear of the United States, which began to contain the Soviet Union in various fields.

In 1962, the Cuban Missile Crisis erupted, and the Cold War came close to turning into a nuclear war. The United States and the Soviet Union also wanted to redraw their spheres of influence, and in a bipolar world, the relationship between the United States and the Soviet Union could only be a zero-sum game; the United States could only go into the Soviet sphere to expand its influence, and the Soviet Union could only go into the U.S. sphere to find opportunities.

But the rise of the great powers may not necessarily fall into the "Thucydides trap", the rise of the United States is a typical example. According to the logic of the "Thucydides Trap", the rise of the United States would cause fear in Britain, which would inevitably lead to the siege of the United States by Britain and other European countries and eventually lead to a major war. However, in the process of America's rise, except for a war with the declining Spanish Empire, which seized some territories, the United States did not compete with Britain and France for colonies. The United States chose another way of development — the open market and free trade approach to seek common development with the European powers. The U.S. market offered greater opportunities for the European powers to develop, both in terms of investment and trade, and the U.K. and France had much to gain from the U.S. This created a logic of **Variable Sum Game**. The United States can also provide investment and products to the United Kingdom and France. In the logic of a variable sum game , the interests of the parties to the game are not fixed, so confrontation and conflict lose their basis, and only cooperation can gain greater benefits.

China's rise is also a game of variable sum, as it does not compete with the U.S. or other developed countries for profits or territory, and it has developed rapidly within the framework of world free trade. After the 1960s, China has not aligned itself with any country and does not make others feel threatened. China's rapid development has not only provided export and investment markets for other countries, but Chinese investment in the United States and Europe has also provided them jobs and momentum. In recent years, giant and well-known

U.S. companies have made far more money in the Chinese market than they have in the U.S. market. It's a classic game of variable sums.

The United States Cannot Contain China's Development

Since 2018, there has been trade friction between the United States and China, and some politicians in the United States are very paranoid and want to use various means to contain the development of China and Russia. U.S. public opinion believes that the United States won the Cold War against the Soviet Union and therefore can also contain China's development and regain American majesty.

Learning from the past, when we understand the reasons for the Soviet Union's defeat in the Cold War, we realize that it is impossible for the United States today to contain China's development.

At the beginning of the Cold War, the industrial development of the Soviet bloc lagged significantly behind that of the Western bloc. At that time, the countries of the Soviet bloc were bent on criticizing the market economy and equating it with capitalism. The criticism of market economy led to a dogmatic planned economy where everything had to be done according to plan and all industrial production could only have one standard. In the absence of competition, the whole industrial system is inefficient and produces "stupid" products that consumers do not like, but there is no alternative.

In the late 1950s, China and the Soviet Union diverged on the path of development, and China's leaders did not recognize the Soviet model of development. Even in the era of planned economy, China did not make all industrial production into a monopoly, as the Soviet Union did. In China, there were manufacturers with similar products in Beijing, Shanghai, Tianjin, and several other major cities, and there was a degree of competition in the quality and branding of products.

After the reform and opening up, the Chinese government has deepened its understanding of market economy and planned economy and has continuously explored ways to control the macroeconomy under the market economy model. On the one hand, China has used the market mechanism to promote individual initiative, facilitate the rational allocation of resources, maintain market competition, and improve efficiency. On the other hand, China has adopted an open-door policy, introducing advanced production equipment and increasing labor productivity. Through reform and opening up, Chinese products entered the international market, China gained access to more resources and technology, and at the same time regulated the behavior of domestic operators, truly unified the domestic market, and brought the economies of scale of this mega-market into full play. To some extent, it is China's opening up that has led to this round of globalization, making China the "world factory".

Of course, China is not satisfied with being the "world's factory", so national policy of encouraging technological innovation has become the hallmark of China's development in the new era. The Chinese do not have a single faith, and there are multiple religious cultures in Chinese society. The persecution of heretics in the name of one religion is uncommon in Chinese history. Chinese culture is eclectic, and the current socialist market economy is not determined solely by the market. In contrast, in Western societies, since the 1980s, neoliberalism has reigned supreme, and "market fundamentalism" has become a dogma for both internal and external purposes.

This neoliberal theory has misled some developing countries and led them to fall into the debt trap one after another. "Market fundamentalism" has also had a negative impact on developed countries. The fans of neoliberalism criticized industrial policy, state intervention and preached market omnipotence. Following this path, many developed countries have suffered from industrial hollowing out, widening gap between rich and poor, shrinking middle class and other problems, and they finally fell into a vicious circle of stagnant economic growth and increasing social unrest. It was not until the financial crisis broke out in 2008 that developed Western countries, led by the United States, again used state intervention to intervene directly in the market, stabilizing it through nationalization and other measures and implementing stimulus programs to promote growth. In the wake of the financial crisis, some Western analysts have realized the problems of neoliberalism.

The competition between China and the United States should be a benign competition, promoting each other, complementing each other's strengths and making greater contributions to human development. But some U.S. politicians see China's rise as a threat and try every possible way to prevent China's development. These politicians ignore the interdependent relationship between China and the U.S. Hindering China's development will ultimately harm the interests of the U.S. U.S. politicians should understand that technology cannot be sustained without application to the market, that research cannot last without labor support, and that alliances cannot be sustained without the support of allies. If the U.S. insists on standing against China, it will only end up isolating itself, being thrown off by the tide of globalization and eventually falling into recession.

The United States lists both China and Russia as its competitors. However, China and Russia are rapidly developing cooperation, which is different from the logic of Sino-Soviet cooperation back then. China has no intention to control other countries, and therefore, with the rise of China, Sino-Russian relations will become more balanced.

China's Reform and Innovation v. the United States of America's Stagnation

Since the outbreak of the international financial crisis, China's development has attracted widespread attention from international public opinion, while in contrast, the development of the United States, Japan and European countries has stagnated. China's development over the years is the result of reform and innovation, while the stagnation of the United States and other Western countries is the result of stuffiness.

Since the reform and opening up, China has abandoned the dogmatic socialist planned economic system and introduced the competitive mechanism of market economy, which has activated various forms of economic agents in the market. State-owned enterprises, private enterprises, foreign enterprises, and individual households, all forms of economies have developed comprehensively, with both competition and cooperation, giving China's economy an endless vitality.

In 2008, China's economic growth rate was somewhat lower than that in previous years, due to the decline in exports following the international financial crisis. But in a horizontal comparison, China's economy stood out from the international financial crisis and the quality of its economic development is getting better, consumption of energy and raw materials is declining, and environmental pollution is improving. Compared to 2008, China's GDP nearly tripled in 2018, while the U.S., which was regarded as the most "robust" economic recovery by the Western media, has seen its GDP grow by only about 9 % in 10 years.

In recent years, China's per capita income has grown faster than the country's GDP, and the people's happiness index is rising as the social security system continues to improve, poverty alleviation progresses, and the construction of subsidized housing continues to advance. The improvement of the pension and health insurance systems has alleviated the worries of Chinese people and led to rapid growth in consumption. In the first three quarters of 2017, consumption contributed 64.5 % to China's economic growth, and the service sector has surpassed the primary and secondary industries as a share of GDP, becoming a strong backbone to support economic growth. China is the world's largest single market, and with the restructuring of the Chinese economy, external shocks will have less and less impact on the Chinese economy. The resilience of China's economy has once again been demonstrated in the face of a sluggish global economy.

On the contrary, in the West, economic growth has stagnated, social problems are prominent and ethnic conflicts are intensified. In the midst of the economic crisis, Western governments mobilized public finances to bail out financial institutions but kept reducing social welfare spending because of the debt crisis. According to Trump's report in his State of the Union address, 94 million people in the United States are without jobs and more than 43 million are in poverty, living on government-issued food stamps. The U.S. development model benefits only capital and ultimately leads to unsustainable production and a polarized distribution of wealth that benefits only 1 % of Americans. In many European countries, the economic recession has become more pronounced because of the debt crisis, and the social welfare system was under huge risk.

In recent years, the main reference for the development of the U.S. economy is the stock market, as long as the stock market is high, everything is good, and the stock market is considered a barometer of economic conditions. It is this gambling type of behavior that has harmed the U.S. economy, because the stock market only reflects capital gains. For this reason, U.S. companies have to take a lot of their profits out to please the market. According to the Stanford Business Journal, public companies on the S&P 500 record typically use 54 % of their profits to buy back their own stock and 37 % of their profits to pay stock dividends, all to satisfy the stock market. Ultimately, companies are left with only 9 % of their profits to invest and reward their employees. Against this backdrop, U.S. companies have little money available to encourage employee innovation and little money to spend on technological renovation and renewal.

In contrast, Chinese companies have enough time, energy and money to invest in new technologies and new business models and to encourage employees to innovate. For example, Huawei does not need to raise capital from the capital market at all; every time it expands its capital, it simply raises money internally, and employees will enthusiastically subscribe to it because the company gives its employees a good share of the profits. As a result, Huawei is able to invest 15 % of its annual profits in technology research and development, continuously developing new products and becoming the world's most innovative communications equipment company, leading the way in new technologies.

After the Soviet dismemberment, Western public opinion touted the "democracy plus market" model of development, and some scholars even argued that

Western democracy was the end of human ideological development and constituted the "end of history". But just over 20 years later, both the market economy and democracy in the West are in crisis. In recent years, the U.S. Congress has been at war with the government, making it difficult to implement effective policies, and public opinion in the U.S. sees Trump's election as a victory for populism. A similar political phenomenon has emerged in European countries, where populism has become the archenemy of democratic elections.

Populism is growing in the West because people do not agree with the establishment politicians in power. However, populism can plunge the Western world into an even more serious crisis. Before World War II, the Nazi Party of Germany and the National Fascist Party of Italy were elected and came to power on the wave of populism.

In China, on the contrary, reforms are still underway; state-owned enterprises have to be reformed; the government has to be reformed; and to reform is to continuously break the established interest groups, to make the society more equitable and the development more balanced.

The United States Is Losing the Moral High Ground in the International Arena

Although Trump met with Xi Jinping at the G20 summit in Osaka, Japan in June 2019 — when both sides agree to continue trade talks—by August, Trump tweeted that the negotiations were not going well and that the U.S. wanted to impose 10 % more tariffs on $300 billion worth of Chinese exports starting Sept. 1st. Trump was being aggressive and was losing the political credibility that the United States has built up since World War II. Internationally, the U.S. has lost its moral high ground, and even experts at U.S. think tanks are calling the U.S. a potential "rogue super power."

The multilateral free trade system, represented by the WTO, was developed with the participation of the U.S. and has been an important institution in maintaining stability and development in the world since the end of the Cold War. However, after the Trump administration launched unilateral trade sanctions against many U.S. trading partners, the WTO's arbitration mechanism has become a moot point. The U.S. has also threatened to withdraw from the WTO, and it has ignored the rules of multilateral trade by imposing sanctions on its trading partners at every turn. The U.S. has imposed additional tariffs on Chinese exports and denied India preferential tariff treatment for developing countries; it has also used the illegal immigration issue to pressure Mexico to impose additional tariffs on Mexican exports; and it has threatened to impose additional tariffs on European and Japanese auto exports to the U.S. Since the end of World War II, the United States has been a fan of free trade, with open markets to attract Western European countries and Japan and other allies to maintain good relations with the United States. Now, with the U.S. government imposing sanctions on its trading partners, who would dare to trust it?

The United States has preached free market economy everywhere, giving advice to other countries and helping them take the path of market economy. The United States believes that its own development and prosperity are the results of the implementation of the free-market economy and open their own markets to attract other countries to develop a market economy. The "rules of the market" has become a principle that all countries in the world have to follow. However, the United States is now taking the lead in undermining the principles of market economy. The Trump administration has blatantly violated the rules of the market economy and increased government intervention in trade on the grounds that the U.S. trade deficit is too large. In addition, the Trump administration has imposed tariffs on products exported to the U.S. by various countries without any respect for other sovereigns. The U.S. government has also directly ordered that U.S. semiconductor companies be banned from supplying Huawei and several other Chinese technology companies. U.S. companies supply Chinese companies according to market demand, and Chinese companies account for 70 % of the global market for semiconductors. The U.S. direct order prohibiting companies from acting in accordance with market demand is completely contrary to the tenets of a market economy.

The United States once boasted of being the representative of a nation governed by the rule of law. The reason why a market economy needs the rule of law is that laws and regulations are needed to maintain order in the market and investors need predictable development and returns. The Trump administration is forcing U.S. companies to default on their contracts and breaking commercial contracts, all of which are serious violations of the rule of law and come at a heavy price. When U.S. companies default on their contracts, they have to pay liquidated damages, which can run into billions or even tens of billions of dollars for these large contracts. In addition, U.S. companies no longer supply to Chinese companies, Chinese companies can only find other alternative services. Once the U.S. companies have lost this large market in China, it is difficult to get back, and the future development of these U.S. companies is gloomy.

The United States also prides itself on being a model democracy. But its elected leaders are bent on personal preference, regardless of the interests of American businesses and consumers. A study by the Peterson Institute for International Economics shows that trade frictions are already costing the average American $650 more per person. If Trump were to impose additional tariffs on Chinese exports, each American would spend more than $2,500 more per year. Trade frictions have already put hundreds of American farms out of business, real investment in manufacturing has plummeted, and many small and medium-sized businesses that depend on Chinese imports have gone out of business. The democratically elected leaders of the United States seem to be treating the interests of the American people like a child's play.

In 2019, a Federal Reserve economist and two professors from Columbia University and Princeton University analyzed the damage to the U.S. economy from the trade sanctions launched by the Trump administration. The study shows that the U.S. economy is not really that important for the world economy, and they also analyze the impact of the U.S. tariff increase, and the conclusion is clear: to see if the tax increase benefits the U.S., it is necessary to see if the U.S. tax increase can affect world market prices, thus depressing import prices through the tax increase. Usually, large countries can benefit through this method. But the results show that this tax increase by the Trump administration did not affect world market prices, which means that the U.S. economy did not have as much impact on world market prices as it thought. Therefore, the U.S. tax increase only raises prices in the United States, and the cost of the tax increase must be borne by U.S. consumers and businesses, which in turn reduces social welfare in the United States.

In this regard, it is not necessary for China to focus all its efforts on responding to U.S. trade sanctions. China should actively respond to the challenges while developing cooperation with other trading partners to build an international multilateral free trade system in the "post-U.S." era. From this perspective, more active promotion of bilateral investment agreements — with the EU, working with the EU, Japan and other G20 members to promote WTO reform, maintaining the authority of the WTO arbitration mechanism — should be the main direction for the Chinese government to work toward in international trade in the future.

Sino-US Competing Relations and World Economic Development

If the U.S.-China relationship is a game of variable sum, it can also be summarized by the term "Co-Opetition," which comes from the theory of cooperative competition. Both China and the United States compete in science and technology and economic development, but it is a peaceful competition. On many global and regional issues, there is much cooperation and common interest between China and the United States, and there will be more cooperation in the future.

In fact, competition between China and the United States in the global market may not be a bad thing. Why do both China and the United States pursue market economies? That is because the market mechanism brings competition, and competition can promote efficiency and continuous innovation in enterprises and countries. A certain degree of competition between China and the U.S. will motivate both countries to promote scientific and technological progress and make greater contributions to the development of mankind.

China and the United States are in competition for economic development, both wanting to develop faster and better to prove that their own development models are superior. Although there is a certain degree of ideological competition behind this competition, it is still more beneficial than harmful as long as it is kept within certain limits. Other countries can see that different societies can adopt different social management systems, and that economies at different stages of development do not necessarily have to adopt the same development model. Human societies should have different development models as choices. Considering that different societies have different historical backgrounds, social structures, development stages, cultural characteristics, and ethnic relations, each country should draw experience from different development models to form a unique development model that suits the characteristics of its own society.

The United States thinks it has "won" the Cold War and is confident in its own development model. It claimed that the U.S. model represented by "democracy plus market" was the best model for human society and wanted to form a "coalition of democratic countries" to replace the United Nations, promoting a new world order. However, after the wars in Afghanistan and Iraq, the United States did not succeed in getting these countries to replicate the American model. The U.S. then joined forces with European countries to fight the war in Libya, overthrowing the Gaddafi regime, and riding the wave of the Arab Spring to bring the war to Syria. Contrary to U.S. expectations, after a series of wars that toppled the regimes of these countries, these countries not only failed to follow the U.S. model, but also opened Pandora's Box, and terrorism grew stronger and stronger. The U.S. and its allies have again had to spend tremendously to combat terrorist forces.

Just as the U.S. was scrambling to deal with terrorism, the U.S. financial markets went haywire again. The real estate bubble burst, the financial markets went into turmoil, a number of major financial institutions went bankrupt, and the financial system of the United States and its allies was in jeopardy. The financial crisis triggered an economic and social crisis, which in turn led to the rise of political extremism and populism, and the American public began to wonder if their political system was in trouble.

In fact, after the end of the Cold War, if the U.S. government had been less arrogant and more thoughtful in maintaining and strengthening the functions of multilateral cooperation institutions such as the United Nations, the international order today might have been a little more stable.

China's "One Belt, One Road" initiative and its proposal to build a "community of shared future" have given a new impetus to world economic growth and provided an alternative approach to international cooperation. If the U.S. can see the opportunities instead of provocations, China and the U.S. can find many opportunities of cooperation to stabilize the existing international system and make it more equitable and balanced.

When we recognize the logic behind this game of variable sum in Sino-U.S. relations, we will know how to control this rivalry so that it becomes a competitive mechanism for development rather than a reason for confrontation and conflict.

10

Constructive Partnership between China and the EU in the Process of Globalization

According to Chinese diplomats, bilateral relations between China and the EU have been qualified by China as the most important partnership. However, despite China's willingness of developing a fruitful relationship with the EU, China has not got a positive response on the key issues of Sino-European relations, such as lifting arms' embargo, or granting the market economy status to China. Why are those relations considered asymmetric by both Europeans and Chinese? I tried to analyse this sort of paradoxes several times. Some of the analyses have been written in 2007, others in 2016. Generally speaking, Chinese people can hardly get a satisfactory response from Europe, because the EU's decision making process is so complicated that Chinese government and Chinese diplomats cannot handle it. Some European countries have taken EU's specificity as an useful diplomatic instrument. When it can get some real advantages by bilateral relations, they will promote their relationship with China as strategic partner, while they will put the blame on EU, when they cannot meet China's demand.

The EU's diplomatic relations with China are, in Chinese diplomatic terms, of the highest order and can be defined as a comprehensive strategic partnership. Yet there are still some dissonances in this relationship, such as the fact that the EU still maintains a regulation that is not very fair to China, which is a ban on the sale of military-related products to China. In addition, the EU still does not recognize China's market economy status, which is a time-bound provision in the treaty China signed with other WTO members when China joined the WTO[1].

If the relationship between China and the EU is so important, why do obstacles repeatedly arise in practice? In order to answer this question, we need to sort out the complex relationship between China and the EU.

Lessons from the Failure of the EU's "lifting embargo"

The ban on arms sales to China has not been lifted since it was announced by the European Community in 1989. Despite the fact that China and the EU have made great progress in their relations in recent years, with an increasing range of cooperation and common interests, both China and the EU find the ban a delicate matter in their bilateral relations. The EU has tried to lift it, but such efforts ultimately failed. From this failure, we can see that today the EU is still not so "independent" in terms of common foreign and defense policy.

The EU is still far from being a mature pole in the world's political landscape; it has not actually found a way to develop a common foreign policy, and each member state still has a strong incentive to protect its own diplomatic sovereignty. In the foreseeable future, the EU may not be able to reach unity in foreign policy either. Therefore, we should have an objective understanding of the EU's integration development, evaluate more appropriately the EU's role in dealing with international issues, and better understand the EU's decision-making mechanism in foreign policy to avoid misjudgments about the future.

We should summarize the EU's failure to lift the embargo on arms sales to China in the following four aspects.

First, some European researchers argue that both China and the EU are to blame for the EU's failure to successfully lift the ban on arms sales to China. They argue that China has not been sophisticated enough in promoting the EU's lifting of the ban and lacks the ability to influence the EU at key moments in its decision-making. For example, during Prodi's presidency of the European Commission, China did a lot of work in the hope that the European Commission would play a greater role in lifting the ban. However, the conflict between the Council of Europe and its member states has been deep, and Prodi's desire to lift the ban on arms sales to China and expand the Council's mandate, which coincides with China's interests, may have caused opposition from some Council members, not necessarily because they are hostile to China, but because they do not want to expand the Council's diplomatic powers. The lack of understanding of this internal contradiction by Chinese diplomats has given the Council of Europe member states the impression that China's actions are "interference in their internal affairs". In fact, this is neither in line with China's diplomatic principles nor its true intentions.

Second, the governmental structures of key EU member states make foreign policy decisions more difficult. From time to time, European countries are governed by a coalition of several political parties, and at such times, the efficiency of their foreign policy is often greatly compromised. In France, where President Jacques Chirac (de Gaulle's faction) and Prime Minister Jospin (leader of the French Socialist Party) were in a coalition, the government changed in 2002 with Chirac as president, Raffarin as prime minister and de Villepin as foreign minister, all of whom were in the same camp, and both Raffarin and de Villepin had demonstrated friendship with China. It was at this point that China began formally proposing to France that it help China lift EU's ban on arms sales to China. German Chancellor Gerhard Schröder also actively cooperated with French President Chirac in pushing for the lifting of the ban. Since Germany was a coalition government at the time, Schröder needed to join forces with Foreign Minister Fischer (a member of the German Green Party) to push the process forward, but Fischer was less enthusiastic about lifting the arms sales ban and repeatedly suggested linking the issue to the "human rights" situation in China. The structure of the German coalition government made these efforts ultimately "bankrupt".

Once again, the United States has a lot of influence over the EU and can exert influence on EU decision-making. After the EU decided to discuss whether to lift the ban on arms sales to China, the U.S. used various forces to lobby the EU's decision-making bodies. The U.S. President, Secretary of State, Deputy Secretary of State and other political figures visited Europe and continuously pressured the leaders of EU member states to change their views. The U.S. Congress has also put pressure on the European Parliament, repeatedly stating that lifting the ban on arms sales to China would lead to a gap between Europe and the United States. The U.S. military-industrial community has also put pressure on EU member states, using a combination of "carrot and stick." The U.S. also used its relationship with its allies to encourage Japanese politicians to step in and convince European leaders. From the example of the U.S. offensive to force the EU to abandon the lifting of the ban, the EU's foreign policy has two major characteristics. One is that the EU's foreign policy is still very influential in the international arena and has some symbolic significance. New Zealand and other countries belonging to the same Western camp have long lifted the ban on arms sales to China, but they simply failed to attract the attention of the United States. And when the EU wants to lift the ban on arms sales to China, the U.S. attaches great importance to it, even going so far as to use all kinds of diplomatic power to push the EU to abandon this decision. Second, the EU's foreign policy has a certain degree of stability, once it has determined a certain direction of foreign policy, it is very difficult to change. In other words, it is not easy to make the EU change its decision positively, but it is easier to make the EU maintain its original decision.

Finally, despite the EU's efforts to unify its foreign and security policies, the EU has so far failed to establish an effective common diplomatic and security mechanism, let alone a European global strategy. Thus, a comprehensive strategic partnership between China and the EU seems to be only an expectation, and the EU—which is unable to develop a global strategy—cannot understand China-EU relations in a larger perspective and cannot consider them in a strategic vision as a whole EU. Only a few major powers in the EU have political ambitions and strategic diplomatic planning, such as the UK, France and Germany, which participated in the Iranian nuclear negotiations, and only these powers have shown interest in regional security issues, including the North Korean nuclear issue. In 2011, the U.K., France and the U.S. supported the establishment of a "no-fly zone" for Libya in the U.N. Security Council, and then used it as a reason to launch air strikes against Libyan government forces and help the Libyan opposition overthrow the Qaddafi regime. All this was not based on the EU's common foreign policy resolution, but directly through the UN Security Council. This shows that the EU powers do not take the EU's Common Foreign and Security Policy seriously at all, and they know that the decision-making process of this mechanism is too long and complicated, and they would rather use the traditional framework of international relations, such as the UN and NATO, when practicing foreign policy decisions.

European integration is still a long-term process, and while we should support the efforts of European integration, we should not take the possible future of Europe as the current reality.

The EU Does Not Recognize China's Market Economy Status

When China joined the WTO, there was a special provision in the agreements it signed with the EU and the US. This is Article 15 of the Protocol on China's Accession to the World Trade Organization. This provision provides that within 15 years from the date of China's accession to the WTO, because China is not a full market economy, when the EU or the U.S. considers that Chinese enterprises' exports to these regions are suspected of "dumping," they can use the prices of similar products in third countries as a reference to determine whether Chinese enterprises are "dumping".

At the end of 2016, the 15-year deadline was reached, but the EU and the US still refuse to recognize China's market economy status. The EU is a full strategic partner of China and such attitude makes the Chinese public feel that European countries are not righteous and reliable enough. Moreover, EU member states also question China's motives for increasing its investments in Europe. Is all the above because China is developing too fast, causing the EU to worry, or is the EU unable to keep up with the situation and ignore China's changes?

The EU's attitude towards the recognition of China's market economy status has been in a process of change. When China applied for WTO accession, the EU considered that China did not fully meet the conditions of market economy, so it came up with a transitional approach (i.e. Article 15 mentioned above) and gave China a 15-year transition period. The EU promised to recognize China's market economy status when it expires.

Why was the EU so "generous" at that time? Because the EU recognizes Russia's market economy status and there is a special clause in the agreement between the EU and Russia. This clause stipulates that when the EU finds two prices for Russian products exported to the EU (i.e. one external price and one internal price), the EU can refer to the prices in third countries, and if the price of Russian products is higher than the price in third countries, the EU can still impose "anti-dumping" duties on Russian exports. Therefore, the EU believes that even if China's market economy status is recognized, the EU may still impose duties on China if the EU finds pricing difference for Chinese products.

However, things have since changed. Similar provisions were included in the EU's free trade agreements with Indonesia and Venezuela. When trade frictions occurred between the two sides, the EU tried to use third-party prices for measurement, so Indonesia and Venezuela took their case to the WTO, and the EU eventually lost the case. The EU then panicked and realized that if it recognized China's market economy status, it would face more similar problems in the future, and Chinese exports to the EU would get out of control. After the change of the European Commission, the new trade commissioner stopped discussing whether to recognize China's market economy status as scheduled.

In 2016, protests by steel workers broke out in several EU countries, arguing that China was dumping steel into the EU. Some members of the European Parliament then launched a campaign against the recognition of China's market economy status and eventually got the Parliament to adopt a resolution. Considering the increasing role of the European Parliament in EU decision-making, the European Commission probably could not completely disregard the resolution of the European Parliament and had to adopt some compromise. China believes that the EU should recognize China's market economy status because it is really unfair to measure Chinese exports by third country prices, which is tantamount to not recognizing China's competitive advantage in controlling production costs. Many Chinese companies have suffered from the unfair imposition of "anti-dumping duties". Although the trade involving "anti-dumping" is only a small part of China-EU trade (3 %–4 %), it is very unfair for Chinese companies, because exports to the EU may be critical for some companies. Once deemed "dumping" by the EU, their exports to the EU may be sentenced to "death". Therefore, taxing Chinese companies in the name of "non-market economy" is simply a kind of political discrimination. China has been practicing a socialist market economy and attaches great importance to its trade relations with the EU. However, if China's strategic partners do not recognize the Chinese government's efforts in practicing market economy and even put China in a different category, this will be very detrimental to the healthy development of bilateral relations.

Of course, as old Chinese saying teaches, "Those who suit their actions to the times are wise," when China noticed that the EU institutions were divided on whether to recognize China's market economy status, it began to take steps to prevent things from getting out of hand, even though it was unhappy with the EU's attitude. While the European Parliament's resolution cannot be retracted, the heart of the matter lies in the provisions of Article 15 of the Protocol on China's accession to the World Trade Organization. As long as the EU fulfills this provision and stops measuring Chinese exports to Europe with third-country prices, China can also make appropriate concessions.

However, there are still some people within the EU who want to make a fuss over this clause. They think that if China's market economy status is not recognized, they can still use third-country prices to measure the prices of Chinese exports to the EU. However, these attempts are futile, because if in the future the EU finds Chinese companies "dumping" by referring to third-country prices, Chinese companies can go to the WTO and sue, and China will definitely win.

However, even if the EU no longer arbitrarily identifies Chinese enterprises as "dumping", the future of trade relations between China and the EU may not necessarily be bright. Since the EU is still worried about Chinese products being too competitive and subsidies from the Chinese government on export enterprises, "countervailing" measures might be the focus in future trade friction between the EU and China.

The Protocol on China's Accession to the World Trade Organization mentions two "preventive mechanisms", namely "countervailing" and "anti-dumping". After the expiration of the 15-year transition period, the "anti-dumping" measures will expire, but the "countervailing" measures have no time limit. Therefore, if the EU believes that Chinese companies' exports are suspected of being subsidized by the government, they will also request a "countervailing" investigation. If it is true, the EU will impose "countervailing duties" on such products.

"Countervailing" will be an important part of international trade in the future. Some years ago, the EU proposed the principle of "competition neutrality", the core of which is "anti-subsidy". "Competition neutrality" emphasizes complete freedom in the market, and any government subsidies will undermine this principle and will be punished after the ruling. "Competition neutrality" involves tax neutrality, debt neutrality, rule neutrality, and so on. In other words, if the government—in any form, such as tax incentives, debt interest subsidies, policy preferences, etc.—gives preferential policy to Chinese enterprises, whose exports are investigated and subject to "countervailing duties".

However, the EU has greatly underestimated the competitiveness and innovation capacity of Chinese companies, which they instead attribute to the support of the Chinese government. In fact, although government policies played a role in the rapid development of China's economy since the reform and opening-up, the critical role in this booming is actually taken by a group of Chinese entrepreneurs who dare to innovate and persevere in innovation. Chinese brands like Huawei and Haier gained their reputation domestically and internationally, indeed, because of their consistent innovation, rather than government subsidies.

China is carrying out a new round of reforms, including enterprise reforms, financial reforms, and trade system reforms. China has established a number of "free trade zones" in several coastal cities to experiment with finance and trade reforms. If the reforms in these areas are successful, their experience will be shared throughout the country and elevate China's economy to a new level.

Competitive Relations between China and Europe

The perception of China in the EU countries seems to be changing with the dynamic balance of the bilateral powers in globalization.

The EU is not only the world's largest economy, but also its member states Germany, France, Italy and the UK were once ranked second only to the US and Japan in terms of GDP. In recent years, these countries have been overtaken by China one after another, which disturbs their inner equilibrium.

Public opinion in the EU countries believes that China is the biggest beneficiary of globalization and that the Chinese are taking away the jobs of many Europeans. Many EU countries believe that the Chinese economy has achieved so much because China has violated trade rules. At the same time, although most of China's trade surplus with EU countries comes from foreign companies, public opinion sees this trade surplus as a sign of China's violation of trade rules and uses it to increase "anti-dumping" lawsuits against Chinese companies.

In the past, EU countries have been the largest exporters of technology products to China. Europeans are not too worried about exporting and transferring technology to China, as they believe that China has many years behind Europe in technology and it will take a long time for China to catch up. But in recent years, the momentum of the Chinese economy has impressed the Europeans. A study commissioned by the European Commission and conducted by the European Research Council shows that some Europeans believe that China will surpass Europe in terms of technology within 10 years. As a result, the topic of intellectual property rights has become much more relevant in the dialogue between China and the EU.

Many European countries, especially Germany, have always been big exporters of machinery. But in recent years, China's machinery exports have grown rapidly and have a tendency to overtake Germany. At present, China is still an important market for European machinery exports, and British public opinion believes that the extraordinary growth of German exports in 2010 is mainly because the Chinese market absorbed a large number of German machines. However, in terms of exports to other parts of the world, China has caught up. For example, in 2010, China's machinery exports to Brazil surpassed those of Germany, becoming the second largest exporter of machinery to Brazil after the United States. The competition between Germany and China has made European countries, especially Germany, particularly wary of, and even repulsed by, China's development. And when referring to its development, European countries always shift the focus to Chinese domestic social problems, as if they ignore that China's economic development has first and foremost benefited the Chinese people.

Since 2007, the attitude of EU countries toward China has been changing. For example, in 2007, China overtook Germany to become the world's third largest economy, and in the same year German Chancellor Angela Merkel proposed to adhere to "values diplomacy," whose so- called values became the premise of Germany's policy toward China. In the same year, Merkel met with Dalai, which strained Sino-German relations. Also in 2007, French President Nicolas Sarkozy visited China, and in a speech at Tsinghua University, he recognized China's development. Sarkozy's trip to China brought more than 20 billion euros business order back home. What a fruitful return! However, Sino-French relations hit a low point in 2008 when Sarkozy met with Dalai and expressed his intention to boycott the Beijing Olympics. Germany, on the other hand, started to improve relations with China again in 2008, and in the spring of 2009, Chinese purchasing delegation went to Europe, signing 13 billion euros orders in Germany and the UK, but bypassing France. To summarize, if we carefully analyze the policies of the EU countries on China in recent years, we may find two sides of these countries: on the one hand, they cannot cut off China as a huge market, especially in the context of the financial crisis where EU countries are deeply in debt and need to cooperate with China to promote their economic development; on the other hand, they always like to "teach" China a lesson with European values, in order to maintain their European pride. Thus, we see the phenomenon of European countries taking turns to accept orders from China but looking back to criticize China.

Sino-European relations have also been plagued by other factors over the years, especially by EU countries' blocking of China's plans to aid Africa. Many major European powers have established colonies in Africa. Today, the official languages of many African countries are English and French, and education is basically in English and French. The spread of European culture in Africa is also the result of colonization. After the end of the Second World War, African countries set off a surge of independence movements and declared their independence. However, for a long time, African countries remained very close to their former suzerain states in Europe, and European enterprises in fact controlled the economic lifelines of African countries. For example, the mineral and energy resources of Africa were basically in the hands of these European companies. The political influence of European countries can be seen in the regime change of many African countries. To some extent, Europe has always regarded Africa as its own backyard and considered Africa as a space reserved for development by European countries.

However, Chinese investments in Africa and Chinese aid to Africa in recent years have caused consternation among Europeans. With the rapid development of China's economy, its demand for energy and raw materials has grown rapidly. Securing the supply of these materials, and especially their price stability, has become an important basis for China's economic development. Therefore, in recent years, China has stepped up its investments in resource development in African and Latin American countries. The rapid economic development of these developing countries in recent years is strongly related to China's investments in these countries.

In fact, China's healthy relations with African countries can go way back. In the late 1950s and 1960s, China actively supported African countries in their national liberation movements for independence, and in the early 1970s, African countries played a key role in China's return to the United Nations. During the Cold War era, China's diplomacy, guided by the "Three Worlds" theory, has been focused on strengthening ties with the Third World, thus expanding China's influence in Africa. It has also helped African countries to strengthen their infrastructure development. Today, Chinese aid sites and iconic Chinese buildings can be found in many African countries, and cheap Chinese goods have improved the living standards of Africans. It is in this context that a certain resistance to Chinese investment in Africa has suddenly emerged in Europe.

Certain European media criticize China's investment behavior in Africa, which is a microcosm of the conflict between China and Europe. In the future, the US and European countries may use their influence in Africa to create uncertainty between China and African countries. However, the effectiveness of the "Chinese model" is confirmed by the fact that China's investment and development in Africa has contributed to the rapid economic development of African countries. Chinese investments in Africa are then elevated by the European media to the level of an ideological and developmental battle, and Africa may become the focus of conflicts between China and European countries.

The Negative Impact of EU Decision-Making Mechanism on China-EU Relations

The key to significant progress in Sino-European relations may still lie in the veto system in the EU decision-making process, which makes it impossible to remove several obstacles in Sino-European relations. As the financial crisis deepens, if EU member states do not find a way to overcome this lengthy and ineffective way of decision-making, the economic stability of the eurozone will be threatened.

The financial crisis in 2008 started with the bursting of the real estate bubble in the United States, and Europe was only an indirect victim. But with the development of the financial crisis, the debt crisis in the eurozone broke out frequently, and the debt crisis in European countries soon became more serious than that in the United States. Why did this happen? From an objective point of view, the overall debt level in Europe is lower than that of Japan and the United States, because when the European Economic and Monetary Union was established, the Maastricht Treaty at that time (i.e., the Treaty on European Union) stipulates that the budget deficit of EU member states should not exceed 3 % of GDP and that government debt should not exceed 60 % of GDP. These standards were breached successively during the economic crisis, but because of these red line limits in the past, the total debt of the eurozone countries did not grow very fast. The debt crisis in Europe is lingering because the eurozone's system is flawed. The eurozone only has a unified monetary policy but no unified fiscal arrangements, so when a crisis strikes, EU member states lack unified support at the EU level and their debts cannot be restructured, which will lead them in trouble.

Before the financial crisis, some peripheral countries in the eurozone, i.e. those with less robust economies, were able to borrow in the market at lower interest rates thanks to the power of the euro. The level of interest on the national debt of these countries was almost negligible compared with that of the core eurozone countries such as Germany and France. However, after the outbreak of the financial crisis, the financial situation of the peripheral countries in the eurozone deteriorated rapidly, and the interest differential between their national debt and the German national debt of the same period widened rapidly. In the case of Greece, for example, the interest spread between Greek and German government bonds widened to 274 basis points after the outbreak of the financial crisis.

The peripheral countries of the eurozone are facing a structural recession. If they do not reduce their fiscal deficits substantially, it will be difficult for them to pay their debts on time, and the interest on their debts will become higher and higher. But if they adopt a tight fiscal policy, the economies of these countries will experience an even more severe recession since there is no public spending stimulus.

The euro is appreciating because the core eurozone countries are highly competitive globally, and the eurozone has a solid external position[2] and a solid currency. The peripheral eurozone countries have fallen into another trap: they cannot use currency depreciation to quickly build external surpluses, cannot easily restart private sector borrowing, and cannot easily maintain their current fiscal deficit levels. Their debt situation will continue to deteriorate, as the real debt burden in euro terms will increase as nominal prices and wages continue to fall. This could lead to a new wave of private sector (or even public sector) defaults.

At the same time, the core country of the eurozone, Germany, is also dissatisfied with the development of the eurozone. German public opinion believed that, in order to keep the euro strong, the Germans have been "tightening their belts" for 10 years, with limited wage growth and government services. After the outbreak of the debt crisis in Greece and Ireland, the German public is outraged because they believe that the taxes—which Germans scrimp and save—may be used to fund early retirement in Greece, or to support Ireland's ultra-low corporate taxes.

As the financial crisis evolved, nationalistic tendencies emerged among the leaders of the eurozone and EU countries. Take German Chancellor Angela Merkel as an example: when the debt crisis broke out in Greece and Ireland, Merkel chose to blame the victim countries together with the German media, and even said that if the crisis continues, the eurozone should be divided into two, with the countries of debt problems forming a separate eurozone, while Germany and the countries without debt problems forming another eurozone. This attitude is in sharp contrast with the former German Chancellor Kohl. Back then, in order to promote the euro and let the Germans give up the Mark—the pride and symbol of the Germans—Kohl repeatedly presented evidence to the German parliament. He tried to convince other German politicians that the euro is crucial to European integration and the future of Germany. In 1989, Kohl seized the historical opportunity to unify Germany, and his reputation turned as high as the sky. In order to unify the European currency, he put his personal political reputation on the line to convince the German public to accept the euro. In contrast, the leaders of European countries today do not have Kohle's spirit of struggle, nor do they have the kind of mind to build European integration. When the crisis is at the head, they only blame each other, unwilling to promote integration or to find a way out of the crisis. In fact, the designers of the Maastricht Treaty did take into account the weaknesses of the internal structure of the eurozone. Former French President Francois Mitterrand's economic adviser Jacques Attali participated in the whole process of the Maastricht Treaty, and many of the criteria of the treaty came from his hand. In an interview, Attali said frankly that a system designed with only a unified monetary policy and no unified fiscal policy would certainly lead to a crisis, but that is the beauty of the Maastricht Treaty. The construction of European integration has always been driven by economic integration, with the aim of reaching political integration, and in fact its goal was to form a federal system. This is an unprecedented attempt. If there is a crisis, the leaders of the EU must find a way out. Since there is no future for regression, it is necessary to further unify fiscal policy. That is, to build an "economic government". If the establishment of a European economic government is successful, the next step to promote the establishment of a political government will meet less resistance. However, despite the thoughtfulness of the designers of the system, they did not anticipate that the leaders of European countries today would be so unmotivated, and that they would cater to nationalist sentiments, leaving the European integration unattended.

According to the current trend, the structural weaknesses and contradictions of the EU will continue to develop in the future, even endangering the existence of the EU. This also means that the debt crisis will always haunt the eurozone and affect the development of the European economy. In the future, China is likely to become the target of attacks by European countries, because the leaders of European countries do not have the ability to guide the people or the will to convince them, but only cater to public opinion and use it as a pretext to defend themselves. And when the country's economic development is weak, they are likely to use China as a scapegoat.

Looking ahead, while it's hard to see any breakthroughs in China-EU relations, the demand for China from EU member states is growing. Thus, when Chinese leaders visited France, Germany and Portugal in 2010, they were warmly welcomed and several cooperation agreements were signed. From this perspective, the EU's dual approach to China will continue.

China should look at what is happening in Europe realistically and objectively, understand the logic of European policy towards China, and not imagine the current situation in other countries according to our own logic and way of thinking. In fact, there is no fundamental conflict of interest between China and the EU, nor are there geopolitical contradictions. On the contrary, China and the EU share common interests and concerns, so China and the EU should work together to tackle global challenges. However, if the decision-making process in the EU countries is dominated by other factors that prevent rational cooperation and common benefits, then it will be difficult to maintain a healthy development of China-EU relations.

Prospects for China-EU Relations

After more than 40 years of friction, a variety of dialogue, consultation and cooperation mechanisms have been established between China and the EU, covering political, economic and trade, humanities, science and technology, energy, environment, and other fields. The China- EU Leaders' Meeting, the highest-level political consultation mechanism between the two sides, was established in 1998. On July 16, 2018, Li Keqiang co-chaired the 20th China-EU Leaders' Meeting with European Council President Donald Tusk and European Commission President Jean-Claude Juncker in Beijing. The China-EU High Level Economic and Trade Dialogue, the highest-level dialogue mechanism between China and Europe in the field of trade and economy, was officially launched in 2008 and is led by the Chinese Vice Premier for Trade and Economic Affairs and the European Commissioner for Trade and Economic Affairs. The Dialogue is held once a year, alternately in China and Europe. In addition, another annual dialogue, the China-EU High Level Strategic Dialogue, which was upgraded in 2010, is led by the Chinese State Councilor for Foreign Affairs and the Vice-President of the European Commission for Foreign Affairs.

The focus of China-EU relations is on economic and trade relations. Since 2004, the EU has been China's number one trading partner, and China is the EU's second largest trading partner. Trade has been the cornerstone of China-EU relations, and bilateral investments between China and EU member states have been growing, and the exchange of goods and capital has been stable. There are frequent cultural exchanges between China and many EU member states, and various cultural festivals and cultural exhibitions have enriched the exchange of ideas and culture between the two sides.

At the same time, trade is the main source of conflict between China and Europe. The trade imbalance between China and the EU has caused concern in EU countries, and European manufacturers are increasingly worried about competition from China. In addition, European companies have increased their lobbying efforts for governments to step in and negotiate reciprocal market access standards with China. Both Chinese companies and the Chinese government are also frustrated by the EU's refusal to recognize China's market economy status. Many Chinese companies have had to navigate with EU institutions to avoid them judging Chinese exports to Europe as "dumping" at third-country prices.

In addition to bilateral trade, the China-EU partnership is crucial for maintaining the international multilateral trade order. China's rapid development cannot be separated from an open international trade environment. However, the multilateral trade order has been fraught with uncertainty in recent years. China's economy is transitioning from a phase of rapid development to one of high-quality development, while many EU member states are struggling to recover from the shocks caused by the financial and debt crises. At such a critical time, the United States has threatened to withdraw from free trade agreement negotiations and announced its withdrawal from the Trans-Pacific Partnership Agreement, while negotiations on the Transatlantic Trade and Investment Partnership Agreement have been suspended due to opposition within the EU. Trump also threatened that the U.S. would withdraw from the WTO if its demands were not met.

Against this background, China's cooperation with the EU is particularly important. China is keen to work with the EU to promote reform of the existing international trade system and to retain the multilateral consultation mechanism. Through international cooperation, China hopes to avoid turning the world towards protectionism. China also hopes that the EU will be more active in China's "Belt and Road" initiative and find new ways of cooperation between China and the EU through increased investment in infrastructure in developing countries. So far, the EU has remained an important force in support of globalization. At a time when the United States is becoming increasingly isolationist and protectionist, China and the EU can work together to promote globalization and world economic cooperation.

In addition to strategic cooperation, China and the EU are also important technology partners, and in the future China and the EU can strengthen their cooperation in the field of sustainable development. The Chinese government considers solving environmental problems as a top priority in development, and many EU countries have advanced technologies for environmental protection and management, rich experience and many standards related to environmental protection. China and the EU can try to cooperate on sustainable development issues, and China can provide a larger market for European companies to promote the development of green industries. In 2012, China and the EU signed the Joint Declaration on China-EU Partnership on Urbanization, which aims to promote exchanges on urban development issues.

On an international scale, cooperation between China and the EU on climate change issues has become more important as the US announced its withdrawal from the Paris Agreement. China and the EU are ranked first and third in the world in terms of carbon emissions, respectively. In international negotiations, China represents developing countries, while the EU represents developed countries. If China and the EU can reach an agreement and establish a cooperative relationship on addressing climate change, China and the EU can become leaders in global action to reduce emissions and set an example for other countries.

In the past, the EU has been the largest source of advanced technology transfer to China. European companies' investments in China are characterized by the fact that they seek to open markets on Chinese soil and use the Chinese market to consolidate their development. Therefore, European companies do not hesitate to take their latest products and latest technologies to the Chinese market for development. The automotive industry is a good example. Initially, the French company Peugeot brought some of its outdated models to China, because Peugeot thought that these less fashionable models were more "robust" and better adapted to the Chinese road conditions at the time. However, car companies from other countries pushed more fancy models to China, which became popular. Later, the French Citroen Motor Company learned its lesson and produced the "ZX" car in Wuhan, the latest model launched in parallel with France. After the merger of Citroen and Peugeot, Citroen introduced the latest models to the Chinese market and gradually expanded its share in the Chinese market.

As China's foreign exchange reserves have risen to the top of the world, the country has begun to consider how to make better use of them. Stimulated by the policy of encouraging Chinese companies to "go global", many Chinese companies have increased their outbound investment, and Europe has become a popular market for Chinese companies. Chinese companies' investment in Europe is different from European companies' investment in China after the reform and opening up. Today, Western European countries have long been industrialized, and it is difficult to find greenfield investment opportunities there. But since corporate transactions in the Western European market are frequent, Chinese companies can enter the European market by buying all, majority or partial equity. After acquiring European companies, Chinese companies can acquire the technology of these companies and also use the sales network of these companies to enter the European and other developed markets.

In terms of Chinese companies investing in Europe, we can cite many successful cases, such as Geely Automobile Group's merger with Volvo Group, which revitalized a European car company on the verge of bankruptcy. After the merger with Volvo Group, Geely took a big step up in terms of technology and appearance improvement, as the production technology of Volvo Group had a positive spillover effect on Geely's production. Another famous case is Sany's merger with German Putzmeister. When Putzmeister was merged by Sany, the employees of the company were worried that they would lose their jobs and that the Chinese company would walk away after acquiring the German technology. But this did not happen, Sany Heavy Industry opens the Chinese market for Putzmeister. In a few years, Putzmeister's turnover increased by almost 1/3, so it had to expand production and recruit more employees. It is such two-way exchange between Chinese and European companies that has led to a continuous achievements, improving technology, increasing profits, and creating more and more jobs on both sides.

However, as Chinese companies are investing more and more in Europe, some European countries have new concerns about the consequences of Chinese investments. They fear that Chinese companies will acquire more technology and become more powerful by merging with European companies, threatening the future development of European countries. Therefore, some European countries want to imitate the U.S. by pushing the EU to establish a review system for inward investment, which would review and block foreign mergers and acquisitions of European companies in the name of national security. However, because many EU member states need Chinese investment, this proposal has not been adopted. We need to improve communication with the governments of EU member states to make them realize that cross-border investment and technology exchange between Chinese and European companies can be a win-win situation and bring greater benefits to both sides.

The development of China-EU relations can be approached in four ways. During his visit to Brussels in March 2014, Xi Jinping clearly proposed to view China-EU relations from a strategic perspective, proposing to combine the two major forces, two major markets and two major civilizations in China and Europe, and to jointly build the four major partnerships of peace, growth, reform and civilization between China and Europe, so as to give new impetus to China-EU cooperation and make a greater contribution to world prosperity. In July 2018, when European Council President Donald Tusk and European Commission President Jean-Claude Juncker were in Beijing for the 20th China-EU Leaders' Meeting, Xi Jinping met with them again and reiterated the importance of the four major China-EU partnerships as following.

First, China and the EU should be partners in peace and take the lead in the path of peaceful development. China and the EU have an important strategic consensus on building a multipolar world. Both sides should respect each other's social systems based on their independent choice, take care of each other's core interests, and support each other's path of peaceful development. The two sides should strengthen communication and coordination in international and regional affairs, jointly resolve regional hotspot issues and participate in the construction of relevant international regulations.

Second, China and the EU should be partners in growth and provide each other with development opportunities. We should negotiate a good investment agreement as soon as possible, start a feasibility study on a free trade agreement, and jointly improve the quality and level of trade between China and the EU. We hope that the European side will expand high technology trade with China. We should combine China-EU cooperation with major intercontinental cooperation initiatives such as the Silk Road Economic Belt, aim to build a large market in Asia and Europe, and strengthen infrastructure connectivity. We should adhere to market opening, join hands to safeguard the multilateral trading system, and work together to develop an open economy of the world.

Third, China and the EU should be partners in reform, learning from and supporting each other. At present, both China and the EU are entering uncharted water in their reforms. Both sides should strengthen exchanges, share experiences and deepen cooperation on reforms in macroeconomics, social governance, public policies, agriculture and rural areas, employment and social welfare, environmental protection, and other important areas.

Fourth, China and the EU should be civilizational partners and provide more nourishment for each other's progress. Sino-European relations have civilizational attributes and historical depth. The two sides should enhance mutual understanding through equal dialogue and exchange, strengthening cultural exchange and media communication, expanding tourism and the scale of exchange students, and jointly supporting research on China-EU relations.

In 2014, Xi Jinping pointed out—during his talks with concurrent European Council President Van Rompuy in Brussels—that China-EU relations have developed into a complex relationship with a high degree of interdependence. China-EU relations are not only about the respective development of China and the EU, but also have a significant impact on the development of the world political and economic landscape. China views and attaches importance to the EU from a strategic perspective, firmly supports the construction of European integration, and is willing to continuously expand and deepen the comprehensive strategic partnership with the EU.

All in all, China and the EU share many common interests and can find more ways to cooperate through consultation and promote a development dynamic of joint participation and mutual assistance. China and the EU can achieve a more constructive dialogue among civilizations and make a greater contribution to the progress of humanity.

Notes

1 Article 15 of the Protocol on China's Accession to the World Trade Organization provides that WTO members shall terminate the practice of "substitution" of anti-dumping against China 15 years after the date of China's accession to the WTO. Editor's Note

2 In finance, a position is the amount of a particular security, commodity or currency held or owned by a person or entity. In financial trading, a position in a futures contract does not reflect ownership but rather a binding commitment to buy or sell a given number of financial instruments, such as securities, currencies or commodities, for a given price.

11

The Rise of the BRICS

The chapter about BRICS countries development has been written originally on the request of a French news magazine in 2017. The story about BRICS is just like a fairy tale. Nothing predestined those countries to come together, but similar claims and similar international positions rendered those countries solidary. Over time, the cooperation mechanisms of BRICS countries have become very effective and attractive, and its' open and inclusive characters have made BRICS+ mechanism a practical tool to work with more and more emerging economies. Western media may be wrong by underestimating BRICS countries contribution to global economic development and its importance in shaping the future global economic position. That's why I like to remind readers outside BRICS that the world is changing faster than people may expect, so a better knowledge of BRICS may allow people to better master the orientation of world movement.

In recent years, the international media has paid a lot of attention to the BRICS countries. BRICS countries not only regularly participate in current international forums, but also create opportunities to hold institutionalized meetings and organize international cooperation, such as annual summits, ministerial meetings, meetings of national security representatives, meetings of chambers of commerce, meetings of research institutes, meetings of youth leaders, meetings of various working groups, etc.

In addition, BRICS countries have established international entities such as the New Development Bank for financial cooperation.

How do countries as geographically distant as Russia and Brazil, and countries as vastly different as India, China and South Africa come together in the same international stage? There seems to be no commonality that can bring these countries together in the international community. They have neither much historical connection nor ideological commonality, and are at different links in the global production chain. The concept of BRICS was introduced by Jim O'Neill, chief economist at Goldman Sachs, and refers to the world's emerging markets. Today, Brazil, Russia, India, China and South Africa seem to have formed a community of destiny in many aspects of international cooperation.

Born in the Wave of Globalization

Although the leaders of the BRICS countries are keen to promote international cooperation, they did not invent the concept of BRICS. The cooperation between these countries is entirely out of coincidence.

Jim O'Neill, a chief economist at Goldman Sachs, first mentioned Brazil, Russia, India and China (BRIC) in his November 20, 2001 global economic analysis entitled "Building Better Global Economic BRICs". (BRIC, an acronym for the four countries, pronounced similarly to the English word brick)[1]. O'Neill's intent was that we need to build better "bricks" for the "big house" of world economy. In October 2003, Goldman Sachs published a report entitled "Dreaming with the BRICs: The Path to 2050", which predicted that the BRICs would dominate the world economy in the future — Brazil will overtake Italy in GDP by 2025 and France by 2031; Russia will overtake the United Kingdom in GDP by 2027 and Germany by 2028; China will overtake the United States as the world's largest economy by 2041; and India will overtake Japan in GDP by 2032[2]. In total, the BRIC economies will surpass the current six largest economies in the world (U.S., U.K., Germany, France, Japan, and Italy) by 2041. By 2050, the six largest economies in the world will be China, the United States, India, Japan, Brazil, and Russia.

This report made the BRIC countries famous, and the international media started to pay attention to these countries. As the BRICs seem to represent the future of the world economy, they have also become increasingly popular with countries around the world. 2005 saw the first G7 Finance Ministers meeting to which representatives from the BRICs were invited. Large multinational corporations began to reorganize their strategies for emerging markets. Former South Korean President Roh Moo-hyun led a delegation of Korean large business on a diplomatic mission to the BRICs.

It should be said that these emerging market countries have indeed accelerated their economic growth through globalization, and the financial crisis that erupted in 2008 hit the global market hard, leading to a massive recession in many countries. But the crisis also raised the international community's awareness of the BRICS countries. In order to better cope with the new challenges, the BRICS countries demanded a more equitable international economic order. That is to say, the international economic order needs to cater to the demands of developing countries.

In June 2009, the first BRICS Summit was held in Yekaterinburg, Russia, which focused on international economic and financial issues, energy security, environmental protection, disarmament, nuclear non-proliferation, international trade, and reform of international institutions. The BRICS countries issued a joint statement at the end of the meeting, expressing their common position on development and international security issues.

Institutionalized Cooperation of BRICS Countries

In April 2010, BRIC leaders held the second BRIC summit in Brazil to discuss the world economy, the international financial system reform, the coordination mechanism for policy construction and cooperation among BRIC countries, and other topics. It should be said that after this meeting, the cooperation mechanism of BRICS countries was officially formed.

In November 2010, the G20 summit was held in Seoul, South Korea, during which South Africa formally applied to join the BRICS. After South Africa's application was accepted, the number of BRICS member countries officially increased to five.

In 2011, the leaders of the five BRICS countries met for the first time in Sanya, China, where discussions focused on expanding cooperation in the areas of energy, trade, agriculture, and food security. The BRICS leaders exchanged views on international issues, focusing on the reform of the international monetary system, coordinated their positions at the G20 Summit in France, and discussed issues such as climate change and sustainable development.

India hosted the BRICS Summit in 2012, and the Delhi Declaration expressed the willingness of the BRICS countries to coordinate economic policies between developed and developing countries through the G20 platform. In addition, at the summit, the BRICS countries planned to establish a new development bank.

In July 2014, BRICS leaders announced in Fortaleza, Brazil, the establishment of the BRICS New Development Bank, headquartered in Shanghai, China. The BRICS countries are all developing countries and are downstream in the global production chain. They produce large quantities of raw materials and manufactured goods that are exported to international markets and use the foreign exchange to buy bonds of developed countries.

In response to the financial crisis, developed countries adopted extremely loose monetary policies, and their hedge funds borrowed loans at very low interest rates, which are eventually invested in the BRICS countries. The increase in trade surpluses and foreign exchange reserves of the BRICS countries led to higher inflation and currency appreciation, resulting in a de facto reduction of foreign exchange reserves. Since the Fed's decision to discontinue quantitative easing, capital outflows and currency depreciation in BRICS countries have exacerbated the vulnerability of the financial systems of these countries. The volatility in international financial markets has also affected the economic development of BRICS countries.

To get rid of their dependence on the hegemony of the US dollar, the BRICS countries have jointly established the BRICS New Development Bank (NDB). Through the contribution of the BRICS central bank, a portion of foreign exchange reserves can be pooled. Likewise, by issuing bonds on the international financial markets, the pooling of idle funds can serve the infrastructure development of BRICS countries.

In fact, the existing international financial system is no longer able to meet the demand for infrastructure investment in BRICS countries. 2008–2012, the World Bank provided a total of $52 billion in loans to BRICS countries, of which Russia received only $515 million.

Until the end of 2011, the ADB (Asian Development Bank) lent a total of $25.9 billion to China and less than $27 billion to India. The other BRICS countries did not receive any development funds from the ADB. The BRICS NDB was apparently created to restructure and consolidate government savings in China and Russia — it hedges the current account deficits of India, Brazil and South Africa to improve financing for infrastructure development in the BRICS countries. The BRICS NDB has the following advantages:

First, the central banks of the BRICS member countries must contribute to the BRICS NDB, which will reduce the issuance of currency by the central banks and ease inflationary pressures; second, the BRICS NDB will gain far more from real economic investment than the BRICS central banks gain from purchasing developed country treasury bonds, and infrastructure investment can also boost domestic demand in these countries and boost economic growth; finally, the BRICS NDB will promote the use of the currencies of BRICS member countries and facilitate domestic trade and reciprocal investment in these countries, thus reducing dependence on the US dollar and the unfair international economic order. In conclusion, the establishment of the BRICS NDB reflects the willingness of BRICS countries to make better use of their foreign exchange reserves, which is conducive to reducing inflation risks and more beneficial to the development of the real economy of BRICS countries.

BRICS and G20

At the third meeting of BRICS leaders in Sanya, China, in 2011, BRICS member countries made it clear that BRICS would not replace the G7 or G20 coordination mechanisms. Instead, the BRICS countries will use the G20 platform to advance the development agenda.

In terms of cooperation goals, the BRICS countries should establish a new platform for South-South cooperation and build bridges for cooperation between North and South countries. With a population of more than 3 billion, BRICS countries have an obligation to contribute to building a fairer world. BRICS countries can also play a more active role in promoting global economic growth, democratizing international relations, upholding multilateralism, and maintaining world peace and stability and global security.

In terms of forms of cooperation, the BRICS countries insist on progressive cooperation, hoping that international cooperation will be more pragmatic, transparent, and mutually supportive. Inclusive and non-confrontational are the two words most often used to describe BRICS cooperation. BRICS can strengthen the role of the G20 in global governance in the post-financial crisis era, as well as the role of the UN in addressing new challenges to global security. The BRICS countries attach great importance to the implementation by member countries of resolutions and consensus adopted at G20 summits and UN conferences, and are willing to assist developing countries in fulfilling them.

When discussing the development agenda in the post-financial crisis era, the G20 insisted on balanced growth of the global economy and reduction of the huge trade surplus of the developing countries; the EU insisted on green and sustainable development with a focus on solutions to climate change; and the BRICS countries insisted on strong economic growth as the basis for all development, especially the recovery of the global economy. In the end, the G20 reached an overall framework agreement to promote strong, sustainable, balanced and inclusive growth in the world economy. As for the implementation of the overall framework agreement, the United States and the European Union advocated the establishment of a mechanism to evaluate G20 members. The BRICS countries, on the other hand, proposed a constructive and non-binding assessment of implementation measures, taking into account the development differences between developed and developing countries. Finally, the G20 has adopted a reference guide for the mutual evaluation of macroeconomic policies of member countries. This indicates that the BRICS countries do not oppose global governance measures advocated by developed countries, but the BRICS countries propose richer and more inclusive measures to improve the global governance agenda and coordinate public policies of member countries.

The London G20 Summit resolved to establish a Financial Stability Board to replace the Financial Stability Forum, expanding the Board from 10 to 20 members. BRICS countries maintain the G20's G-SIFI (Systemically Important Financial Institutions) report to reduce moral hazard for financial institutions globally. Hedge funds, shadow banking, offshore financial derivatives and rating agencies are regulated for the first time.

On international trade issues, the BRICS countries urged G20 members to refrain from protectionist measures in the short term and to recognize the WTO as the only long-term multilateral trade body. 2008 saw G20 members commit to a free trade agenda for 2008–2013 at the G20 Washington Summit, and again in 2013 at the G20 St. Petersburg Summit for 2014–2016. In late 2013, at the Ninth WTO Ministerial Conference in Bali, Indonesia, BRICS countries pushed WTO members to reach a multilateral agreement that consolidated the Doha Round of negotiations.

At the G20 Seoul Summit, the BRICS countries promoted a consensus among G20 members on a development agenda. The BRICS countries believe that the global economic imbalance is characterized by unbalanced development between the North and the South. That is, there can be no balanced global development without the development of the majority of developing countries. There can be no global shared prosperity if the poorest countries are unable to escape poverty. Developed and developing countries should establish a new type of global development partnership, avoid mutual accusations and confrontations, and strive to reach mutual understanding and coordinate to solve global problems and address new challenges.

"The Seoul Development Consensus for Shared Growth," adopted at the G20 Seoul Summit, consists of six key principles: prioritize growth, develop partnerships, focus on systemic issues, encourage private sector participation, work with each other, and provide incentives for positive outcomes[3]. The nine pillars of the consensus are: infrastructure development, private sector investment and employment, human resource development, trade, inclusive finance, resilient growth, food security, domestic resource mobilization, and knowledge sharing.

It is evident that BRICS countries are more insistent than ever on developing equal partnerships. They advocate creating an atmosphere of cooperation between developed and developing countries, allowing different countries to choose the path that suits their development.

BRICS and Counter-Globalization

In recent years, the world has been going through a process of "reverse globalization". The United States and some developed countries, fearing of their own decline, are actively promoting the establishment of high-standard free trade areas, such as the "Trans-Pacific Partnership Agreement" (TPP) and the "Transatlantic Trade and Investment Partnership Agreement" (TTIP).

It is certainly no coincidence that all BRICS countries have not been invited to participate in the negotiations to construct these free trade areas. The BRICS are not intended to replace the G7, but we cannot be sure that the developed countries will leave the BRICS out of their development agenda.

Since the Fed's change in monetary policy, there has been tremendous turmoil in international commodity markets and a development gap among BRICS countries. Brazil, Russia and South Africa, as major producers and exporters of raw materials, have been affected by the drop in commodity prices. Brazil and Russia experienced negative economic growth. India and China, importers of raw materials and exporters of manufactured goods, are not directly affected by commodity price fluctuations, but they are also affected by capital flight and currency depreciation. Still, they both have found ways to sustain economic growth and have maintained relatively high economic growth rates (7.2 % in India and 6.9 % in China in 2017).

Are Differences of Development Stages among BRICS Countries Creating Centrifugal Forces among Them?

Brazil's economic recession caused a social backlash, and in 2016, the Brazilian parliament initiated an impeachment motion against then-President Dilma

Rousseff, which immediately sparked popular protests in defense of the president. In the end, however, Rousseff was removed from office, although this did not affect Brazil's commitment to other BRICS countries. The fact that the BRICS cooperation mechanism has withstood the test of regime change in Brazil shows that it is a mature mechanism for international cooperation.

In response to their economic woes, consultation and cooperation among the BRICS countries have intensified. The year of 2014 saw Russian President Vladimir Putin come under intense pressure from the West over Crimea at the G20 summit in Brisbane, Australia. The BRICS countries did not isolate Russia; they insisted that the primary mission of the G20 is to coordinate macroeconomic policies and promote global economic recovery, and the BRICS countries maintained this original intention.

China was the host of the 2016 G20 Hangzhou Summit, where it sought to advance the development agenda on a global scale. In fact, the G20 was born in the wake of the international financial crisis, and it began as a crisis management and emergency management mechanism. After years of cooperation, the BRICS countries hope to push the G20 to become a coherent global long-term development and governance mechanism.

The G20 Will Be the Necessary Platform for BRICS Countries to Express Their Positions on Global Governance

G7 was also a product of the economic crisis of the 1970s. Although the G20 grew out of the G7, the G7 still exists and the world's industrial powers still need this mechanism to coordinate their global interests and consolidate their position. The same logic applies to the BRICS countries. Therefore, we can foresee that the BRICS will remain a force to be reckoned with on the international stage in the future.

BRICS Countries Lead the World Economic Development

The BRICS countries held a summit conference in Xiamen, China, on September 2017, laying out an ambitious development plan for the next decade. The declaration issued at the end of the conference demonstrates the willingness of representatives of these emerging economies to make a greater contribution to the sustainable and inclusive development of the global economy and to the improvement of global governance.

In recent years, the BRICS countries have taken an ever-increasing share of global economic growth. According to estimates by the International Monetary Fund, the contribution of the BRIC countries to global economic growth was about 60 % in 2016. The IMF also estimates that in 2017, emerging economies and developing countries will contribute more than three-quarters of global economic growth. And in the next few years, the contribution of these economies will still account for about 70 % of global economic growth.

Emerging economies have not only made great contributions to the global economy in terms of growth, they have also been successful in promoting the growth of international trade. According to estimates by the World Trade Organization, from 2000 to 2015, imports from developing countries increased from 27 % of world trade to 41 %, and exports increased from 30 % to 43 %. In 2005 developing countries contributed 24 % of global service exports. In 2015, this figure was 39.4 %. Goldman Sachs predicts that by 2050, the top five economies would be composed of the BRIC countries (China, India, Brazil, Russia), and the United States.

As the structure of the global economy changes dramatically, the BRICS countries have expressed a strong desire to participate in and take action on global economic governance. With regard to the existing international system, the BRICS countries have supported multilateralism and promoted domestic reform to make the system more equitable. Whether within the framework of the United Nations, or the G20, the BRICS countries are actively collaborating, seeking to speak with one voice. The BRICS countries have played an active role in promoting global economic growth, fighting the return of protectionism, and strengthening cooperation in the supervision of financial markets.

At the same time, the BRIC countries have created new cooperation mechanisms, like the creation of the new development bank, and emergency mutual aid provisions. This has created a new base of cooperation among emerging countries based on equality. In these new mechanisms, there is no room for intimidation or vetos; equality prevails, with each country entitled to one vote. It is a model of consultative cooperation.

At the Xiamen Summit, BRICS leaders invited several leaders from other emerging economies, to show that the BRICS group is not a closed bloc. Indeed, the new trend of the world economy is the collective rise of emerging economies.

The BRICs Also Face Significant Challenges. If They Can Overcome These Challenges, the Future Development of These Countries Would Be Even Brighter

Since the dollar is still the hegemonic currency of the international monetary system, the Federal Reserve's monetary policy has a major impact on the economy. After the end of quantitative easing in 2014, the Federal Reserve entered a cycle of interest rate retrenchment. The changing value of the dollar has caused sharp fluctuations in the international commodity market, and commodity-exporting countries among the BRICS have suffered tremendously from the Federal Reserve's "spillover effects". In the future, the Federal Reserve will reduce its position on the debt market. In addition, the interest rate will be raised as well. All this will cause a big fluctuation in the value of the dollar, the international capital markets, and the markets of the primary products. Only by strengthening monetary cooperation and adopting a swap for the settlement of their international trade could the BRICS countries mitigate the negative impact of the dollar's turmoil on their economies.

Among the BRIC countries, China, Russia and India are major land powers in Eurasia and would inevitably be suspicious of each other. In the past, China's "Belt and Road" initiatives were regarded by Russia with suspicion, particularly its plan to construct an "Eurasian Economic Union". Later, President Vladimir Putin proposed connecting the plan for the Eurasian Union with the Chinese Belt and Road initiative, reducing mistrust between the two powers. China and Russia have cooperated on aviation, spaceflight and arms development. Russia has advantages in industrial design and technologies, but has weaknesses in industrial processing and market exploitation. Cooperation between China and Russia is win-win. The lessons of Sino-Russian cooperation can be translated to Sino-Indian cooperation. If India can join its international development strategy with the Chinese "Belt and Road" initiatives, this will certainly bring more development opportunities to South Asia.

Emerging economies have enormous needs for infrastructure, and the development of consumption and services. Emerging economies have better demographics, are more open minded, more willing to participate actively in international cooperation, more ready to build reasonable coordination mechanisms. On the whole, emerging economies are the main force for promoting a new version of globalization. The BRICS countries have created a new model of mutually beneficial cooperation among emerging economies. This model of South-South cooperation would have effects on other emerging economies.

Cooperation among these developing countries will significantly change the outlook of global growth, also affecting the structure of the global economy.

Notes

1 https://www.goldmansachs.com/insights/archive/archive-pdfs/build-better-brics.pdf
2 https://www.goldmansachs.com/insights/archive/:~:text=%20Dreaming%20with%20BRICs:%20The%20Path%20to%202050,quite%20different%20in%202050.%20The%20largest...%20More
3 https://www.oecd.org/g20/topics/development/Annex1-Seoul-Development-Consensus-Shared-Growth.pdf

12

How Could China Contribute to The Development in Africa?

China's presence in Africa is not new, can date back to its support to African people's struggle for their national liberation and independence. Nevertheless, China's growing investment in Africa in 21st century has changed completely Africa's visage. When the bipolar world disappeared, international media paid their attention only to Eastern European countries, Africa has been neglected as a forgotten corner of history during 1990's. What is more dramatic, is that some European countries even wanted to impose what happened to Eastern European countries to Africa, forcing them to undertake multiparty democratic reform. People may easily imagine what happened next. As African countries' boundaries have been decided by European colonial powers, contradictions and frictions among different ethnic groups were checked by strong men politics during those years of national liberation struggle. However, with democratic revolution introduced in Africa, those contradictions and frictions among different ethnic groups have been released, and national solidarity has been forgotten, replaced by deeply rooted ethnic anger and hatred. I wrote a series of papers on Africa in 2016 and 2017, hoping that when China started investing massively in Africa, we should take account of this historic context. We should not only help African countries get into development path, but also help African countries build their State. The State building process will be as important as the development, for the first will give Africa a sound framework of development, while the last will give African people incentives to endeavour for a better life.

Sub-Saharan Africa has grown rapidly in recent years, and in the 1990s, when the world economy entered the era of globalization, Africa became the "forgotten corner". It was not until the 21st century, when Chinese investment in Africa increased dramatically, that Africa re-emerged as the "continent of hope" and the new star of 21st century world economic development. With the exception of Ethiopia, the vast majority of African countries were colonized by European countries and have been poorly modernized since regaining independence. In recent years, terrorism has been expanding rapidly in Africa, and most African countries have limited capacity to deal with it, both in terms of military capability and national financial capacity. In the future, Africa's development will largely depend on their ability to successfully complete the construction of public authority.

Africa in the Cold War

The boundaries of the modern African state were largely inherited from the demarcation by the colonial powers, and the management model of the African state was designed according to the framework of the European nation-state, so the problems faced by the African state were almost "innate." In other words, the creation of modern African states did not take into account the ethnic and cultural differences in Africa, and the colonial demarcation created a great deal of potential problems. Different tribes in Africa had different religious and cultural traditions, and the colonizers artificially grouped them together and eventually developed them into modern states, where inter-tribal conflicts became frequent. How to overcome these "original sins" and find a framework for the establishment of a modern African state for the stable development of society is the top priority for Africa.

After achieving independence, the most pressing task facing African countries was nation-building, and therefore strongman politics was the norm in African countries. Until the 1960s and 1970s, the ideological struggle between socialism and capitalism became dominant in the bipolar world, and the rest of the conflicts, including tribal and religious conflicts, were overshadowed by the ideological struggle. Moreover, the leaders of the newly independent African countries were aware of the current situation in Africa, knowing that the national boundaries drawn during the colonial period were not in line with cultural traditions, but new demarcation would cause new conflicts and wars. So, in May 1963, 31 African countries met at a summit in Addis Ababa, the capital of Ethiopia, and decided to form the Organization of African Unity (OAU) to recognize the national boundaries that had been drawn and to stop fighting over the demarcation of borders.

During the Cold War, when the arena of the two superpowers' confrontation was mainly in Europe, Africa experienced a period of stability. France had a unique African policy that enabled France to maintain a special relationship with French-speaking countries in Africa (mostly former French and Belgian colonies). France stationed troops in several African countries to provide security for these countries, provided financial and monetary support to West African countries, and created a separate West African franc zone in West Africa. The French franc became a nominal anchor for the currencies of these countries, whose currencies were pegged to the franc for currency stability. The United States, although unhappy with France's African policy, adopted an accommodating attitude toward France in order to maintain the unity of the Western world.

There are exceptions, however, for African countries. For example, after gaining independence from Portuguese colonial rule in 1975, Angola was embroiled in a protracted civil war, with the United States and the Soviet Union supporting each side, neither of which could control the situation alone. The war lasted 27 years, killing about one million people and displacing about one-third of Angola's population.

There are some African countries that are calm on the surface, but there are undercurrents that are ready to explode into conflict at any time. Rwanda, for example, is a country where 85 % of the population are Hutus, who are mainly engaged in agriculture, while 14 % of the population are Tutsis, who are mostly pastoralists, and another 1 % are Twa. The division of labor between the different ethnic groups constitutes a source of ethnic conflict in Rwanda, as cattle are a more valuable asset than crops. In 1860, the Tutsi Laubugli established a feudal dynasty, with the Tutsi as rulers and the Hutus as servants. When the Belgians made Rwanda their colony, the Belgians took full advantage of the country's ethnic differences. They openly supported the "more intelligent, active, and educated" Tutsis by providing them with superior education, administrative positions, and political rights, while the Hutus were left to sell their labor under Tutsi rule.

In March 1957, nine influential Hutu intellectuals published a pamphlet called the "Bahutu Manifesto", calling for the establishment of a "democratic system". This manifesto promoted a typically racist rhetoric, claiming that the "foreign invaders", the Tutsis, were to be driven out. The Rwandans finally drove out the Belgians in the late 1950s in a wave of anti-colonialism. However, ethnic vendettas soon engulfed Rwanda[1]. After a Hutu politician was attacked by Tutsis, a popular Hutu uprising quickly spread throughout the country. Groups of 10 Hutus looted, set fire to, and killed Tutsis. Subsequently, in the 1960 elections, the majority Hutu population won 90 % of the top government posts. Since then, more than 20,000 Tutsis have been forced into a mass migration, and many more have been massacred and exiled. In 1973, Hutu general Habyarimana seized power in a military coup, calling for an end to violence against Tutsis and including some in his "rubber stamp" parliament. The Tutsis boosted Rwanda's economy, and Habyarimana ruled for more than 20 years in what Westerners saw as a corrupt, totalitarian state.

There are numerous African countries similar to Rwanda. Many African countries are ruled by strongmen and maintain a superficial stability, while in reality various tribal and local factional conflicts are suppressed.

Democratization and Social Collapse in Africa

After the end of the Cold War, the West thought it had won. In the meantime, the West has been pursuing a strategy of democratization all over the world. Japanese American political scientist Fukuyama summarized this political belief as "the end of history". At that time, Fukuyama was convinced that a political democracy combined with an economic market economy was the ultimate form of human society, and that there could be no other new form.

Former French President Francois Mitterrand, linked French aid to Africa to the democratization of African countries after the East European upheaval. In the 1980s, France experienced several setbacks in its economic development, with several new prime ministers and various government attempts to stimulate economic development. In the past, the French government had assumed a tremendous number of subsidies to African countries, but financial difficulties stretched the French government's public spending, so Mitterrand decided to scale back the aid to Africa. In June 1990, at the Franco-African Summit in La Baule, France, Mitterrand proposed that French aid to Africa would depend on the state of democratization in African countries. Subsequently, at the G7 summit in July 1990, Western countries explicitly listed human rights, democracy, and market economies as prerequisites for aid to Africa.

The democratization of Africa has resulted in explosion of various conflicts that were previously under the disguise of ideological conflicts. During the Cold War period, independent African countries were largely ruled by strongmen. In the years following independence, Africa experienced some economic and social development, but tribal conflicts persisted. The result of strongman rule was that only the tribes and certain tribes to which the rulers belonged were given preferential treatment, which created great injustice. Democratization has intensified tribal conflicts and led to large-scale riots, which in some countries can even be called civil wars. At the same time, the rich resources of African countries were coveted by many countries, which exacerbated the unrest in African countries.

Let us take Rwanda as an example. After the wave of democratization in the 1990s, both the United States and France put pressure on Rwanda. As a result, President Habyarimana had to agree to abandon the totalitarian regime and promote pluralism and multi-party democracy. However, the implementation of pluralist politics opened a Pandora's box of tribal hatred. Since the introduction of "free elections" in 1990, Hutus have been spreading anti-Tutsi slogans. In a mass movement known as the "Hutu Power Movement", Hutus even portrayed Tutsis as "enemies of democracy" In the face of Hutu atrocities, an armed force led by Tutsis, calling themselves the Rwandan Patriotic Front (RPF), invaded Rwanda from neighboring Uganda to wage a fight against the Hutus[2].

In 1994, after the death of Rwandan President Habyarimana, the Hutu Power Movement issued a national call to a bloody campaign against the Tutsis. In just 100 days, the Hutus killed some 800,000 to 1 million Tutsis. Most Westerners insist that the Rwandan tragedy had nothing to do with the push for democratization. While Rwanda's Hutus and Tutsis have a history of violence, political unrest was clearly the catalyst for the massacre. According to Amy Chua, a professor at Yale Law School, "The fact remains that the majority of the Rwandan masses supported, and indeed physically carried out, the unspeakable atrocities of 1994. In a terrible sense, these atrocities were an expression of the 'will of the majority' in a context of mass poverty, colonial humiliation, manipulation by political demagoguery, and resentment toward an extremely wealthy 'foreign' minority"[3].

China's Aids to Africa

African countries urgently need to establish effective national governance systems, without which they cannot successfully modernize themselves.

In the last two or three decades, African governments have faced a crisis of legitimacy. As for the elections, the elected governments have been usually accused of bribery, corruption and other charges for a variety of reasons. James Madison, the "Father of the Constitution" in the United States, famously argued that it is important for a government of men to establish authority before we can talk about monitoring it. The difficulty for African countries is that although governments can be elected, they often do not have sufficient authority and are often overthrown by various forces, such as military coups and foreign military interventions, because of tribal and religious conflicts.

At the same time, the market of African countries is too small to achieve economies of scale, and regional economic integration is an inevitable choice to expand the market. The Economic Community of West African States and the West African Franc Zone are attempts to promote integration.

African governments are faced with the dual task of nation building and regional integration building: on the one hand, they need to establish and protect national sovereignty; on the other hand, they need to cede some sovereignty in due course to form regional organizations in order to improve management efficiency and create economies of scale. The difficulty lies in the fact that African regional organizations are often unable to provide a platform for mediation or a tool for intervention in the political unrest or a military coup.

As a last resort, many African countries still need to return to their former suzerain states (such as France) to intervene when they are in trouble— this provides an excellent excuse for foreign powers to intervene in the internal affairs of African countries. For example, French troops in Côte d'Ivoire, along with other UN peacekeeping forces in Africa, were involved in the fight against Gbagbo in Ouattara, eventually overthrowing the government that had been elected and claimed a majority of votes. While French public opinion claims that Gbagbo committed electoral fraud, some studies suggest that the French military retaliated against the Gbagbo government for "harming" French businesses during its time in power.

After the outbreak of the Arab Spring, extremist religious and terrorist forces soon spread from North Africa to West Africa, and African countries felt the need for transnational cooperation and the urgency of nation-building.

Africa's development urgently needs to solve the problem of the lack of human resources in the process of nation building, and urgently needs to train a large number of engineers, legal personnel, economic managers. It also needs to build a modern army loyal to the country and overcome tribal conflicts, and only by training a large number of inter-tribal technical personnel can nation building be truly on track.

China can help more to train African technicians. The Chinese government could offer more scholarships and provide long-term or short-term training opportunities for African students and technicians. Chinese companies have invested a lot in Africa, and the Chinese government should encourage more training of African employees and help African countries strengthen their "hardware" as well as their "software". African governments should also make efforts to overcome tribal conflicts in their countries and send students and technicians from different tribes to China for training in a more balanced way, so as to promote the harmonious development of their societies and the modernization of their countries.

As Chinese aid and investment in Africa has increased, African countries have become increasingly close to China. However, both domestic and international public opinion has expressed concern about this trend. The Western media seems jealous. Some Chinese public opinion also concerns that China's aid to Africa will be "wasted", because many African countries are still politically unstable and strongly dependent on external aids. African countries, on the other hand, believe that China's success has much to learn for their late-developing countries.

In fact, the purpose of Western-led international aid to Africa does not help Africa develop for two reasons: on the one hand, Westerners want Africans to be grateful to the West, and on the other hand, Western left-wing intellectuals want psychological comfort from the aid. Thus, Western-led international aid is often a trap that sometimes hurts Africa more than it helps.

Historically, international aid has generally only occurred between allies, and only after World War II did international aid become synonymous with institutionalized help for the economic development of some "backward" countries.

After the end of World War II, the Marshall Plan pioneered international aid. Shortly thereafter, Western European countries also launched a certain scale of "international aid" to former colonial countries, and also signed the Lomé and Yaoundé Agreements, granting special trade preferences to African countries.

However, this international assistance was based on the background of the Cold War. Beginning in the late 1950s, national independence movements in Asian and African countries were on the rise, with many countries declaring independence from their European sovereign powers. In this background, the countries in the socialist camp morally supported the independence movements of these countries, while the Western countries feared that all African countries would join the socialist camp, so the international aid of the Western countries was not really spent on training the labor force and developing the productivity of African countries, and much of the money was spent on lobbying. For example, if there are politicians in African countries who side with the West, the West spends money to support them. In fact, some dictators in African countries who came to power by military coups have received assistance from the West. But this has not helped African countries to develop their human resources or build their industrialization systems.

In addition, much of the international aid provided by Western countries is loans to explore the natural resources of African countries. Western countries need overseas resources and markets, and much of the international aid to Africa is aimed at opening up new markets and developing new suppliers at the same time. However, the price of resources on the international market fluctuates, and the market price is determined by the demand of developed countries and the dollar exchange rate. It is hard to balance the investment of the resource development in African countries: due to excessive investment, the overflowing market supply of resources leads to price competition and profits losses. On the other hand, insufficient investment cannot sustain economies of scale, so that the development of resources cannot even recover the cost. Studies by economists in some African and Latin American countries have found that developing countries often experience a deterioration in the terms of international trade: when resource prices continue to fall, the more resources developed, the more prices fall, the less profit they can make, while the debt owed for the development of resources continues to rise. Economists attribute this phenomenon to the inequality of the international economic structure (order).

In order to improve the disparity between the rich and the poor in the world, the United Nations has proposed several "development decade" plans since 1961. In the plan for the Decade, which began in 1981, developed countries were required to provide 0.7 % of their GDP each year as development assistance to developing countries in order to alleviate the widening gap between the North and the South, according to Resolution 2626 adopted by the 25th session of the United Nations General Assembly. The United Nations Development Programme(UNDP) and the United Nations Conference on Trade and Development (UNCTAD), established in the mid-1960s, have also done much good work in this regard.

The UNDP, who aims to provide technical assistance to developing countries, is currently the largest international provider of multilateral technical assistance, and 80 % of its funding going to least developed countries with a per capita GDP of less than $600 per year. The UNCTAD, an international economic organization that coordinates North-South relations and considers issues related to national trade and economic development, has given special attention to the trade and development of developing countries in its agenda. "Globalization" became the theme of the tenth session of the UNCTAD, held in Bangkok in February 2000. The Bangkok Declaration and the Plan of Action adopted by this Conference are two important documents that fully reflect the strong desire of developing countries for a more just and reasonable international trade order under the situation of accelerating globalization, and at the same time put forward a series of concrete proposals that are conducive to the balanced, healthy and sustainable development of the international economy.

Until the 1970s, international aid was mainly focused on the economic sphere. However, in the 1980s it began to broaden into the social sphere, involving multilateral and bilateral technical assistance programs. The reasons for this are that in the 1980s, some developing countries had already achieved economic take-off and the demand for economic aid declined; in addition, numerous studies in development economics have shown that economic growth is strongly related to overall social progress. International aid must be tilted toward other areas in order to help developing countries grow better. Therefore, health, education, women, population, environment, and resources are gradually becoming important aspects of development programs.

During the Cold War, although Western countries granted large amounts of development aid loans to African countries, African countries were not able to embark on the path of development. Many countries also fell into the debt trap, and the profits from the exploitation of resources were not enough to pay off their debts.

Developed countries often require developing countries to carry out political and economic reforms in accordance with the wishes of Western countries in the name of economic aid, and make these reforms a condition attached to the aid. For example, some Western countries use the domestic political, economic and social conditions of recipient countries, and even their human rights records and democratic processes, as important indicators and bases for whether to grant aid loans. The harsh political conditions of donor countries have led to a decreasing amount of development assistance to some developing countries.

International aid is increasingly tied to other requirements or foreign intervention of domestic affairs. An increasing number of donors are linking international aid to the purchase of commodities and the use of labor, and "restricted procurement" is becoming a growing proportion of aid disbursements. More than half of the bilateral aid provided by DAC member countries requires recipients to purchase goods and use services from the donor country. This "restricted procurement" of aid forces recipient countries to import poor quality but expensive goods and services, as well as unsuitable and outdated technology and equipment, which not only weakens the impact of aid but also increases the debt burden of recipient countries.

In the late 1980s, with the rise of reforms in some socialist countries and the dramatic changes in Eastern Europe, Western countries began to make "democracy, multi-partyism, and privatization" a prerequisite for providing development assistance to developing countries. During the Cold War, among the Western countries, France was "assigned" to administer Africa. France had a military presence in many African countries and the currencies of many countries in West and Central Africa were pegged to the franc. The West African franc is still the currency of eight West African countries, while the Central African franc (CFA) franc is the currency of six Central African countries. France gives financial subsidies to these countries that use the CFA franc to help them peg the franc. After the end of the Cold War, France was financially strapped and could not afford to subsidize African countries. French aid to Africa began to be tied to democratization, and many African countries began to introduce multi-party elections. Such strategy reduced French financial subsidies on the one hand, and gave France the moral high ground to seemingly promote the development of African countries on the other. As a result, the democratization of Africa has fueled local conflicts between different tribes. It was in this context that the Rwandan massacres took place.

The 1960s and 1970s were the high point of international aid, and after the 1980s, the scale of international aid did not grow significantly and even stagnated somewhat.

In the case of the member countries of the Organization for Economic Cooperation and Development (OECD), for example, the aid by the organization's member countries increased from $6.986 billion to $27.296 billion during 1970–1980, which is an increase of 290.72 %; although the aid in 1980–1990 increased from $27.296 billion rose to $53.356 billion, the growth rate dropped by 95.47 %; after the 1990s, the growth of international aid entered a stagnant phase, with the amount of aid in 1993 increasing by only $1.097 billion or 2.06 % over 1990. While the growth of developed countries' aid to developing countries was declining, the number of LDCs in need of emergency assistance increased from 25 in 1970 to 48 in 1998, and the number of countries in extreme poverty eligible for IDA assistance increased from 42 in 1990 to 70 in 1996. The contradiction between the stagnant growth in the scale of international aid and the growing number of poor countries has become increasingly pronounced. Against this backdrop, Chinese aid and investment in African countries has become increasingly prominent as we enter the 21st century.

In fact, in the 1960s and 1970s, when China was not rich, China has been supporting the construction of African countries. The Tanzanian Railway is the best proof of China's "belt-tightening" support to African countries. In 1971, many African countries voted for China when Albania and Algeria proposed to the UN General Assembly to restore China's legal seat in the UN. At that time,

China's production capacity was limited, so Chinese aid and investment in Africa was also limited at that time.

In 21st century, China announced the first-time debt relief for African countries, forgiving the debts of 31 poor African countries and some of the debts of other least developed countries in the world, totaling about RMB 10 billion. From 2000 to 2011, China provided economic support (in the form of economic aid, interest-free loans, concessional loans, commercial loans, etc.) to 51 African countries, funding 1,673 projects totaling $75 billion. China's assistance to Africa is based on the needs of African people and can meet the needs of local social and economic development.

China decided to further expand the scale of aid to Heavily Indebted Poor Countries (HIPCs) and Least Developed Countries (LDCs), and to forgive or otherwise cancel the debts of all HIPCs with which China has diplomatic relations through bilateral channels. China decided to grant all 39 LDCs with which China has diplomatic relations zero tariff treatment for some goods, including most of their exports to China. China also decided to provide $10 billion in preferential loans and preferential export buyer's credits to developing countries, including African countries, to help them strengthen infrastructure development and promote joint ventures and cooperation between enterprises of both sides.

In addition to investment in economic construction, China has also provided Africa with materials and medicines for malaria prevention and treatment, and helped African countries improve medical facilities and train medical personnel. In some recent years, China has helped African countries train many talents.

A Chinese diplomat who has worked in Africa for many years said that China has provided about $26 billion in various interest-free and low-interest concessional loans to Africa. At first glance, the Chinese government's financial subsidies appear to be enormous, but Chinese companies have also received $548.2 billion in contracts for projects in Africa. There are many private companies and more than one million Chinese laborers in Africa. Thus, Chinese aid and investment in Africa is mutually beneficial.

Western public opinion believes that China is only interested in Africa's resources and that Chinese investment in Africa is only focused on resource development. In fact, China's investment and assistance in Africa is comprehensive. In many African countries, Chinese investment is mainly focused on the manufacturing sector, which can help African countries truly industrialize. For example, Ethiopia is one of the poorest countries in Africa because it does not have much mineral resources. In recent years, China has helped Ethiopia to establish the Eastern Industrial Park. Some Chinese manufacturing companies have partnered with Ethiopian companies and helped them train many skilled workers. Ethiopia's economy has been growing at an annual rate of about 10 % for five consecutive years, making it a shining new star in Africa. Wang Wen, executive director of the Chongyang Institute at Renmin University of China, visited a Chinese-owned garment factory in Ethiopia. The monthly salary of local workers is about 700 yuan, the cost of producing garments is only 1/7 of that in China, and the quality of products is up to standard. Although accessories and sewing equipment need to be imported from China, Ethiopia has no restrictions on exports to Europe and the United States, offsetting the trade risks of exporting directly from China.

In Tanzania, the cooperation between Chinese and local enterprises has produced very positive results, providing much-needed materials such as steel and cement for local infrastructure construction, as well as many industrial manufactured products. In Dar es Salaam, the former capital of Tanzania, China J.D. United Manufacturing Corporation invested $16 million in a factory employing more than 1,600 local workers and exporting $18 million, mainly to the United States and Europe[4].

Western public opinion accuses China of not attaching conditions to its aid and investment in Africa, which is detrimental to the democratization of Africa and the transparency of public governance. The reality is that China's aid to Africa is predicated on the development of the African people and can promote economic growth, social progress, and improve the living and working conditions of African people across the board, from education to health. China's assistance to Africa over the past decade or so has been more effective than decades of international aid from Western countries.

In recent years, competition between Western countries and China in terms of aid to Africa has intensified. This has put new challenges and pressures on Chinese aid and investment, but it has also forced Chinese companies to do better and be more disciplined in Africa.

Western countries have become less "generous" in terms of foreign aid. Some Western policy researchers argue that emerging economies (such as China and Southeast Asian countries) have "graduated" and should no longer enjoy aid. There is also public opinion that since aid money has made African countries dependent, and many countries are caught in a vicious circle of more debt the more they develop, it is better to encourage private investment, as long as they create a friendly environment for foreign investment, they can attract more money. In addition, developed countries' aid to African countries has gradually deviated from the original purpose of development assistance, and increasingly emphasizes assistance in areas such as political reform, democracy, human rights, and private economic development, and makes these as prerequisites for aid. If recipient countries do not adjust their economic structure according to the requirements of the donors, it will be difficult to get more aid funds.

While aid funding is being scaled back, more and more Western countries are implementing pro bono aid programs, with a focus toward improving the quality of the population and a shift toward human resource development.

The Development Assistance Committee (DAC) of the OECD, the central body for coordinating Western aid policies, has in recent years continuously called on Western countries to pay attention to strengthening the institutions of recipient countries, improving their administrative capacity, and engaging in multifaceted policy coordination and dialogue. This means that the developed countries' development assistance will more deeply penetrate into the administrative decision-making process of the recipient countries.

The future of Chinese aid and investment in Africa faces triple challenges:

First, building discourse. Although aid from developed countries to developing countries is declining, they still have a lot of advantages in terms of the discourse of international aid. For example, their aid is mainly used to train human resources, although the money spent is not much, it has played a more effective role. The African political elites they have trained often occupy key positions in African countries, and these individuals have occasionally published articles in the Western mainstream media expressing skepticism about China's aid and investment in Africa, which have been widely reproduced in the Western media.

To counter these fallacies, China needs to focus on developing both hard and soft power. If we only focus on investing in hard power, although we could help African countries build their infrastructure efficiently, we might easily neglect public opinion and end up being misrepresented and criticized despite our efforts. In fact, without "software" building, it is difficult to make the modern infrastructure and modern industrial production equipment to maximize the benefits. When I was visiting Africa, I heard more than once that Africans expressed their concern about infrastructure management. After many modern hospitals and schools are handed over to Africans, if there is no qualified managers and technicians, the modern equipment may soon fall into the predicament of being left unattended. Therefore, in recent years, the Chinese government has been granting more scholarships to African students, and the number of African students enrolled in Chinese universities has been increasing, all of which has laid the foundation for enhancing China's soft power in Africa.

Second, there is a need for good coordination among Chinese enterprises investing in Africa. Chinese companies should unite closer, as if clenching fingers together into a fist to make a more powerful punch. Sometimes, in order to compete for the African market, the competition among Chinese enterprises is quite fierce, and the way some of them communicate with the African side is not proper, which sometimes even leads to aborted projects. To better promote Chinese aid and investment in Africa, the Chinese government must do a better job of coordination, and Chinese embassies in African countries should play more of a role in coordinating corporate activities. To this end, Chinese companies should cooperate with the government and build a good image of the Chinese government in Africa. Chinese aid and investment in Africa just gave a strong push to the short term development of Africa, but whether this aid can contribute to the sustainable development of Africa depends on whether Chinese enterprises can be modest and prudent, respect local customs and traditions, and bring the capital, technology and talents that are urgently needed for the development of the African people in the interest of the African people.

Chinese investments in Africa also face competition from the United States, Japan and European countries. With the rise of Africa, more and more countries and companies are setting their eyes on Africa. Africa is attracting rapid growth in foreign investment.

While global cross-border investment is declining, Africa remained one of the fastest growing regions for FDI in 2015, with a growth rate of 7 % and a higher number of jobs created than the global average for 2010–2014. In 2015, the United States carried out 96 investment projects in Africa, investing a total of $6.9 billion, making it the largest foreign investor in Africa that year. Traditional investors such as the UK, France and the UAE have also revived their interest in investing in Africa. In addition, the industrial mix of foreign investment in Africa has changed from a concentration in a few countries and resource-based industries to a more decentralized and diversified one, with business services, automotive, environmental technology and life sciences becoming new investment hotspots.

With China investing heavily in Africa and holding the Forum on China-Africa Cooperation with African countries, Japan has followed suit by holding the Tokyo International Conference on African Development (TICAD) and Abe's visit to Africa in 2016, which also stated that Japan would give $30 billion in aid to Africa, it is clear that Japan also wants to develop African markets and compete with China for influence in Africa.

China cannot prevent other countries and regions from being interested in the African market. Increased investment in Africa by the United States, European countries and Japan also has a positive effect on China.

On the one hand, the more investment Africa absorbs, the faster it will develop, the more stable the political situation will be, and the easier it will be for China's investment to pay for itself. With increased investment, African economies will grow rapidly, which will provide a bigger market in return. On the other hand, with more foreign companies investing in Africa, Chinese companies will feel more competitive pressure to do better in order to keep the African market. This will form a "push-back" mechanism, forcing Chinese companies to improve efficiency and improving their social image. Chinese companies will rely on superior products and services to convince Africans of the advantages of "Made in China".

China Should Expand Its Soft Power Influence

According to statistics published by U.S. research institutions, China's aid to Africa from 2000–2011 totaled $75 billion. This aid was so extensive that 51 of the 54 African countries received aid from China.

China's aid to African countries covers a wide range of areas, including debt relief, infrastructure development, education, health and so on. Undoubtedly, China's aid to African countries has brought many benefits to African countries, and has also led to significant investment by Chinese companies in Africa, which has boosted Africa's economic growth. 2012 saw growth rates in major global economics (including China) lower than in 2011, while the economies of sub-Saharan Africa grew strongly for several years in a row. The growth rate in 2012 was higher than in 2011. In addition to its direct aid to African countries, China has granted many concessional loans to African countries to finance their development. According to World Bank research, China's lending to African countries exceeds the World Bank's lending to African countries. 14 % of China's overseas investment from 2005–2010 went to African countries, creating jobs and boosting their economic development, and contributing to the rapid expansion of trade between China and Africa, which exceeded the value of trade between the two sides in 2010. The investament has created jobs in African countries, boosted their economic development, and contributed to the rapid expansion of trade between China and Africa, with trade volume exceeding $120 billion in 2010.

At the present developing rate, Africa is likely to become China's largest trading partner in the next 10 years.

China's aid and investment in Africa has not only boosted the economic development of African countries, but has also brought great benefits to China. First, aid and investment in Africa has eased the overcapacity of Chinese enterprises. Aid has promoted investment, and aid plus investment has improved the effectiveness of investment. China's aid to African countries for infrastructure construction has extended the service life of Chinese machinery and equipment. Then China's export market expanded when Africa developed. After the international financial crisis broke out in 2008, many developed countries were plagued by debt problems, economic growth stagnated, and the shrinking of traditional export markets seriously affected China's economic growth. China's aid and investment in developing countries such as Africa boosted China's exports to these regions, compensating for the negative impact of China's reduced exports to developed countries.

Of course, along with the rapid development of China-Africa economic and trade cooperation, there are also some "growing troubles". As China's national strength grows, African countries' expectations for China-Africa cooperation are increasing, but China's capacity is still insufficient. Chinese companies have not been out of the country for a long time, and they still lack experience in international operation, and they need to improve their localized operation and fulfill their social responsibility.

China's economic cooperation with Africa is an important guarantee for future global economic growth, and Chinese companies should respect and train their African employees with a long-term perspective. In the past, Chinese technicians have lived and eaten with their African counterparts, teaching them engineering and management methods by hand. We should revisit these successful experiences.

China's assistance to Africa benefits both sides, and Chinese business executives should see this. Moreover, countries around the world are optimistic about Africa's development prospects, and other BRICS countries are increasing their aid and investment in Africa, as are developed countries such as the United States. Chinese companies in Africa not only have to face the challenges of operating locally, but also competition from companies in other countries. For example, studies by U.S. research institutions show that U.S. aid to Africa is comparable to, and perhaps even higher in absolute terms than, that provided by China. In this highly competitive environment, Chinese companies should understand that our aid and investment in Africa is beneficial to the development of China's soft power and the long-term development of China-Africa cooperation.

Accelerate the Pace of Investment in Africa with RMB

China's investment in Africa has been very successful in recent years. China's infrastructure investments in Africa have contributed to the development of local economies, increased employment and greatly improved the quality of life of local people. Chinese companies have been making great strides in Africa, investing in many areas and expanding their business scope, bringing wealth and employment opportunities to local people while reaping huge profits. However, there are some pitfalls in their success, one of which is the habit of Chinese companies to invest in US dollars. If we don't accelerate our investment in Africa with RMB, the dollar investment may become the trigger of African debt crisis.

First, there is a huge exchange rate risk for U.S. dollar investments for China. The cyclical changes in the dollar exchange rate depend on the U.S. economic development cycle, and also on the Federal Reserve's judgment of the U.S. economic trend. However, the development cycle of the economies using dollar investments may not be synchronized with the U.S. economic development cycle, and in case of deviation, many countries using dollar investments will be "collateral damage" by the Fed's policies. In the 1970s, when the oil crisis led to the devaluation of the dollar, many Latin American and African countries borrowed large amounts of dollars to develop oil, which allowed them to enjoy a few years of great wealth.

However, in 1980, Federal Reserve Chairman Volcker used a sharp increase in interest rates to curb inflation, trying to get the U.S. economy out of the "Stagflation". As a result, countries that borrowed dollars to develop oil fell into the dollar debt trap one after another in the 1980s. As the interest rate on dollar debt rose sharply and the price of oil fell due to the spike in the dollar exchange rate, these countries became unable to make ends meet and had difficulty servicing their debts. As a result, many Latin American and African countries experienced debt crises in the mid-1980s, and in the 1990s, Southeast Asian countries pegged their currencies to the U.S. dollar and opened their financial markets to foreign investors. These dollar investments created an economic miracle in Southeast Asia. However, in the mid-1990s, the Federal Reserve decided that the Internet bubble was too big and raised interest rates to curb speculation in the financial markets, which also caused the dollar exchange rate to rise sharply and capital to leave Asia. As a result, a financial crisis broke out in Asia in 1997.

In the late 1960s, the Bretton Woods system, which was pegged to the U.S. dollar, exposed Western European countries to the negative effects of the dollar's exchange rate fluctuations. During a visit to Western Europe by former U.S. Treasury Secretary Connally, Western European leaders complained to him about the dangers of the dollar. Connally made the supreme statement, "The dollar is our currency, but it's your problem." This quote aptly describes the harm caused by the dollar hegemony to other countries. The investment in Africa with the dollar has not escaped this logic to this day.

Second, African countries face many difficulties in managing their dollar assets. Dollar investments are external debt for African countries, and the ability to service external debt depends on the ability of African countries to exchange their exports for foreign currency. African countries are generally resource-exporting countries, and their ability to exchange their exports depends on both the demand for raw materials in manufacturing countries and the trend of resource prices priced in U.S. dollars. When manufacturing demand is strong and demand for raw materials is strong, African countries benefit from high resource prices in international markets. However, since the outbreak of the international financial crisis in 2008, consumer markets in developed countries, which are often the final markets, have been sluggish, so demand for industrial manufactured goods in international markets became less robust. Sometimes, the prices of raw materials (including energy) might skyrocket and plummet, and that is mainly the result of financial speculation by investors in the international futures markets. Or, certain international geopolitical factors can cause investors in international financial markets to believe that future markets will be tight or oversupplied, which can also spur prices to rise or fall.

After 10 years of extremely accommodative monetary policy, the Federal Reserve and Western central banks have entered a process of tightening monetary policy. Although this process is long and developed countries may still phase in loose monetary policy, the overall tightening of monetary valves in developed countries should be the general trend in the future development of the world economy. This trend will cause the appreciation of the U.S. dollar and other currencies, and the price of assets priced in hard currencies such as the U.S. dollar rose, which will attract more investors. While the withdrawal of investors from the resource market will cause the price of resources to fall, African countries that borrowed U.S. dollar debt to develop resources will face great risks.

Many African countries do not have direct control over their foreign exchange reserves, making it difficult for them to manage their external debt. For example, member states of the Economic Community of West African States use a common currency, the West African franc, which was once pegged to the French franc and is now pegged to the euro, and under their agreement with France and the European Central Bank, their foreign exchange reserves are placed under the management of European countries, which is the price of having Europeans manage their currency for them. Therefore, when receiving foreign investment, the future repayment of foreign debt is an important issue. In normal times, the World Bank and the IMF also have to say something about the various ratios of debt borrowed by African countries in order to prevent debt mismatch.

In the event of a debt crisis, in order to rescue these debtor countries, these international institutions are likely to force the debtor countries, on behalf of their "major shareholders" (European and American countries), to offset their debts by selling off national assets or using national assets as collateral for larger foreign exchange loans to repay their debts. The IMF's harsh lending conditions have been criticized countless times by developing countries, but when it comes to crises, these rules are still tried and true. Much of China's investment in Africa is denominated in U.S. dollars, and African countries will have to repay in dollars in the future. If the above phenomenon occurs in the future, China will be blamed for the debt crisis and become the "scapegoat" when African countries are unable to repay their debts due to the currency mismatch of their foreign debt. Therefore, it is necessary to switch from USD investment to RMB investment from now on.

Third, there are many benefits of investing in Africa in RMB. (1) Chinese companies can avoid exchange rate risks by investing in RMB and can also unify the two domestic and foreign markets, which is beneficial for their comprehensive development planning. (2) The Chinese government can encourage African countries to accept Chinese companies to purchase their resources and other products in RMB, which can promote the internationalization of RMB. Now that the RMB has been officially included in the IMF's SDR currency basket, it has become part of the foreign exchange reserves of some African countries, and they will be willing to accept RMB to settle their exports to China. (3) Once African countries receive RMB, they can use it to pay for Chinese companies' investment projects in Africa, and the remainder can also be used to invest in China's bond market or to invest profitably in offshore RMB markets such as Europe. (4) After African countries use a large amount of RMB, even if there is a temporary debt service matching problem, there will not be a currency crisis. As the RMB is China's sovereign currency, China can reschedule and restructure the RMB debts of African countries, which is just a delay in debt repayment and a little bit more interest. China can explain to African countries the benefits of borrowing in RMB and encourage them to accept RMB investments.

On the issue of RMB internationalization, China used to focus on developed countries in Europe and the US, with bilateral trade with these countries settled in RMB being an important part of RMB internationalization. However, as Chinese companies' investments in Africa and countries along the "Belt and Road" continue to grow, the "RMBization" of these investments should also become an important part of RMB internationalization, and over time, a more important part.

In summary, Africa has tremendous opportunities for development. With the growth of Chinese investment in Africa, the "forgotten corner of history" has become a sought-after investment destination in the second decade of the 21st century. China needs to increase coordination between government and business, and Chinese companies must continue to improve their investments and operations in Africa to retain their advantage in the region. On the other hand, if this race to increase investment in Africa forms a healthy competition, it may allow Africa to emerge from the shadow of needing international aid and embark on a sustainable development path, becoming a new engine of growth for the world economy.

Notes

1 BAHUTU MANIFESTO (1957), https://www.blackpast.org/global-african-history/bahutu-manifesto-1957/
2 Human Rights Watch and the International Federation of Human Rights Leagues (FIDH), Leave None to Tell the Story: Genocide in Rwanda (New York: Human Rights Watch, 1999).
3 Amy Chua, *World on Fire: How Exporting Free Market Democracy Breeds Ethnic Hatred and Global Instability*, Knopf Doubleday Publishing Group, 2004
4 Roosing/J.D. United Sustainability Report 2017, http://www.roohsing.com.tw/data/company_report/15622972407IXNX.pdf

13

Building a Community of Shared Future

I have been invited to make a speech at an international forum in Switzerland to explain China's proposal of building up a community of share future for mankind in the summer of 2019. So on the basis of this speech, I wrote a series of papers that try to explain the reasons and philosophy behind China's proposal, and how we can envisage to reach this objective by concretes means. I hope that by reading these analyses, people may have a clearer picture of China's "grand strategy" in the world.

The dilemma facing the world today is the apparent contradiction between the global issues and the current solutions following the framework of the nation-state. For example, climate change affects all countries, but some countries do not contribute significantly to climate change, yet they suffer from its harmful effects. Another example is the spread of international terrorism in various countries and the difficulty for many countries to contain the growth of terrorist forces on their own. When we try to solve these problems within the framework of nation-states, many of them are insoluble. How can we find solutions to these global problems and how can countries reach a consensus to solve them? International public opinion should pay attention to China's idea of building a community of common destiny or of shared future, which can be seen as a Chinese solution to global problems.

A Community of shared future Breaks the Shackles of National Groups

Throughout human history, there have been countless wars and conflicts between different countries and groups of countries fighting for power. In the 20th century alone, there were two world wars, World War I, which killed more than 10 million people, and World War II, which killed nearly 70 million people and injured countless others. After World War II, the two superpowers, the United States and the Soviet Union, faced each other in a bipolar world, and the Cold War began. Although nuclear deterrence prevented the outbreak of a new world war, the bipolar world prevented communication between countries.

After the end of the Cold War, with the development of globalization, the transnational flow of capital, technology, information and people has accelerated, and the degree of interdependence among countries has deepened. A bond of interest has been formed between countries, and each country must maintain this bond and maintain an international order that everyone is willing to accept in order to maximize its own interests.

In the bipolar world, countries belong to different state groups such as G20, and there is a hierarchy within each group. The leading states not only have the power to dominate the other member states, but they also have an unequal relationship with each other, and the hegemonic states enjoy great rights and interests through the division of labor within the state group. Waging wars is a form of fighting for redistribution of power, and the purpose of wars is either to break the balance of power within the group or to gain some member states from other groups in order to gain more benefits.

However, after entering the era of globalization, peaceful competition has become mainstream, replacing extreme means such as "hot war" to achieve national development goals. The economic interdependence of countries contributes to the de-escalation of the international situation, and countries can also maintain and regulate interdependence and safeguard common interests through the international system and multiple global mechanisms.

The outbreak of the international financial crisis in 2008 brought about a deeper understanding of the solidarity of the global economy. In 2000, the finance ministers of ASEAN countries and China, Japan and South Korea (10+3) signed the Chiang Mai Agreement — after the 1997 Asian financial crisis had affected all East Asian countries, this agreement is the most important institutional outcome of Asian monetary and financial cooperation. When the international financial crisis broke out and the global economy fell into recession, the

G20 summit adopted a decision to implement a "stimulus package" to prevent a return of protectionism and prevent a precipitous depression in the global economy. It is conceivable that if countries do not cooperate with each other during this crisis, but rather try to implement beggar-thy-neighbor policies and transfer the crisis outward, the crisis may lead to the formation of national blocs, as in the Great Depression of the 1920s and 1930s, and may even lead to a world war, bringing disaster to human society again.

Of course, there are many people in the world who prefer to see things in a dichotomous way. In the face of China's rapid rise, some U.S. strategists have begun to worry that the U.S.-China relationship will fall into a "Thucydides trap". In other words, they believe that out of fear of losing its hegemonic status, the United States might find ways to join other countries in besieging China, which would inevitably lead to Chinese resistance and a huge conflict between the United States and China. But that is not what China's leaders think.

In early 2017, during his visit to the United Nations headquarters in Geneva, President Xi Jinping said, "Countries should foster partnerships based on dialogue, non-confrontation, and non-alliance. Major countries should respect each other's core interests and major concerns, manage their differences, and build a new model of relations characterized by non-conflict, non-confrontation, mutual respect, and mutually-beneficial cooperation. As long as we communicate and treat each other with sincerity, the 'Thucydides trap' can be avoided"[1].

In 2011, the white paper "China's Peaceful Development" proposed to seek new connotations of common interests and values of mankind through the new perspective of "community of common destiny"[2]. The report of the 18th Party Congress proposed—"in promoting mutually beneficial cooperation, we should raise awareness about human beings sharing a community of common destiny. A country should accommodate the legitimate concerns of others when pursuing its own interests; and it should promote common development of all countries when advancing its own development"[3].

In late March 2013, Xi Jinping made his first visit to Russia after assuming the presidency. In a speech at the Moscow Institute of International Relations, he proposed the concept of a community of common destiny. in late September 2015, during the 70th anniversary summit series of the United Nations, Xi Jinping visited the UN headquarters in New York and delivered a speech entitled "Join hands to build a new partnership for win-win cooperation and build a community of common destiny", which was the first time that China's top leader proposed the concept of a community of common destiny on the occasion of a major international organization. This is the first time that China's top leader has put forward the concept of a community of common destiny and explained in detail its core ideas in a major international organization. This is reminiscent of 1974, when Deng Xiaoping led the Chinese delegation to the sixth special session of the UN General Assembly, where he comprehensively elaborated on the "Three Worlds" theory and the principles of China's foreign relations.

The world today faces many global problems: food security, resource shortages, climate change, cyberattacks, population explosion, environmental pollution, epidemics, transnational crime, etc. These global non-traditional security issues pose a serious challenge to the international order and the survival of mankind. Regardless of where people are located, what their beliefs are, or what their economic conditions are, they all face these problems, and all of humanity must work together to find solutions to them. Therefore, China has proposed the idea of a community of common destiny, which has received the attention of international public opinion and has gradually gained the recognition of international organizations and been included in the resolutions of the United Nations.

The *Datong* World Is the Ideal Form of Human Society in Chinese Culture

The concept of building a community of common destiny embodies a profound Chinese cultural connotation. During the Spring and Autumn Period and the Warring States Period, Chinese philosophers already began to discuss how to build an ideal society. The Confucian classic "The Book of Rites" describes the ideal society as "*Datong*" (common good).

> When the Grand course was pursued, a public and common spirit ruled all under the sky; they chose men of talents, virtue, and ability; their words were sincere, and what they cultivated was harmony. Thus men did not love their parents only, nor treat as children only their own sons. A competent provision was secured for the aged till their death, employment for the able-bodied, and the means of growing up to the young. They showed kindness and compassion to widows, orphans, childless men, and those who were disabled by disease, so that they were all sufficiently maintained. Males had their proper work, and females had their homes. (They accumulated) articles (of value), disliking that they should be thrown away upon the ground, but not wishing to keep them for their own gratification. (They laboured) with their strength, disliking that it should not be exerted, but not exerting it (only) with a view to their own advantage. In this way (selfish) schemings were repressed and found no development.

> Robbers, filchers, and rebellious traitors did not show themselves, and hence the outer doors remained open, and were not shut. This was (the period of) what we call the *datong* (the Grand Union/the common good)[4].

During the Spring and Autumn Period, wars between vassal states were incessant, small states were dying and large states were struggling for supremacy, and the ideal of building a "commonwealth" reflected people's hope for peace in a chaotic world.

The Book of Rite also speaks of "xiaokang"(well-off), the social order that needs to be regulated by institutions and rituals before a "common good" society can be achieved. In Confucianism, "Xiaokang" represents a state of relative stability and satisfaction of the basic needs of the people, a concept that has been applied to the practice of socialism in modern China.

The "world for the common good" mentioned in *the Book of Rite* means that the world is the world of all people and is shared by all. The realization of "the world for the common good" will eliminate the evils caused by selfishness, fill the society with light, and make the people happy. When the Chinese say that a person is public and selfless, it is also a tribute to his personal qualities. Chinese traditional culture emphasizes that people should not think only for themselves, but also for others, for society, and for nature; only when there is a country can there be a family, only when the country is safe can the people be safe, only when the country is rich can the people be rich, and only when the society is developed can the individual be developed.

This cultural tradition of China determines the China's orientation of development. Throughout history, both reformists and revolutionaries, such as Kang Youwei and Sun Yat-sen, has always set their goals to build a world of common good. Because of this cultural tradition, the concept of social development with communism as the ultimate goal was quickly accepted by the Chinese after Marxism entered China.

Nowadays, the world has entered the era of globalization, and China cannot be complacent about its domestic well-off, because its development also depends on the external environment. At present, the construction of socialism with Chinese characteristics has entered a new stage, and China's national power has greatly increased, therefore, China can not only "be good to itself", but also wants to "be good to the rest of the world". In other words, China can influence the development of the world — by sharing China's development experience with others, developing countries can all enjoy the dividends of development. In an era when global interests are intermingled and China's development is profoundly affected by globalization, China can only develop better if all countries in the world develop in a balanced way.

Improving the Global Governance

The challenges to building a community of common destiny come from five main dimensions: economic, political, security, cultural and ecological.

In the economic field, only by cooperating with each other and giving full play to their respective comparative advantages can different countries achieve complementarity. Through closer cooperation between countries in the southern and northern hemispheres, countries could jointly promote the globalization in a fairer and more balanced direction, and they could move world toward common prosperity, common wealth and common progress.

In the political sphere, all countries in the world should respect each other, consult on an equal footing, live together peacefully, and jointly promote global governance in a more democratic, just and balanced direction. The world's major powers should share responsibilities, consult together and govern these global issues together—the big powers should not form new blocs, tear each other down, or undermine international cooperation.

In the field of security, countries should refrain from infringing on each other, and they are supposed to respect the right of each country to independently handle its own security affairs. Great powers should refrain from interfering in the internal affairs of other countries and avoid intervention or threat of force. At the same time, all countries should promote multiple forms of security cooperation to maintain regional and global security and peace.

In the field of culture, China has always advocated harmony and differences under the primary theme of peace. China advocates that all countries should exchange and learn from each other, and promote and protect the cultural diversity, pluralism and nationalism of all countries and ethnic groups in the world. China hopes that all countries in the world will adopt a spirit of openness and tolerance, inheritance and innovation, and encourage "the blossoming of a hundred flowers"(百花齐放) and "the contention of a hundred schools of thought"(百家争鸣).

In the field of ecology, we all live on the same planet, and if we destroy it, all of humanity cannot survive. All countries in the world should help each other and work together to promote environmental protection, jointly address the global ecological and environmental crisis and climate change crisis, build a world of "unity of man and heaven", jointly follow the path of green development, and jointly take care of the global home on which human beings depend for survival.

To solve these global problems and build a community of shared future, it is necessary to form a corresponding international system and international system. China supports the existing UN system and actively participates in various activities of the UN. China hopes that the UN will play a more active role in global governance. China actively cooperates with UN peacekeeping operations. In fact, China is the country with the largest number of peacekeeping troops among the permanent members of the UN Security Council. China supports the WTO and the multilateral trading system, and actively organizes and participates in the regional multilateral trading system that runs parallel to the world multilateral trading system. China is a strong supporter of the Paris Agreement and actively cooperates with the global plan to reduce CO2 emissions. It can be said that China is at the forefront of the world in developing renewable energy and an environment-friendly eco-economy.

When the existing international system fails to solve the current global problems, China is also actively exploring other ways of international cooperation. For example, realizing that the World Bank could not meet the needs of developing countries for infrastructure development, China initiated the establishment of the Asian Infrastructure Investment Bank (AIIB), which received positive responses even from European countries, to make up for the shortcomings of the existing system.

China does not want to create a new international system to compete with the existing one, but it does intend to make up for the shortcomings of the existing international system and provide services that the existing one cannot satisfy. This echoes Mao Zedong's idea of "walking on two legs" in "On the Ten Major Relationships"[5]. When the objective conditions are not sufficient, China cannot sit and wait for the pie to fall from the sky, but should strive to build various mechanisms that can promote the development of the community of common destiny.

The "Belt and Road" Initiative Promotes the Construction of a Community of share future

It is not enough to have an ambitious vision, but also to have a concrete plan for implementation. China's "One Belt, One Road" initiative (i.e., the cooperative initiative to build the "Silk Road Economic Belt" and the "21st Century Maritime Silk Road") is a solution for building a community of human destiny as a solution.

After the "Belt and Road" initiative (BRI) was put forward, from 2013 to 2018, the total trade between China and countries along the "Belt and Road" has exceeded US$6 trillion, and Chinese enterprises have invested more than US$90 billion in the countries along the "Belt and Road", with an average annual growth rate of 5.2 %. Direct investment by Chinese enterprises in countries along the Belt and Road exceeded US$90 billion, with an average annual growth rate of 5.2 %. The total value of new contracts signed by countries along the Belt and Road exceeds US$600 billion, with an average annual growth rate of 11.9 %. 126 countries and 29 international organizations have signed the "Belt and Road" cooperation document with China.

The "Belt and Road" initiative has been questioned by some Western countries' public opinion. However, the fact is that Chinese enterprises have not only built up a good corporate image and brand image, but also developed foreign markets in the process of participating in the "Belt and Road" construction. For example, in recent years, Chinese companies have cooperated with Kazakhstan to build a lot of infrastructure, such as roads and railroads, which have greatly improved the local transportation conditions, and also opened up the local automobile market. Some Chinese auto companies see this business opportunity, not only to export the China-made cars into the Kazakhstan market, but also to use the auto parts shipped from China to assemble new products suitable for the local market demand.

Among the projects related to the Belt and Road, many of them are carried out through bilateral or multilateral cooperation. China cooperates with foreign governments in financing, and Chinese enterprises play the role of project contractors and builders. For example, Bangladesh is an important country along the "Belt and Road" route. Chinese companies have been contracted to build seven bridges in Bangladesh, of which the Padma Bridge is a huge and very successful project. The Padma River is located in the north of Bangladesh, and the torrent is so strong that it takes at least 5 hours for local residents to cross it by ferry. Previously, the Bangladeshi government had also requested assistance from European companies such as France and Germany to build the bridge, but these companies eventually gave up the project after doing trials because of the difficulty of the bridge design and construction. So, the China Railway Bridge Bureau took up the challenge, and decided to drive more than 100 steel pipes with a circumference of 3 meters diagonally into the riverbed at a depth of 100 meters to anchor the bridge that can resiste the floods. Local residents have high hopes for this project, calling the Padma Bridge "the bridge of dreams".

Many of the infrastructure projects built by Chinese companies in Central Asian countries and Southeast Asian countries have become local landmarks. Whether it is roads, ports, or urban sewage treatment systems, these projects have greatly improved the local infrastructure and living conditions of local people. For example, in Malaysia, Chinese companies have built sewage treatment systems that have improved the local environment and the living and working conditions of the residents, and the real estate prices around the project have risen rapidly. These projects have greatly enhanced the visibility of Chinese enterprises abroad and the prestige of China in the countries along the Belt and Road.

The projects related to the BRI also have huge benefits for Chinese companies, employees and even all Chinese people. For example, China's exports of raw materials, machinery and equipment, and daily necessities to countries along the Belt and Road have been increasing significantly as the projects progress. The global economy has been sluggish since the outbreak of the international financial crisis, but China's exports have recovered slightly after a major downturn. In the first decade of the 21st century, China's economic takeoff was directly related to the rapid growth of international trade. If world demand for Chinese products shrinks significantly, then China's future economic growth, employment stability and social development will encounter new difficulties. The countries along the Belt and Road provide new markets for China and open up a new world for Chinese exports, which is very important for China's economic development.

Guangdong Province, for example, is the largest exporting province in China. After the financial crisis, Guangdong Province's exports to traditional markets (mainly developed countries in Europe and the United States) have been slowing down. However, with the introduction of the BRI, Guangdong's exports to countries along the "Belt and Road" have grown rapidly. Guangdong's exports to countries along the Maritime Silk Road is now experiencing an annual growth rate of over 18 %. The growth rate of Guangdong Province's investment in this region is even faster, with an annual growth rate of about 30 %. Guangdong's cross-border investment has greatly boosted international trade and exports, as well as the economic development of other countries.

For individuals, participating in the "Belt and Road" project has enabled Chinese young people to exercise themselves, broaden their horizons and enrich their experience, and laid a solid foundation for China's deeper involvement in global activities and global governance in the future. For Chinese young people and the whole nation, participating in the Belt and Road construction is a valuable experience.

For Chinese enterprises, the "Belt and Road" has not only maintained their international competitive advantage, but also greatly enhanced their ability to open up new markets. Some Chinese enterprises have also made great gains in contracting projects, establishing brands and training employees. Many landmark buildings in countries along the "Belt and Road" are designed by Chinese designers. For architects, it is very important to participate in the design of landmark projects in the countries along the Belt and Road, and to leave a strong mark in history — the best way to realize one's artist dream.

Revitalizing the Silk Road Provides a Solution to the Problem of Dealing with Chaotic Times

The revival of the Silk Road offers a new window into the world and a solution to the problems of a troubled world. For a long time, many countries in the 30° N region have been mired in war or democratic revolutions. But whether it is democratic revolution or war, in these countries the need for human survival comes first. For example, after 30 years of war in Afghanistan, the country needs to start from almost zero, from public infrastructure to livelihood economy to industrial restructuring, but Afghanistan cannot restore productive order and redevelop its economy quickly on its own. Who can help? The U.S. military presence in Afghanistan has maintained somehow its social order, but the U.S. is not capable of reorganizing the country's economic production either. The Belt and Road Initiative can help these countries revive their economies and stabilize the lives of their inhabitants. The Chinese thinking is that only when social and economic development is achieved and the local population is given a better vision of the future will they have something to look forward to and begin to pursue a new life. Only when the local people are pursuing a new life will the society gradually stabilize and the economy will have a basis for development.

After the end of World War I, developed countries in Europe and the United States have long supported some forces in the Arab region to combat and contain others, which also brought about a lot of war, and the people of the Arab region have thus developed a sense of dislike for Western countries, which has led to some obstacles for Western companies to enter these regions. But China does not have such historical baggage, and the people of the Arab region are welcoming China, especially Chinese companies. The development of the Silk Road Economic Belt could lead to rapid development agreements between China and the countries along the route. From this perspective, the Belt and Road Initiative has special significance in promoting the economic development and national renaissance of the region. From a global perspective, this region is also a densely populated area. For example, Pakistan and India are populous countries; Iran, Syria, Iraq, Egypt, Libya and other countries are still populous countries despite the large number of deaths caused by wars. The total population of the Middle East and North Africa is more than 600 million, which is more than the population of the entire European Union. With a huge market, there will be a huge demand. The construction of the Silk Road Economic Belt can develop local demand to a great extent and open up a huge market.

More than 10 years have passed since the outbreak of the international financial crisis in 2008, but the impact of the crisis is still there, especially for the developed countries in the United States and Europe. In this context, many developed countries have no time to take care of the emerging economies. China is now the world's largest manufacturing country, with not only a complete industrial manufacturing system, but also ample capital and advanced production technology. Therefore, when China joins the economic reconstruction and economic development of these regions in a cooperative posture, it is warmly welcomed. Therefore, China's revitalization of the Silk Road also provides a solution to deal with the difficult problems of a troubled world.

Building the Silk Road Economic Belt Is in Line with China's Geopolitical Interests

Why is building the Silk Road Economic Belt important for China? Because it is in China's geopolitical interest. China is a land power whose borders and their extensions are particularly important for its defense security and economic development. However, in modern period, China has been threatened mainly from the southeast, from the sea — the Opium Wars, the Sino-Japanese War, and the Japanese War of Aggression against China, all of which originated at sea. But as long as the western and central parts of China are stable, China can withstand the pressure from the southeast and from the sea. For example, during World War II, the Japanese army quickly occupied the coastal areas of China, and the Kuomintang (KMT) government kept retreating to the central region, finally retreating to Chongqing. Despite the war power of the Japanese army at that time, the KMT government was able to resist the Japanese invasion because of the Yunnan-Myanmar Highway and Indian support to the west. As we can see from historical experience, the construction of the Silk Road Economic Belt helps to consolidate China's great rear area, through which China can connect the vast Eurasian continent and use the whole continent as a support for China's continued development. This is China's geopolitical advantage, its geographical advantage.

China is a major foreign exchange reserve country, with more than $3 trillion in foreign exchange reserves. How to make better use of this resource is a challenge for China, but it is also an ace in the hand. The debt of economies such as the United States, the European Union and Japan is unsustainable in the long run. For example, Japan's government debt is over 200 % of its GDP, and the U.S. government's debt has reached about 105 % of U.S. GDP. In the European Union, although the debt to GDP ratio of the eurozone countries has not yet exceeded 100 %, it is also approaching, and some EU member states have very high debt, which has exceeded 120 % of GDP, or even close to 140 %. Therefore, several sovereign debt crises have erupted in Europe in the past few years. According to historical experience, when a country's debt is too high, the ultimate solution is to rely on inflation to deflate the debt in real terms, which is the best way to "peacefully default". If inflation occurs, the purchasing power of these hard currencies in our hands will be significantly reduced. From this perspective, if all these developed countries reduce their debt through inflation in the future, then China's foreign currency holdings will shrink. How to deal with this prospect? The only way at this point is to use existing foreign exchange reserves to better invest abroad and diversify future risk.

If China uses its foreign exchange reserves to help other countries develop, direct investment in economic projects in those countries may be a better option. This is because the return on direct investment is much greater than the return on bond investment. In addition, China has now become a major foreign direct investment country, and the amount of China's foreign direct investment has exceeded the amount of foreign direct investment received by China, which used to be the largest destination country for foreign direct investment. Taking foreign exchange reserves for direct investment not only increases the revenue but also helps other countries to develop better, and at the same time cultivates China's export market, making the relationship between China and these recipient countries a win-win model. Therefore, using the huge foreign exchange reserves to promote the economic construction of countries along the "Belt and Road" is a major strategic choice for China, by which China could promote the development of the world economy and solve the shortage of demand in the world economy.

International System Building Could Benefit the Construction of the Silk Road Economic Belt

Russia is also a country on the Silk Road Economic Belt. Russia has an ambitious plan to build the "Eurasian Economic Union", that is, to re-establish economic ties between Russia and Central Asian countries: to build a common market, to open up production chains between them, to further expand the economy, to reduce costs, and to ensure the future development of the region. It can be said that the Eurasian Economic Union is very important for the development of Russia and Central Asian countries.

After the outbreak of the Russia-Ukraine crisis in 2014, Russia was subjected to economic sanctions by Europe and the United States, and its strategic focus shifted more to Asia. Strengthening ties with China and Asian markets is the most reasonable way for Russia to cope with the economic sanctions imposed by Europe and the United States. In this context, the construction of the Silk Road Economic Belt is beneficial for the development of all countries in Eurasia. President Vladimir Putin has publicly stated that Russia welcomes China's plan to build the Silk Road Economic Belt, that Russia will participate more actively in its construction, and that Russia hopes to connect the Eurasian Economic Union with China's Silk Road Economic Belt. The construction of the Russian-Chinese high-speed railroad provides new possibilities for the connection between the Chinese Silk Road Economic Belt and the Russian Eurasian Economic Union.

The Shanghai Cooperation Organization (SCO) can become an important coordination mechanism for building the Silk Road Economic Belt. In terms of the general development environment, the current international environment is very favorable for China to promote the construction of the Silk Road Economic Belt.

To certain extent, the construction of a new international system is very useful to promote the Belt and Road Initiative. Since the outbreak of the international financial crisis, there has been a growing trend for emerging economies to unite and work together on development plans. In 2015, the BRICS New Development Bank (NDB) was established to create a common financial safety net to provide financing for developing countries.

In 2013, China initiated the establishment of the Asian Infrastructure Investment Bank (AIIB) because of the huge demand for infrastructure development in Asia and the inability of the existing international development institutions—both the World Bank and the Asian Development Bank—to meet the needs of Asian countries in terms of infrastructure investment. The process of China's initiative to establish the AIIB did not go smoothly either, but during the formal process of its establishment, not only Asian countries but also many European countries actively applied to join, and eventually more than 50 countries became founding members of the AIIB, which is as large and enthusiastic as the situation after the end of World War II when the United States initiated the establishment of the Bretton Woods system. In terms of the number of founding members, the AIIB even surpasses the size of the Bretton Woods system. From this perspective, it is clear that China's appeal in the international economic arena is still very strong, and it is also clear that the idea proposed by China caters to the needs of many countries. In fact, since the outbreak of the international financial crisis, many countries are expecting to find a way out of the downturn.

Therefore, immediately after China proposed the initiative, it received support from many countries. In addition to Japan, the most prominent allies of the United States, including Australia and Canada, are members of the Asian Infrastructure Investment Bank.

This shows that China's initiative to strengthen infrastructure development has a broad base. People do believe that building infrastructure projects can boost the world economy out of its current sluggish state. The countries' enthusiasm for economic revitalization coincides with China's BRI. In 2014, while attending the Shanghai Cooperation Organization summit in Dushanbe, Tajikistan, Xi Jinping and Russian President Vladimir Putin actively discussed cooperation on high-speed rail and satellite navigation systems, as well as joint development of long-range wide-body passenger aircraft and heavy helicopters, and joint energy development. New progress has been made, and cooperation between the two countries in technology, science and economy has entered a broader field. In the future, China and Russia will cooperate more in the construction of the Silk Road Economic Belt, and the construction of the Silk Road Economic Belt will bring rich economic benefits to the countries along the route, which will significantly change the pattern of the world economic development.

The Reconstruction of the Silk Road Is an Important Symbol of the Revival of Chinese Civilization

Since China proposed the "One Belt, One Road" initiative, the scale of China's outbound investment has grown rapidly, and in 2015, for the first time, China's outward foreign direct investment (OFDI) exceeded that of foreign direct investment, with the "One Belt, One Road" initiative driving significant growth in outbound investment. Projects along the Belt and Road Initiative have become the focus of China's OFDI.

China's economy has contributed significantly to world economic growth, and after the outbreak of the international financial crisis in 2008, China became the main force driving world economic growth, and now China still contributes 1/3 of the growth share to the global economy every year. China's contribution to world economic growth is even greater if we include the rapid growth of Chinese outward foreign direct investment over the years. But as China's outbound investment grows, so does the risk of investment. China has to make a more accurate assessment of the investment risks in the countries along the Belt and Road, so it could avoid and resolve the risks in the future development and make China's outbound investment sustainable.

1. Risk of infrastructure investment. In recent years, there have been many projects in which Chinese companies have traded resource development for infrastructure investment overseas. In other words, some countries rich in natural and energy resources have used their own resources as capital, in exchange for Chinese companies' investment in local infrastructure. Chinese companies have been given the right to develop some local mines and oil fields for a period of time to compensate for the investment in infrastructure projects. However, resource development is a long-term project, and the payback period for infrastructure investments is also long, which involves many investment risks.

When Chinese companies have to take into account the fluctuation of resource prices in the international market to develop resources, how can they hedge the risk of falling resource prices? Five years ago, when Chinese companies started to develop resources overseas, the prices of resources in the international market were very good and energy prices were high. The investment-to-revenue (ROI) ratio for developing resources was very cost-effective, and Chinese companies made a lot of money developing overseas resources. However, since 2014, resource prices in the international market have plumped and may remain low in the near future. Chinese companies are investing in resource development projects with a 20- or 30-year expectation, and future resource prices in the international market may not allow these overseas resource development projects to break even.

Resource development and infrastructure construction are both long-cycle investment projects that require a stable political environment. Therefore, Chinese companies also need to deal with possible political risks. How do you ensure that project contracts can still be fulfilled when there is a change of government in certain countries? China's investments in Latin America and Asia have encountered difficulties in the performance of contracts due to changes in government (some projects were later agreed to continue after negotiations between the parties). But this is a reminder that we need to sign bilateral investment protection agreements with some countries along the Belt and Road to ensure that contracts are honored in the event of a change of government. We can also use mechanisms such as BRICS to set up commercial arbitration institutions to resolve such problems through international arbitration.

2. Risk of hard currency and weak local currency. Chinese companies generally invest overseas using hard currencies, such as U.S. dollars and euros. However, the gains obtained are often settled in the local currency of the recipient country. When the local currency depreciates, Chinese enterprises, as overseas investors, have to bear the loss of falling exchange rate; as the investment is borrowed in hard currency, there may also be the risk of sudden increase in debt. The Fed's increase in interest rates has caused the dollar to rise, leading to currency depreciation of up to 20 % or even 30 % in some countries. If a Chinese company borrows dollars for investment, it is likely to fall into a debt crisis as a result.

One way to hedge exchange rate risk is to denominate in RMB. If Chinese companies invest in infrastructure projects and resource development projects overseas that are denominated in RMB, it can both promote the internationalization of the RMB and, to a certain extent, mitigate the price risks faced by Chinese companies.

3. Risk of external shocks. The scale of trade and investment between emerging economies and developed economies far exceeds the scale of trade and investment between emerging economies. Therefore, emerging economies are very sensitive to changes in developed economies, and macroeconomic policy changes in developed economies can have a huge spillover impact on emerging economies.

The "Belt and Road" ends in Europe. European countries have been in recent years between deflation and recession, some countries have also broken out of the debt crisis. If the European economy is trapped in this vicious circle for a long time, the enthusiasm of countries along the Belt and Road to invest in transportation and other infrastructure will be affected, as well as the enthusiasm of enterprises to invest. In order to deal with this situation, it is necessary to strengthen trade and investment activities between emerging economies, so that they can become important markets for each other, in order to offset the impact of changes in the markets of developed countries.

4. Geopolitical risks. The Silk Road Economic Belt runs through Europe and Asia. The countries along the route have different cultures, races, religions and political systems, and the geopolitical landscape is complicated. Some countries not along the Silk Road Economic Belt are also actively involved in the affairs of this region for their own interests.

The British geopolitician Mackinder famously said, "Who rules East Europe commands the Heartland; who rules the Heartland commands the World-Island; who rules the World-Island commands the world"[6]. Since the 19th century, the hegemonic powers of the world have been maritime hegemons. If the New Asia-Europe Continental Bridge is established and the interests of Europe and Asia are integrated, the role of maritime hegemony will decline and the center of gravity of the world will shift. The United States has also proposed the "New Silk Road" plan, hoping to intervene in the development of Central and South Asian countries, but with little success. Given the volatile situation in the Middle East, we have reason to be concerned about the future development of Central Asian countries. How to deal with the negative effects of social unrest in these countries? The Shanghai Cooperation Organization may be able to play a greater role in ensuring security and stability in the region.

5. The risk brought by the lack of government authority. China follows the principle of "non-interference in other countries' internal affairs" — it generally only negotiates and signs agreements with the central government in terms of foreign investments. However, there are many countries along the Belt and Road that have both ethnic and tribal conflicts, religious conflicts, and conflicts of local interest groups. In many countries, the central government does not have a lot of authority, and the relationship with local governments and tribal groups is very special. Good coordination and balanced distribution of interests are the basis for successful investment. For example, the Myitsone hydropower project in Myanmar was shelved, which was invested by China, and it might partly be responsible for the conflict between the central government and the Kachin people.

In the process of promoting the "Belt and Road" projects, it is necessary to have good relations not only with the central government of the recipient countries, but also with the local or tribal leaders where the projects are located. The "Belt and Road" initiative is not only the cause of the Chinese government and enterprises, but also the cause of Chinese civil society. We need to strengthen public diplomacy, strengthen communication at all levels, build good public relations, do a good job of communication, weave a huge social network, and pave the way for China's investment overseas.

The "Belt and Road" initiative has promoted the rapid growth of China's outbound investment, but we need to keep a clear head and do a good job of risk assessment of projects in countries along the route, so as to lay the foundation for the sustainable development of China's outbound investment. The Silk Road Economic Belt can become a new driving force to stimulate world economic growth, which is also an important symbol of the revival of Chinese civilization.

Historically, the Silk Road was an important trade route, serving as a link between the cultural exchanges between the East and the West. Chinese tea, silk, porcelain, etc. all went to the world through this route. After the Song Dynasty, the porcelain trade developed rapidly. Since porcelain was heavy and fragile, there were many difficulties in transporting it by land, so from then on, a large amount of porcelain and other goods were shipped to the Middle East and Europe through the Maritime Silk Road, which gradually became the main road from China to the Western countries. Many foreign species were introduced to China through the Silk Road, such as wheat, sesame, spinach, grapes, corn, potatoes, tomatoes, etc. Therefore, the Silk Road was very important to the social development of China.

In terms of culture, it was through the Silk Road that Xuanzang went to India to obtain scriptures of Buddhism. In Dunhuang, an important city on the Silk Road, a large number of valuable texts and historical documents were found, which for various historical reasons were scattered around the world, and Dunhuang studies have become a prominent discipline in international academia. As you can see, the Silk Road is an important cultural link.

The construction of the Silk Road Economic Belt has revitalized the ancient Chinese trade route to the West, which is of great significance to the revival of Chinese civilization. From 1868 to 1872, German geographer Baron von Richthofen visited China 7 times, and wrote a book titled "China: Ergebnisse eigener Reisen und darauf gegründeter Studien". He mentioned in this book the concept of Silk Road for the first time. He believed that the Silk Road was an important trade route between China and Western countries, and the reason why it was called the "Silk Road" was because silk was the main trade commodity at the time, a medium of exchange, and a link between East and West.

Ferdinand von Richthofen greatly appreciated the importance of the Silk Road in the history of human civilizational exchanges. According to he and his student Sven Hedin's prediction, "if China can revive the Silk Road and use modern means of transportation, the Chinese government will certainly contribute to mankind and at the same time make a monument to itself"[7]. From this perspective, today we are promoting infrastructure investment through the Belt and Road Initiative, and promoting the interconnection of countries along the route with China, until the market of the entire Eurasian continent is fully developed. To revitalize the Silk Road is a great creation, a major contribution not only to the development of the world economy, but also to the reshaping of the history of human civilization. It is also a major contribution to the reshaping of the history of human civilization. It can be said that the success of the construction of the Silk Road Economic Belt is related to the revival of Chinese civilization and its status in world history.

"One Belt, One Road" Is the Road to a Community of shared future

In recent years, international public opinion has been very interested in China's "Belt and Road" initiative. Initially, the Belt and Road Initiative consisted only of cooperation with countries along the route to build infrastructure and industrial parks to promote regional economic development and integration. As more and more countries expressed their willingness to participate in the Belt and Road Initiative, especially those not located along the Silk Road, the spirit of the Belt and Road Initiative finally took shape. As long as they are willing to cooperate, strengthen infrastructure development and promote connectivity among countries, they can participate in the Belt and Road Initiative.

The "Belt and Road" Initiative Is a Great Practice for Building a Community of shared future

The "Belt and Road" initiative has three principles: co-business, co-construction and sharing, which extends to community of interests, community of responsibilities and community of common destiny. The three words "discuss, build and share" are not just empty slogans, but they are used to promote the docking of economic development strategies of related countries and encourage both sides to give full play to their comparative advantages. The "One Belt, One Road" project cannot be decided by a certain country, but must be discussed by the relevant countries to ensure that the "One Belt, One Road" project can take into account the interests of all parties and reflect the common will of all parties.

The "Belt and Road" planning is not a charity and assistance from big countries to small countries or strong countries to weak countries. Instead, it is a rational division of labor and joint construction based on giving full play to the comparative advantages of the "Belt and Road" countries, so that the original economic development strategies of each country can be integrated into one, achieving the overall synergy of "one plus one is greater than two".

Sharing means that the fruits of the "Belt and Road" project are not exclusively owned by a certain country, but are distributed relatively equally to all countries concerned, thus realizing common interests and common destiny, which also realizes the aspiration of common development.

There is a Chinese saying that "relatives look up to their relatives and neighbors look up to their neighbors". In other words, the Chinese traditionally attach great importance to neighborly love. Extending to country-to-country relations, China also hopes that its neighbors can become rich and prosperous, so that they can achieve common prosperity. Most of the countries along the Belt and Road are developing countries with huge needs for infrastructure investment and industrialization, and China wants to help these countries modernize and integrate into globalization. In this way, these countries form a community of interest, responsibility and destiny with China.

Mutual benefit and win-win cooperation is the most concise summary of the "Belt and Road" projects. In the face of the urgent need for development in neighboring countries, China is willing to integrate its own development more closely with the development of neighboring countries, and welcomes neighboring countries to ride on the "convenient train" of China's rapid development, so that we can live a good life together. Whether it is the gas cooperation agreement signed between China and Russia, or the industrial demonstration park between China and Malaysia, China is solidly promoting mutually beneficial cooperation with neighboring countries in infrastructure construction, energy, industrial park development and other fields.

Of course, to build a community of human destiny, mutual benefit and win-win cooperation are the foundation, but these alone are not enough. Xi Jinping has spoken about China's diplomatic principles on many public occasions, and in 2014, in a speech at Seoul National University in South Korea, Xi quoted the *Great Learning* as saying, "A state does not take profit for profit, but also take righteousness as profit"[8]. In international cooperation, we need to focus on profit, and more importantly, on righteousness. Only by balancing righteousness and profit can we achieve both righteousness and profit, and only by balancing righteousness and profit can we win together. In ancient China, there are also famous quotes about friendship, such as: "Friendship for profit will be scattered when profit is exhausted; friendships for influence will be broken when influence is tilted; friendships for power will be abandoned when power is lost; friendships for desire will be hurt when desire is quenched; only friendships with heart will be long lasting." In order to build a community of human destiny, China must establish ties with countries beyond economic interests, and constantly strengthen exchanges and communication among peoples, so that mutual understanding can be enhanced, friendship can be consolidated, and the community of human destiny can grow and expand.

Notes

1 Xi Jinping's Speech at the United Nations Office at Geneva, *Working Together to Build a Community of Shared Future for Humankind*, January 18, 2017 http://en.qstheory.cn/2021-01/05/c_579937.htm

2 Information Office of the State Council, The People's Republic of China, *China's Peaceful Development*, September 2011, Beijing. http://english.www.gov.cn/archive/white_paper/2014/09/09/content_281474986284646.htm

3 Full text of Hu Jintao's report at 18th National Congress of the Communist Party of China (CPC), Nov. 8, 2012. http://www.china-embassy.org/eng/zt/18th_CPC_National_Congress_Eng/t992917.htm

4 *The Book of Rites* (*Li Ji*), Translated by James Legge, https://ctext.org/liji/li-yun/ens

5 Speech at an enlarged meeting of the Political Bureau of the Central Committee of the Chinese Communist Party. Bearing in mind lessons drawn from the Soviet Union, Comrade Mao Zedong summed up China's experience, dealt with ten major relationships in socialist revolution and socialist construction and set forth the ideas underlying the general line of building socialism with greater, faster, better and more economical results, a line suited to the conditions of our country. https://www.marxists.org/reference/archive/mao/selected-works/volume-5/mswv5_51.htm

6 Halford Mackinder. *Democratic Ideals and Reality*. 1919. p. 150

7 Ferdinand von Richthofen. *Über die zentralasiatischen Seidenstrassen bis zum 2. Jh. n. Chr [On the Central Asian Silk Roads until the 2nd century A.D.]*. Verhandlungen der Gesellschaft für Erdkunde zu Berlin (in German). 1877.

8 President Xi Jinping delivers an important speech in ROK's Seoul National University, stressing that China will always be a country that maintains peace, promotes cooperation and is modest to learn from others, and that China will create the future of China-ROK cooperation and accomplish asia's revitalization and prosperity together with ROK https://www.fmprc.gov.cn/mfa_eng/topics_665678/xjpzxdhgjxgsfw/t1172436.shtml

Index

www.ingramcontent.com/pod-product-compliance
Ingram Content Group UK Ltd.
Pitfield, Milton Keynes, MK11 3LW, UK
UKHW021836100926
8556IPUK00004B/383

9 781433 193200